# ZEW Economic Studies

Publication Series of the Centre for European Economic Research (ZEW), Mannheim, Germany

# ZEW Economic Studies

Further volumes of this series can be found at our homepage: springeronline.com/series/4041

**Vol. 15:** O.H. Jacobs, C. Spengel
**Effective Tax Burden in Europe**
Current Situation, Past Developments and Simulations of Reforms
2002. X, 131 pp. ISBN 3-7908-1470-9

**Vol. 16:** U. Kaiser
**Innovation, Employment, and Firm Performance in the German Service Sector**
2002. X, 164 pp. ISBN 3-7908-1481-4

**Vol. 17:** J. Köke
**Corporate Governance in Germany**
An Empirical Investigation
2002. VIII, 184 pp. ISBN 3-7908-1511-X

**Vol. 18:** E. Wolf
**What Hampers Part-Time Work?**
An Empirical Analysis of Wages, Hours Restrictions and Employment from a Dutch-German Perspective
2003. X, 174 pp. ISBN 3-7908-0006-6

**Vol. 19:** P. Cecchini et al. (Eds.)
**The Incomplete European Market for Financial Services**
2003. XII, 255 pp. ISBN 3-7908-0013-9

**Vol. 20:** C. Böhringer, A. Löschel (Eds.)
**Empirical Modeling of the Economy and the Environment**
2003. VI, 326 pp. ISBN 3-7908-0078-3

**Vol. 21:** K. Rennings, T. Zwick (Eds.)
**Employment Impacts of Cleaner Production**
2003. VIII, 322 pp. ISBN 3-7908-0093-7

**Vol. 22:** O. Bürgel, A. Fier, G. Licht, G. Murray
**The Internationalisation of Young High-Tech Firms**
An Empirical Analysis in Germany and the United Kingdom
2003. XII, 291 pp. ISBN 3-7908-0120-8

**Vol. 23:** F. Hüfner
**Foreign Exchange Intervention as a Monetary Policy Instrument**
Evidence for Inflation Targeting Countries
2004. X, 175 pp. ISBN 3-7908-0128-3

**Vol. 24:** E. Lüders
**Economic Foundation of Asset Price Processes**
2004. XII, 121 pp. ISBN 3-7908-0149-6

**Vol. 25:** F. Reize
**Leaving Unemployment for Self-Employment**
An Empirical Study
2004. XII, 241 pp. ISBN 3-7908-0168-2

**Vol. 26:** Ch. Böhringer, A. Löschel (Eds.)
**Climate Change Policy and Global Trade**
2004. VIII, 381 pp. ISBN 3-7908-0171-2

**Vol. 27:** K. Jacob et al.
**Lead Markets for Environmental Innovations**
2005. XII, 273 pp. ISBN 3-7908-0164-X

**Vol. 28:** L. Lammersen, R. Schwager
**The Effective Tax Burden of Companies in European Regions**
2005. XI, 251 pp. ISBN 3-7908-1562-4

**Vol. 29:** Ch. Elschner, R. Schwager
**The Effective Tax Burden on Highly Qualified Employees**
2005. VIII, 123 pp. ISBN 3-7908-1568-3

**Vol. 30:** Ch. Lauer
**Education and Labour Market Outcomes**
2005. IX, 286 pp. ISBN 3-7908-1569-1

**Vol. 31:** Ch. Böhringer, A. Lange (Eds.)
**Applied Research in Environmental Economics**
2005. VI, 314 pp. ISBN 3-7908-1587-X

**Vol. 32:** O. Heneric, G. Licht, W. Sofka (Eds.)
**Europe's Automotive Industry on the Move**
Competitiveness in a Changing World
2005. XI, 275 pp. ISBN 3-7908-1590-X

**Vol. 33:** Th. Hempell
**Computers and Productivity**
How Firms Make a General Purpose Technology Work
2006. X, 194 pp. ISBN 3-7908-1647-7

Dan Stegarescu

# Decentralised Government in an Integrating World

## Quantitative Studies for OECD Countries

With 22 Figures and 54 Tables

Physica-Verlag
A Springer Company

ZEW
Zentrum für Europäische
Wirtschaftsforschung GmbH
Centre for European
Economic Research

**Series Editor**
Prof. Dr. Dr. h.c. mult. Wolfgang Franz

**Author**
Dr. Dan Stegarescu
Centre for European Economic Research (ZEW)
L 7,1
68161 Mannheim
Germany
stegarescu@zew.de

ISBN-10 3-7908-1669-8 Physica-Verlag Heidelberg New York
ISBN-13 978-3-7908-1669-3 Physica-Verlag Heidelberg New York

Cataloging-in-Publication Data applied for
Library of Congress Control Number: 2005936127



Physica-Verlag is a part of Springer Science+Business Media

springeronline.com



Cover design: Erich Dichiser, ZEW, Mannheim

SPIN 11579366 43/3153-5 4 3 2 1 0 – Printed on acid-free paper

For Glòria

# Preface

This book provides an empirical and institutional analysis of fiscal federalism in OECD countries, focusing on the impact of economic and political integration on the degree of public sector decentralisation. This work has been made possible through the financial support of the German Research Foundation (DFG) within the Priority Programme "Institutional Design of Federal Systems: Theory and Empirical Evidence" and through different research projects carried out at the Centre for European Economic Research (ZEW).

First of all, I am very grateful to my supervisor Prof. Dr. Robert Schwager for finding interest in this topic and for giving me considerable freedom to write my doctoral thesis. I would like to thank him and Prof. Dr. Thiess Büttner, who kindly accepted to be my second supervisor, for their continuous support throughout this work. Additionally, I am indebted to the Centre for European Economic Research (ZEW) and to Prof. Dr. Dr. h.c. mult. Wolfgang Franz for the excellent working and research conditions. I would also like to express my gratitude to all my colleagues from the ZEW Department of Corporate Taxation and Public Finance for the pleasant working environment and many helpful discussions. Thanks are also due to several anonymous referees and to participants in international conferences who with their critical comments helped to improve the papers written during this time. I am also grateful to the student assistants, and particularly to Lena Lindlar, who provided able help in collecting and processing data and literature.

Last but not least, I would like to thank my wife, Glòria, for her unquestioning support, patience and moral understanding throughout the work on the doctoral thesis. Her affection showed me that life consists of many other important things apart from work. Furthermore, as a sign of my gratitude for the permanent support they gave me during my entire life, I wish to dedicate this work to my family, and particularly to my mother and to the memory of my grandmother.

Mannheim, September 2005 *Dan Stegarescu*

# Contents

1 **Introduction** ... 1
1.1 General Scope ... 1
1.2 Topics and Related Literature ... 4
1.2.1 Existing Studies ... 4
1.2.2 Plan of the Work ... 5

2 **Public Sector Decentralisation: Measurement and International Trends** ... 11
2.1 Introduction ... 11
2.2 Measuring Public Sector Decentralisation ... 12
2.2.1 General Definitions ... 12
2.2.2 Common Measures of Fiscal Decentralisation ... 13
2.2.3 Non-Fiscal Measures of Public Sector Decentralisation ... 16
2.2.4 Different Approaches to Measuring Fiscal Autonomy ... 17
2.3 Corrected Indicators of Revenue Decentralisation ... 19
2.3.1 Tax Autonomy ... 19
2.3.2 Degree of Tax and Revenue Decentralisation ... 21
2.4 A Current Overview of OECD Countries ... 23
2.4.1 Public Expenditures ... 23
2.4.2 Fiscal Autonomy and Revenue Decentralisation ... 25
2.5 Fiscal Decentralisation Trends in OECD Countries ... 31
2.5.1 Public Expenditures ... 31
2.5.2 Fiscal Autonomy and Revenue Decentralisation ... 34
2.6 Discussion and Conclusions ... 39

3 **Costs, Preferences, and Institutions: The Determinants of Fiscal Decentralisation** ... 41
3.1 Introduction ... 41
3.2 Decision-Making Institutions and Government Decentralisation ... 44
3.3 An Institutional Overview of OECD Countries ... 49

3.3.1 Participation of Subnational Entities in Central Decision-Making ... 49
3.3.2 Direct Democracy at the National Level ... 57
3.4 Quantitative Analysis ... 60
3.4.1 Empirical Model ... 61
3.4.2 Institutions ... 63
3.4.3 Costs and Preferences ... 66
3.5 Results ... 71
3.6 Discussion and Conclusions ... 79

**4 Economic Integration and Fiscal Decentralisation** ... 81
4.1 Introduction ... 81
4.2 Theoretical Framework ... 84
4.2.1 Basic Assumptions ... 84
4.2.2 The Optimal Degree of Decentralisation ... 87
4.2.3 Political Integration ... 90
4.3 Empirical Analysis ... 92
4.3.1 Empirical Considerations ... 93
4.3.2 Descriptive Statistics ... 95
4.3.3 Investigation Approach ... 98
4.4 Results ... 101
4.4.1 Basic Estimations ... 101
4.4.2 Sensitivity Analysis and Robustness Checks ... 107
4.5 Discussion and Conclusions ... 112

**5 Long-Term Trends in the Public Sector: An Inquiry into German History** ... 115
5.1 Introduction ... 115
5.2 A Brief History of German Federalism ... 117
5.2.1 The German *Kaiserreich* (1871-1918) ... 117
5.2.2 The Inter-War Period (1919-1938) ... 120
5.2.3 The Postwar Period (since 1949) ... 121
5.3 Quantification of Long-Term Trends in the Public Sector ... 124
5.3.1 Growth of the Public Sector ... 124
5.3.2 The Process of Public Sector Centralisation ... 127
5.4 Determinants of Fiscal Decentralisation in Germany ... 137
5.4.1 Quantitative Approach ... 137
5.4.2 Results ... 139
5.5 Discussion and Conclusions ... 142

**6 Summary and Conclusions** ... 145

**A Theoretical Model** ... 151

**B Tables and Figures** ... 153

**C Data Sources and Definitions** .......... 203

**D Descriptive Statistics** .......... 211

**List of Figures** .......... 214

**List of Tables** .......... 217

**References** .......... 219

# 1 Introduction

*La décentralisation n'a pas seulement une valeur administrative; elle a une portée civique puisqu'elle multiplie les occasions pour les citoyens de s'intéresser aux affaires publiques; elle les accoutume à user de la liberté. Et de l'agglomération de ces libertés locales, actives et sourcilleuses, naît le plus efficace contrepoids aux prétentions du pouvoir central, fussent-elles étayées par l'anonymat de la volonté collective.*
*A. DE TOCQUEVILLE*

## 1.1 General Scope

The design of fiscal relations across levels of government has gained increasing importance in government practice.[1] Since the 1970s and especially during the last decade, in several industrial and developing countries, and, more recently, in the post-communist countries in East Europe, government functions and tax-raising powers have been reallocated from central government to regional or local governments. Formerly highly centralized countries like Spain, Belgium or Italy are increasingly plagued by secessionist trends and gradually evolve into federal or quasi-federal states, and countries with long-standing federal traditions like Germany and Austria currently debate on the reform of their federal structures in terms of larger subnational autonomy and stricter separation of government functions.[2] However, despite these worldwide trends, large differences in vertical government structures still persist and are not likely to disappear in the near future.

Apart from the devolution of fiscal competencies, electoral control over municipal, state, and national governments was also extended in recent times.

[1] See, e.g., Bird (1993) and Oates (1999).

[2] See OECD (1997, 2002b, 2003) for a description of these decentralisation trends.

Accordingly, in several countries democratically elected bodies were introduced at subnational levels, and citizens were increasingly allowed to participate directly in policy-making by means of initiatives and referendums. This process of fiscal and political decentralisation is actively supported by supranational institutions such as the World Bank, the United Nations or the OECD, particularly in developing countries and East European transition countries.[3] By enhancing efficiency, policy innovation and transparency in the public sector, government decentralisation is expected to promote economic and social development.

Different forces are assumed to be at the origin of this decentralisation process.[4] The worldwide spread of democracy is often invoked as an important source of decentralisation, since it gives voice to local demands of specific groups and brings decisions closer to the citizens' preferences. In his famous article, Huntington (1993) pointed to another possible source of the breakdown and increasing decentralisation of countries: the end of the Cold War, which allowed the realignment of people into countries that better reflected homogeneous "civilisations". Another argument states that increasing economic and social prosperity is associated with increasing diversity of local preferences and the desire of citizens to influence financing and supply of public goods, thus fostering demands for decentralisation and local democracy. Whereas these explanations might apply to culturally, ethnically or linguistically heterogeneous countries, they provide no clear understanding of decentralising trends in rather homogeneous countries or long-standing democracies.

Therefore, the observed decentralisation trend may be driven by another force. Increasing fiscal decentralisation and political separatism seem to go hand in hand with the rapid progress of globalisation and integration of the world economy, particularly noticed since the breakup of the Bretton Woods system in the early 1970s. Technological improvements in methods of production, and in the ease of transportation and communication, together with the advancement of worldwide trade and financial liberalisation have reduced the impediments to mobility of goods and factors, thus increasing both the size of the markets and the degree of transnational interdependency.[5] As recently noted by Alesina (2002), among other authors, in the face of this trend, national governments increasingly prove to be too small to cope with globalisation, and too large and inefficient to take account of local or regional requirements and diversities. Some analysts, such as Ohmae (1995), e.g., even predicted the imminent demise of the nation-state in a borderless world.

Though the disappearance of the nation-state is not likely to occur in the near future, two concomitant, though opposing trends in the public sector

---

[3] See OECD (2002a, 2002b) with respect to EU accession countries and, also, the Decentralization Project of the World Bank described at www1.worldbank.org/wbiep/decentralization and www.decentralization.org.

[4] See Tanzi (2001) for an overview.

[5] See Amin and Thrift (1999), e.g., for a description of different aspects of globalisation.

seem to be the result of the same driving force, increasing economic integration. On the one hand, growing interdependencies and increasing commodity and financial flows erode the regulatory capacities of sovereign states, thus requiring centralisation or coordination of national government policies. Since the end of World War II, an increasing number of supranational authorities have emerged both at the global level, such as the United Nations, or the World Trade Organisation, and at the regional level, such as the European Economic Community, NAFTA, MERCOSUR, or ASEAN being the most prominent examples.

On the other hand, globalisation reduces the benefits of country size for economic growth and allows even small local entities to bypass central authorities in order to participate directly in international transactions and to compete for mobile manpower, firms and investors on global markets.[6] Within this context, Straubhaar (1999) speaks of "glocalisation", arguing that free markets and decreasing transport costs reduce the importance of national economies, at the same time strengthening local and regional agglomerations. Consequently, globalisation poses pressures to both political integration of nation-states and fragmentation into regions and cities at the same time. The World Bank recently estimated that localisation, that is the subnational desire for self-determination and devolution of power, and globalisation will be shaping the world.[7]

This parallel is even more striking with regard to European Union countries. In the course of economic and political integration, significant fiscal and political powers have been transferred from the national governments both to a supranational authority and to lower levels of government. This development is particularly associated with a rise of the regional level of government – referred to by Keating (1998) as "New Regionalism". According to the "Sandwich" hypothesis, national governments are expected to be further pushed back in the course of European integration. This process will ultimately lead to a "Europe of the Regions".[8] With the imminent coming into force of the European Constitution, the European Union gradually evolves from an initial customs union into a quasi-federalized multi-level government structure. Yet, despite this overall tendency, the form and pace of regionalisation and decentralisation differ considerably among EU member countries. Whereas Spain, Belgium, Italy, France, and more recently, the United Kingdom represent the most prominent examples of real devolution in terms of expenditure and tax-raising autonomy, other countries like Ireland, Portugal, Greece and Finland created only administrative regions under central government control.

Apart from normative considerations, these issues therefore raise the question about the common factors which determine observed differences in the

[6] See, e.g., Keating (1998) and Scott (1998).
[7] See World Bank (2000) and also Hiscox (2003), among others.
[8] See, e.g., Lammers (1999) and Zimmermann (1990). The latter, however, questions this development.

distribution of spending and taxing powers between levels of government across countries and over time. This work takes an empirical approach to investigate the determinants of vertical government structures and the developments described above. The particular aim is to analyse the causal relationship between those two broad trends, increasing integration of the world economy, and concomitant supranationalisation and decentralisation of government structures. The analysis draws on OECD countries with long-standing democratic traditions, particularly focusing on the process of European integration.

More specifically, the following questions are addressed:

- How decentralized is the public sector in OECD countries and is there a real decentralisation trend observable among them?
- What are the general determinants of cross-country differences in the degree of fiscal decentralisation?
- Is there a causal relationship between increasing economic and political integration on the one hand, and increasing fiscal decentralisation on the other hand, particularly among EU member countries?
- And, finally, which are the long-term trends in the public sector and the factors underlying them, taking Germany as an example?

## 1.2 Topics and Related Literature

### 1.2.1 Existing Studies

The interest in the public finance literature in empirical studies of vertical fiscal structures has considerably grown. This empirical literature deals partly with possible determinants of public sector decentralisation as derived from the theory of fiscal federalism,[9] or tries to detect long-term centralisation trends in the public sector, as suggested by Popitz (1927). Alternatively, other studies focus instead on the possible implications of centralisation for the size of the public sector,[10] economic and productivity growth,[11] or good governance and corruption.[12]

General reference for the analysis of vertical government structures is the theory of fiscal federalism in the tradition of Musgrave (1959) and Oates (1972). According to the "Decentralisation Theorem", the optimal degree of decentralisation of the public sector is determined by the costs and benefits of the decentralized provision of public goods. On the one hand, decentralisation

[9] See, e.g., Oates (1972), Wallis and Oates (1988), and more recently, Panizza (1999), and Strumpf and Oberholzer-Gee (2002).

[10] See the empirical Leviathan literature, e.g., Oates (1985) or Feld et al. (2003). The latter also provides a survey of this literature.

[11] See, e.g., Davoodi and Zou (1998), Thiessen (2003), or Behnisch et al. (2002).

[12] See, e.g., Arikan (2004) and Fisman and Gatti (2002).

allows for the differentiation of public goods according to local preferences and conditions. On the other hand, it implies costs in form of interjurisdictional spillovers and foregone economies of scale.

Recent theoretical work on fiscal federalism has shown that apart from traditional cost-benefit aspects, institutional rules underlying decision-making processes in democracies considerably influence the costs and benefits of decentralisation, and consequently, the choice of the vertical government structure (Besley and Coate, 2003, Lockwood, 2004, Redoano and Scharf, 2004). The delegation of political decision-making to elected representatives is shown to create a common-pool problem, collusive behaviour and vote-trading leading in the end to inefficiently high public spending and centralisation (Brennan and Buchanan, 1980).

Empirical analyses mostly support the "Decentralisation Theorem", showing that particularly heterogeneous countries or jurisdictions are more decentralized. On the other hand, the political-economic considerations and, above all, the implications of specific institutions of collective decision-making for government decentralisation have only partly been tested on a cross-national level. For example, some evidence is provided for a positive effect of local referendums and subnational participation in central decision-making on the degree of fiscal decentralisation (Schaltegger and Feld, 2001, Vaubel, 1996).

While explaining cross-country differences in the vertical government structure, the theory of fiscal federalism fails to give an adequate explanation of the recent process of decentralisation. Inspired by the spread of political separatism and the emergence of new countries throughout the world, a growing new literature (Alesina and Spolaore, 1997, Bolton and Roland, 1997) explores the economic determinants of the creation and disintegration of countries. They show that economic integration lowers the benefits of large jurisdictions by increasing the market size and reducing political and economic transaction costs. As a consequence, integration enhances incentives to secession or to regional autonomy.

However, the resulting implications of integration for the vertical government structure are mostly neglected by the literature on secessions. Apart from this, the possible contribution of political integration among countries to explaining the decentralising tendencies is not taken into account. While the negative relationship between the size of the country and the degree of economic openness is mostly confirmed in empirical studies, there is only little evidence with regard to the impact of integration on the vertical government structure. The results of some studies seem to support a positive relationship between integration and fiscal centralisation (Rodrik, 1998, Garrett and Rodden, 2003).

### 1.2.2 Plan of the Work

Given this background, the present work extends previous analyses in order to focus on other aspects of the positive theory of fiscal federalism which have not been explored empirically. The specific questions formulated above are addressed by dividing the work in four parts.

### Measurement and Description of Fiscal Decentralisation

In order to verify the claim that decentralisation is in vogue, chapter 2 begins with the analysis and quantification of the extent of fiscal decentralisation of 23 OECD countries. We investigate how decentralized the public sector is in OECD countries and whether there is a real decentralisation trend observable among them? The share of subnational government expenditure or revenue in consolidated general government expenditure or revenue as derived from financial statistics is widely used in the literature as a proxy for the degree of decentralisation of the public sector. As already mentioned by Oates (1972), without taking into account the vertical structure of decision-making, the degree of decentralisation of the public sector tends to be misrepresented and both cross-country comparisons and the description of long-term trends might be seriously distorted.

In view of its predominant importance for subnational autonomy, the present analysis focuses on the revenue side of fiscal decentralisation. We start in section 2.2 with a general discussion of existing concepts of measuring public sector decentralisation. Drawing on an analytical framework provided by the OECD, different measures of tax autonomy and revenue decentralisation are constructed in section 2.3. Classifying local taxes according to the degree of discretion of sub-central governments, the degree of fiscal decentralisation is measured by relating revenue from taxes or other resources which are significantly controlled by sub-central government to total tax or other revenue of consolidated general government. Based on this set of fiscal indicators, the development of the vertical government structure in OECD countries is investigated in sections 2.4 and 2.5. Taking account of changes in the assignment of tax raising powers in the course of time, new time series of annual data on the corrected degree of fiscal decentralisation are provided for 23 OECD countries in the time period between 1965 and 2001.

The analysis shows that common measures usually employed tend to considerably overestimate the extent of fiscal decentralisation. Though no uniform pattern of development could be determined, evidence is provided for increasing fiscal decentralisation in a majority of OECD countries during the last three decades.

### Determinants of Vertical Government Structures

In the next step, based upon the decentralisation measures developed in chapter 2, chapter 3 addresses empirically for a panel of OECD countries the question about the general determinants of cross-country differences in vertical government structures. Since the literature provides only limited cross-country evidence, the particular focus is on the contribution of preferences and institutions in explaining the degree of fiscal decentralisation.

For this purpose, section 3.2 starts with a summary of the main theoretical results of recent political-economic work on fiscal federalism. Then, section 3.3 provides a detailed analysis of decision-making institutions of the 23 OECD countries from 1965 to the present. Different institutional rules providing for subnational or citizen participation in central decision-making processes are represented by means of qualitative indicators. Based upon this, we investigate in sections 3.4 and 3.5 the effect of specific decision-making institutions on the degree of fiscal decentralisation, explicitly considering institutional changes over time, and controlling for preference heterogeneity, economies of scale and other possible determinants. More specifically, we test the collusion hypothesis and other propositions laid down in the literature.

The results of the cross-sectional time-series regression analysis indicate that institutions, as well as costs and preferences have a significant impact on the degree of fiscal decentralisation. Only when using a measure of fiscal decentralisation which accounts for the distribution of decision-making powers among levels of government, the evidence strongly supports the collusion hypothesis according to which delegation of decision-making concerning assignment of powers and national legislation to subnational representatives leads to increased centralisation of tax-raising powers. In contrast to this, direct participation of the citizens of the subnational entities is associated with more decentralisation. On the other hand, however, there is some evidence that direct democracy at the national level tends to be associated with increased centralisation.

## Integration and Decentralisation

Once the factors generally determining government structures have been identified, we turn in chapter 4 to the theoretical and empirical investigation of the specific relationship between those two trends described in the introduction, integration and fiscal decentralisation. The question is whether there exists a causal relationship between increasing economic and political integration on the one hand, and increasing fiscal decentralisation on the other hand, particularly among EU member countries? The analysis draws on the new literature on secessions, which mostly neglects the resulting implications of economic and political integration for the vertical government structure and provides no thorough empirical verification.

To begin with, in section 4.2 a theoretical model is set up, which relates the degree of fiscal decentralisation to economic integration, preference heterogeneity, and economies of scale. By lowering the relative costs of local provision of public goods, integration is expected to enhance fiscal decentralisation. Political integration might further contribute to decentralisation, since market integration is intensified and the costs of supplying certain public goods from now on in the competency of the supranational level are reduced. On the other hand, by increasing economic risks, economic integration is also expected to enhance the demand for inter-regional risk-sharing or other policies carried out or enforced by the central government. Then, section 4.3 discusses different empirical considerations and some descriptive statistics on the process of integration and presents the investigation approach. The hypothesis of a decentralising effect of economic integration in general, and of political integration in the European Union in particular, is tested empirically in section 4.4 for the panel of OECD countries, along with controlling for inter-regional heterogeneity, institutions, and other possible factors. In order to focus on the impact of increasing integration and of other factors which are assumed to determine the costs and benefits of decentralisation over time, the model is estimated with country fixed effects.

The results found mostly support a decentralising effect of economic and European integration, particularly in the context of preference heterogeneity, whereas participation of subnational governments in central decision-making is associated with increasing centralisation. Some limited evidence is therefore provided for the "Sandwich" hypothesis postulating a diminishing role of national governments in the course of European integration. Also, circumstantial evidence is reported for a causal relationship between the end of the Cold War and decentralisation of the public sector.

### Long-Term Trends in the Public Sector

The studies carried out for OECD countries in chapters 2-4 have shown that, in spite of few exceptions, vertical fiscal structures and institutional rules barely change over time. Chapter 5 therefore provides a long-term view on the development of the public sector, drawing on the history of Germany from the creation of a unified state in the 19th century until today. First, it addresses the question whether there is an unavoidable long-term centralisation trend in the public sector, as suggested by Popitz (1927). Second, we investigate empirically whether those factors identified above were also determining the development in Germany over a longer period of time. Whereas long-term trends in the public sector have already been dealt with by earlier studies, the determinants of the underlying development have barely been investigated in empirical terms.

The analysis starts in section 5.2 with a brief historical description of Germany's vertical government structure since 1871 until today. Then, in section 5.3, the long-term development of the public sector is quantified in terms of government size and allocation of public expenditure and revenue by fiscal tiers. The regression analysis is carried out in section 5.4. The effects of economic development and of economic and European integration on fiscal decentralisation are tested empirically for the period 1950 to 2001, controlling for other time-variant determinants of the vertical government structure.

Despite significant centralisation and coordination in today's federal system, the German experience provides no clear evidence for a continuous and unavoidable process of centralisation in the public sector, but rather for some distinct developments before and after 1950, caused by the distortionary effects of wars and regime changes. However, the collusion hypothesis is supported by institutional changes in the German history. The results of the time series analysis also contrast with previous predictions, indicating a significant decentralising effect of per capita income growth during this time. On the other hand, there is no clear evidence for a causal relationship between economic and European integration and fiscal decentralisation in the case of Germany.

The last chapter finally provides a summary of the main findings of the different studies, concluding with a discussion of future developments and resulting normative considerations.

# 2

# Public Sector Decentralisation: Measurement and International Trends

## 2.1 Introduction

Motivated by increasing interest in public finance and practice in the comparison of vertical government structures, this chapter focuses on the problems encountered in defining and measuring public sector decentralisation appropriately.

Despite several shortcomings, the share of subnational government expenditure or revenue in consolidated general government expenditure or revenue is widely used as a proxy for the degree of decentralisation of the public sector. However, Oates (1972), among others, already pointed to the limitations of using budgetary shares. Without taking into account the vertical structure of decision-making, the degree of decentralisation of the public sector tends to be misrepresented and both cross-country comparisons and the description of long-term trends might be seriously distorted. It is therefore not obvious that the observed worldwide increase in the subnational government share of public expenditure and revenue actually reflects fiscal decentralisation in terms of devolution of decision-making powers to lower levels of government.

Related to this, erroneous measurement of decentralisation may seriously bias the results of empirical studies and in the end may lead to wrong conclusions. This has been recently confirmed by Ebel and Yilmaz (2003), who replicated previous studies and showed that more comprehensive measures of fiscal decentralisation actually yield deviating results. Within this context, measurement errors concerning decentralisation as the independent variable are more problematic in regression analyses than those concerning decentralisation as the dependent variable.[1] Due to its importance, the measurement of fiscal decentralisation has been recently placed on the research agenda of international organisations like the OECD or the World Bank.

[1] Greene (2000: 375f), e.g., shows that as long as the independent variable is measured properly, measurement errors on the dependent variable are absorbed in the regression disturbance and can therefore be ignored.

The analysis draws on a recent study of the OECD which provides a cross-country comparison of tax-raising autonomy of sub-central governments. Based upon the analytical framework elaborated by the OECD, measures of both fiscal autonomy and revenue decentralisation are constructed which consider tax-raising powers of sub-central governments. The new contribution is twofold. First, more recent figures on subnational tax autonomy, as well as on the different indicators of fiscal decentralisation are presented for 23 OECD countries. Second, taking account of changes in the assignment of decision-making competencies for each tax in the course of time, we investigate the long-term trend providing new time series of annual data on the degree of tax and revenue decentralisation of OECD countries in the time period between 1965 and 2001.

The analysis proceeds as follows. It starts with a presentation and discussion of existing concepts for measuring public sector decentralisation. Then, in section 2.3, different indicators of fiscal autonomy and decentralisation are derived for the revenue side. Based on this, sections 2.4 and 2.5 present new figures on fiscal decentralisation for OECD countries and investigate possible long-term trends. Finally, the results are briefly discussed and some conclusions are drawn.

## 2.2 Measuring Public Sector Decentralisation

### 2.2.1 General Definitions

Public sector or fiscal decentralisation is commonly associated with the assignment of authority for public functions or finances to lower levels of government.[2] Due to the complexity of intergovernmental relations, measuring the degree of decentralisation, however, is a difficult task which bears many dimensions and which can hardly be accomplished by using a single quantitative measure.

Among the multitude of definitions found in the public finance literature, a widely used classification distinguishes between three different forms of fiscal decentralisation:[3]

---

[2] The design of fiscal relations across levels of government is to be distinguished from *political decentralisation*, that is the extension of direct or indirect participation of the citizens in public decision-making through referendums or local elections. This form of decentralisation does not necessarily imply the transfer of real fiscal responsibilities. Also, the transfer of government functions to the private sector (*privatisation* or contracting out), or, more recently, to the non-profit sector can be interpreted as a distinct form of extensive fiscal decentralisation.

[3] See, e.g., OECD (1997), Rondinelli (1999), and the Decentralisation Project of the World Bank.

- *deconcentration*: responsibility for the delivery of certain services is dispersed to regional administrative units of central government without transfer of authority,
- *delegation*: responsibility for the administration of functions is transferred to independent units of sub-central government which have some discretion in administration and implementation, but which, however, are accountable to the central government,
- *devolution*: complete decision-making authority for the financing and administration of functions is transferred to independent units of sub-central government which have corporate status.

Strictly speaking, only the last form can be considered as true fiscal decentralisation in terms of real transfer of powers. This qualification suggests to take account of two important dimensions when comparing vertical government structures across countries.[4] The first dimension comprises the formal division of functional responsibilities and revenues across levels of government. Within this context, the range and the relative importance of the different functions and revenues assigned to subnational governments, as well as the extent to which government functions are performed by the private sector determine the degree of fiscal decentralisation.

The second and most important dimension concerns the vertical structure of decision-making, that is the extent to which decisions regarding functions and resources assigned to lower levels of government are decentralised, too. A system where sub-central levels of government have real autonomy to determine the allocation of their expenditure or to raise own revenue is more decentralised than another system where local or regional government spending and revenue is determined by national legislation, even though the formal assignment of functions or revenues might be the same.

A final aspect which should be noticed, is the geographic dimension of fiscal decentralisation, that is the extent to which the assignment of functions and resources is uniformly implemented across different jurisdictions. The special case where responsibilities are unevenly distributed between sub-central government units belonging to the same level, i.e. when certain jurisdictions enjoy a specific autonomy status as compared to others, is referred to as asymmetric fiscal decentralisation.[5]

### 2.2.2 Common Measures of Fiscal Decentralisation

A common approach to quantifying the degree of fiscal decentralisation is to look at how extensive central and sub-central government activities are. Public output is generally approximated by means of government expenditures and revenues. Accordingly, sub-central government (SCG) expenditure or revenue are related to consolidated general government (GG) expenditure or revenue,

[4] See also Oates (1972) and Riker (1964), with respect to this.
[5] See Bird (2003).

thus weighting each government function and resource with the corresponding budgetary share.[6]

Vertical aggregation of expenditure and revenue across levels of government requires the elimination of intergovernmental expenditure (transfers) and revenue (grants). Therefore, in order to avoid double counting of intergovernmental payments appearing at both the grantor level as transfers and at the recipient level as expenditure, intergovernmental transfers are attributed either to the level of the recipient or, alternatively, to the granting level of government. In the first case, transfers from lower levels of government to the central government are attributed to the latter, the degree of decentralisation thus reporting only amounts spent or administered directly by sub-central government (*direct expenditure*, indicator *ED1* below). By this, we implicitly assume that the decision on the use of the resources is made at the level of the recipient. In the second case, sub-central government spending is adjusted for grants received from central government (*self-financed expenditure*, indicator *ED2* below), thus taking into account all public expenses financed from formally own resources. This seems particularly reasonable when the grantor prescribes the use of these funds (conditional grants). However, in case of unconditional grants, it would be more appropriate to attribute these funds to the recipient. The degree of expenditure decentralisation can then be defined alternatively as:

$$ED1 = \frac{\text{SCG total expenditure} - \text{transfers to other lev. of gov.}}{\text{GG total expenditure} - \text{intergov. transfers}} \tag{2.1}$$

$$ED2 = \frac{\text{SCG total expenditure} - \text{grants from other lev. of gov.}}{\text{GG total expenditure} - \text{intergov. grants}} \tag{2.2}$$

When focusing on the financing of public goods, decentralisation is alternatively represented in terms of revenue shares. Analogous to public spending, one could consider sub-central government revenue from own sources, thus exclusive of received grants from central government (*own revenue*, indicator *RD3* below):

$$RD3 = \frac{\text{SCG total revenue} - \text{grants from other lev. of gov.}}{\text{GG total revenue} - \text{intergov. grants}} \tag{2.3}$$

This approach to quantifying public sector decentralisation, however, suffers from certain limitations. A key methodological problem is associated with the use of aggregate measures. The difficulty consists in distinguishing as to what extent the degree of decentralisation reflects the assignment of functions and

[6] See Oates (1972), Pryor (1968), and Levin (1990). Breton and Scott (1978) propose alternatively to use population shares as weights for the public output provided in each jurisdiction. In the following discussion, we abstract from the problems encountered in the measurement of public output.

resources to different levels of government or, merely, the relative size of sub-central government activities. An increase in the measure of decentralisation might be due to a *ceteris paribus* increase in either the volume, or, in the range of public goods provided by sub-central government. The first effect simply describes a shift in the budgetary shares of the different government functions – in general caused by changing patterns of demand for public goods. In contrast to this, the second effect implies what is generally referred to as true fiscal decentralisation, namely the reassignment of existing government functions or the introduction of new functions in favour of the decentralised provision of public goods.

A second problem is associated with measurement based on fiscal data. Most cross-country empirical studies draw on budgetary data reported in financial statistics.[7] It is widely accepted that budgetary data in general, and expenditure or revenue shares, in particular, are imperfect indicators of the share of public goods supplied by sub-central governments and of the actual degree of decentralisation of the public sector.[8] First of all, the second dimension of fiscal decentralisation mentioned above, that is the vertical structure of decision-making with regard to public expenditure and revenue, is not accurately represented by public finance statistics. These report expenditure and revenue figures at the level of government which ultimately operates or receives them, irrespective of whether it has discretion upon them. Thus, expenditure mandated by the central government or spent on behalf of the central government is reported as subnational expenditure. In addition, no distinction is made between locally determined own taxes, piggybacked or shared taxes, or between conditional and unconditional intergovernmental grants, all being reported as sub-central revenue and grants. It is therefore difficult to interpret the unadjusted subnational share of expenditure and revenue as reported in financial statistics as an indicator of expenditure and financial autonomy.

Apart from decision-making structures, expenditure and revenue shares also fail to capture the extent of legislative and regulatory activities and

[7] Cross-country analyses draw particularly on the Government Finance Statistics (GFS) of the IMF. See, among others, Levin (1990), Panizza (1999), Thiessen (2003), Miñana (1998), and Rahmann et al. (1994). A description of data and methodology can be found in IMF (2001). Some studies also use National Accounts statistics of the UN, such as Oates (1972) and Pommerehne (1977), of the OECD, such as Patsouratis (1990), or the World Tables reported by the World Bank. These statistics, however, encounter certain limitations and generally lack more recent data. Note also that indicators based solely on public consumption data tend to overestimate the degree of decentralisation, since redistributive transfers of central government are not taken into account.

[8] See, e.g., Oates (1972), Levin (1990), Wasylenko (1987), OECD (1999), and Kraus (1983) for a comprehensive discussion of the measurement of decentralisation. With regard to other possible limitations of fiscal indicators based on GFS data, see also Ebel and Yilmaz (2003), and the Decentralisation Project of the World Bank.

other aspects of decentralisation which are not directly reflected in fiscal flows. Legislation and regulation is only partly accounted for by expenses for personnel and implementation.[9] Norms, minimum quality standards, fiscal rules, and other qualitative restrictions imposed by the central government on sub-central levels of government are also not reflected in budgetary data. In addition, coordination among layers of government in the provision of public goods and joint financing are difficult to be taken into account quantitatively. However, it is not obvious whether budgetary statistics will generally tend to under- or overestimate the scope of central government activities, and, thus, the actual degree of fiscal decentralisation.

### 2.2.3 Non-Fiscal Measures of Public Sector Decentralisation

In order to account for the multiple aspects of decentralisation, different non-fiscal measures have been proposed in the literature. Kaufman (1963) compiles a list of indicators measuring the degree of central government control over subnational government, mentioning detailed directives, involvement in the selection of administrative staff, frequency of consultation, and the extent of supervision. A comprehensive discussion of the factors which together describe the extent of government decentralisation is provided by Smith (1979), Bahl (1999), and Treisman (2002), among others. These criterions range from elected local councils, locally appointed chief officers, institutional provisions, size and number of subnational authorities, organisational structures, to fiscal indicators of expenditure, tax-raising and borrowing powers. For example, the extent to which central government controls the deployment of local administrative personnel and supervises local government activity, or the right of sub-central governments to appoint judges or to have separate police forces play an important role. Certain studies therefore employ, as a non-fiscal indicator of decentralisation, the ratio of sub-central government employment to total government employment.[10] Stephens (1974) also constructs a composite index of state centralisation containing information on financial responsibility, delivery, and distribution of public personnel between levels of government, in order to divide up government services in central, local, and joint functions.

Also, a system where sub-central authorities have constitutionally guaranteed statutory rights or autonomy is considered to be more decentralised than a system where powers are delegated by simple national legislation or administrative ruling and the territorial delimitation of jurisdictions is changed by simple law, thus being at central government's discretion. However, this is a necessary but not a sufficient condition for decentralisation, since practice often differs from the legal provisions.

Focusing on the size and number of sub-central authorities, the population-normalised number of sub-central jurisdictions,[11] or even the number of tiers

[9] See, e.g., Zimmermann (1973).

[10] See, e.g., Arikan (2004).

[11] See, e.g., Oates (1985).

of sub-central government have been occasionally used as alternative measures of decentralisation. Larger authorities might be expected to be more autonomous since they have greater political and financial power. On the other hand, the reorganisation of local communities into greater local units has a centralising effect from the point of view of the municipalities involved.[12] It is generally doubtful whether multi-tiered sub-central government systems – which, for example, have an intermediate level – are to be considered as more decentralised than single-tiered systems. It becomes more difficult for the center to control the lower levels of government in multi-tiered systems. From the point of view of the lowest levels of government, however, this implies decisions being taken by a more remote body. Generally speaking, even if providing some information on the number of veto players, indicators of decentralisation which compare the sheer number of sub-central jurisdictions with different statutes and degrees of autonomy across countries seem quite problematic and require stringent common definitions.

### 2.2.4 Different Approaches to Measuring Fiscal Autonomy

A few recent approaches take account of the second dimension of fiscal decentralisation usually neglected by common indicators, the vertical decision-making structure.[13] Fiscal autonomy of subnational governments is generally determined by the legislative competencies and the degree of discretion over spending, and especially by tax-raising powers and debt-raising autonomy. A local unit has complete autonomy if it is not legally obliged to carry out a function or to raise a certain tax, and if the output, or, respectively, the local tax rate and the tax base are not predetermined by a higher unit of government.

With respect to the supply of public goods, the vertical fiscal imbalance, that is the extent to which sub central governments rely on central government grants to support their expenditures, is occasionally used as a measure of expenditure autonomy. However, reliance on own revenues to finance public spending does not necessarily imply that expenditures are made autonomously. A more comprehensive approach would imply breaking down sub-central government expenditure by function and classification according to the degree of local discretion in legislation and execution.[14] Legislative competency refers to the power to pass normative acts, and can be further divided in powers assigned either exclusively or concurrently to the different levels of government and framework legislation on matters of principle as compared to legislation on matters of execution. Administrative or executive competency

[12] See Sharpe (1979).

[13] The approaches described in the following draw mainly on the Decentralisation Project of World Bank, and on Ter-Minassian (1997) and OECD (1997, 2002a).

[14] The Council of Europe (1997) provides a comprehensive discussion of different types of powers.

refers instead to the power to carry out enacted legislation. Here, one may distinguish between discretional and mandatory functions according to the degree of discretion allowed, or between delivery on one's own account or on behalf of another level of government.

Some detailed surveys on the framework regulating sub-central government functions in 15 European countries have been carried out by Pola (1999) on behalf of the European Commission. Sub-central services are classified either as being performed exclusively by the local or regional level of government, as being shared between them, or depending on the degree of involvement of central government.[15] However, no corresponding figures on fiscal decentralisation are reported. The main difficulty encountered in quantifying expenditure decentralisation consists in general in missing data on expenditure categories which are sufficiently disaggregated. Moreover, the adequate assessment of the different degrees of autonomy is quite problematic.

Correspondingly, the share of revenue from formally own resources (*own revenue*), thus exclusive of received intergovernmental grants, in total revenue of sub-central governments is quite often used as an indicator of revenue autonomy. However, it is questionable whether increased reliance on central government grants is to be considered as centralising in terms of reduced autonomy of sub-central governments. Depending on the degree of local discretion over the use of the funds, intergovernmental grants are usually classified as unconditional and conditional grants. The first category comprises general purpose grants and revenue-sharing schemes, whereas matching grants, non-matching grants for specific purposes, and block grants belong to the second category.

These measures of financial autonomy fail to capture decision-making structures especially concerning tax revenue assigned to sub-central governments. Pola (1999) also provides detailed institutional surveys and some figures on the degree of self-financing of local and regional governments in EU countries for 1993. Blankart (2000) uses the share of general government tax revenue which is determined by central government legislation as a measure of fiscal centralisation in order to detect long-term trends in Germany and Switzerland. Aiming at improving the quality of budgetary statistics, the OECD recently provided a comprehensive methodological framework for classifying taxes and tax revenues of sub-central government according to the degree of tax-raising autonomy. Based on the Revenue Statistics, detailed figures are reported for a number of OECD and EU accession countries for 1995/1997 on the revenue structure of subnational levels of government.[16] Drawing on this study, Ebel and Yilmaz (2003) represent fiscal decentrali-

[15] See also Owens and Norregaard (1991) for a similar analysis. Riker (1964) provides a qualitative indicator of centralisation of government functions for US states, which takes into account whether functions are performed exclusively, predominantly or in equal proportions by the respective levels of government.

[16] See OECD (1999). Based on a joint initiative together with the World Bank and the Council of Europe, among others, the OECD started in 2000 surveys on the

sation in terms of the ratio of revenue from taxes which are controlled by sub-central governments to total subnational revenue.

Last but not least, apart from current tax and other revenues, the extent to which sub-central governments are allowed to raise debt is also important in terms of fiscal autonomy. Local borrowing is often subject to restrictions imposed by central government, such as general authorisation and regulation on purpose, amount and structure of borrowing. Accordingly, with rising indebtedness, local government expenditure and revenue-raising autonomy is expected to become increasingly restricted by the supervising level of government.

## 2.3 Corrected Indicators of Revenue Decentralisation

### 2.3.1 Tax Autonomy

In spite of the problems of aggregation and of representation of all aspects of fiscal decentralisation, aggregate measures based on budgetary data which are complemented with information on decision-making powers have the distinct advantage of being operational. Even though local discretion on the supply of public goods may play an important role, it is widely accepted that the provision with own financial resources is a crucial condition for subnational strength vis-à-vis the central government and for real fiscal decentralisation. Both the scope of public spending and the extent of interjurisdictional competition are determined by the degree of subnational control over its own resources. In view of this, the study reported in the present chapter focuses on the revenue side of fiscal decentralisation.[17]

Extending previous approaches to the measurement of subnational tax autonomy, we provide alternative quantitative measures of both tax autonomy and revenue decentralisation which take tax-raising powers of sub-central governments into account. Three aspects seem to be important for the classification of subnational taxes in decreasing order of fiscal autonomy: legislative competencies to determine tax base and tax rate, the attribution of the tax receipts, and tax administration. Only taxes which can be chosen independently, and upon which sub-central levels of government have own legislative and administrative powers ensure complete financial autonomy.

Concerning the classification of tax revenues according to the degree of control of sub-central governments upon them, Pola (1999), e.g., distinguishes between own (autonomous) taxes, devolved taxes managed by the central

design of fiscal systems across levels of government for a group of countries. The first results were presented for six EU-accession countries, see OECD (2002a).

17 Apart from this, as already mentioned, the appropriate quantification of expenditure decentralisation involves serious difficulties related to insufficiently disaggregated data on government functions, and to the selection of appropriate criterions by which to assess the degree of local discretion.

government, but the yields of which accrue to sub-central government, and taxes shared with the central government. The OECD approach mentioned above provides a more detailed classification of tax autonomy (see Table 2.1).

Table 2.1: Classification of subnational taxes (in decreasing order of control over revenue sources)

| | |
|---|---|
| (a) | sub-central government (SCG) determines tax rate and tax base |
| (b) | SCG determines tax rate only |
| (c) | SCG determines tax base only |
| (d) | tax sharing: |
| (d.1) | SCG determines revenue-split |
| (d.2) | revenue-split only changed with consent of SCG |
| (d.3) | revenue-split unilaterally changed by centr. gov. (CG) (legislation) |
| (d.4) | revenue-split unilaterally changed by CG (annual budget) |
| (e) | CG determines tax rate and tax base |

Source: OECD (1999: 11).

In cases (a) to (c), which are referred to as "own taxes" in the OECD study, sub-central government has total or significant control over its taxes, whereas in case of revenue sharing (d.1) to (d.2), it has some limited control through mechanisms of co-decision. For tax revenue categories (d.3) to (e), sub-central government has no control at all, these revenues broadly corresponding to unconditional general purpose grants. Based on the 4-digit classification of taxes by the base of the tax reported in the annual Revenue Statistics,[18] the OECD survey classifies each tax, the receipts of which are assigned to sub-central governments, according to the degree of decision-making autonomy as presented above. The taxes are subsequently weighted with the corresponding share in total tax revenue of sub-central governments. However, the OECD study provides no corresponding aggregate measure of tax decentralisation.

An aggregate measure of *tax autonomy* of sub-central governments can be derived either by using a qualitative scale for the different tax categories (a) to (e), which reflects the decreasing extent of discretion, or, simply by summing up the different taxes which only accrue to sub-central levels of government (own taxes) and which are significantly controlled by them, weighted with the corresponding shares in their total tax revenue. Even if no qualitative distinction is made between the different types of autonomous own taxes, the

[18] Note that the Revenue Statistics attribute the following tax revenues to sub-national governments, irrespective of the degree of local discretion: local taxes collected by them, surcharges on national taxes, and shares of national taxes collected by the central government in their territory which automatically accrue to them.

second method avoids any problems of arbitrary assessment and is therefore preferred here. A value of 100% then indicates full autonomy. Note that this measure is slightly different from the tax autonomy indicator presented in Ebel and Yilmaz (2003) which relates revenues from own taxes to total subnational revenues. The degree of tax autonomy accounting for autonomous own taxes is thus defined as:

$$TA1 = \frac{\text{SCG own tax revenue (a) to (c)}}{\text{SCG total tax revenue}} \tag{2.4}$$

Since especially in federal or quasi-federal countries like Austria, Germany, Spain, Switzerland and, most recently, Belgium, regional or state governments have some influence on the revenue-split of certain shared taxes, one might consider revenue from shared taxes as partly autonomous, too. Unlike intergovernmental grants, tax revenue-sharing is in general fixed by law or constitution and therefore has a more permanent nature. This alternative indicator then denotes the extent to which sub-central governments (SCG) have full or at least some limited control over their tax revenues:

$$TA2 = \frac{\text{SCG own tax rev. (a) to (c)} + \text{shared tax rev. (d.1) to (d.2)}}{\text{SCG total tax revenue}} \tag{2.5}$$

### 2.3.2 Degree of Tax and Revenue Decentralisation

According to the discussion in section 2.2, decision-making autonomy represents only one dimension of decentralisation. The quantitative scope of sub-central activity has to be taken into account, too. Therefore, in the following, the receipts from the different taxes of sub-central governments (SCG)[19] are classified according to the degree of decision-making autonomy and set in relation to tax revenue of consolidated general government (GG) in order to measure the *degree of tax decentralisation*. In the case of federal states where local taxes or regional/local revenue-sharing are determined by regional governments, these are classified as autonomous taxes, since we now focus on the degree of fiscal autonomy vis-à-vis the central government. In doing so, local governments are treated as an integral part of the intermediate level of government and intergovernmental relations at the sub-central level are not taken into account.

The measures of tax decentralisation which account for autonomous own taxes of sub-central governments only (*TD1*), or, additionally, for autonomous shared taxes (*TD2*), are presented below:

$$TD1 = \frac{\text{SCG own tax revenue (a) to (c)}}{\text{GG total tax revenue}} \tag{2.6}$$

19 Regional and local levels of government are consolidated now, local taxes being classified as described below.

$$TD2 = \frac{\text{SCG own tax rev. (a) to (c)} + \text{sh. tax rev. (d.1) to (d.2)}}{\text{GG total tax revenue}} \tag{2.7}$$

In comparison to this, the conventional measure of tax decentralisation represents total subnational tax revenue as reported in financial statistics (*TD3*):

$$TD3 = \frac{\text{SCG total tax revenue (a) to (e)}}{\text{GG total tax revenue}} \tag{2.8}$$

Analogously, extending the analysis to all sources of public revenue, non-tax revenue, such as user charges or operational surplus of public enterprises, and capital revenue could be classified as own autonomous revenue.[20] From the point of view of expenditure autonomy, general purpose and unconditional specific purpose grants attach no constraints on how the funds are spent, and might therefore be classified as own revenues of subnational governments.[21] In contrast to this, conditional specific purpose grants are earmarked for particular purposes and therefore offer only little discretion concerning their use. They might therefore be allocated to the grantor. However, in terms of financial autonomy, it is only relevant whether the revenues are generated autonomously by sub-central governments, and not whether the funds can be spent independently. In contrast to revenue-sharing, general purpose grants are usually not fixed in legislation, but unilaterally during the annual budgetary process, therefore remaining at the discretion of the central government and depending on its financial situation. Since sub-central governments have no control over the amount and structure of these revenues, it seems reasonable to classify all types of intergovernmental grants as non-autonomous revenue corresponding to the OECD category (e) of tax autonomy.[22]

For reasons of aggregation across different levels of government, the corresponding *degree of revenue decentralisation* is then derived excluding intergovernmental grants received from other levels of government. Again, we can consider apart from non-tax and capital revenue only autonomous own taxes of sub-central governments (*RD1*) or autonomous own and shared taxes (*RD2*):

$$RD1 = \frac{\text{SCG own tax rev. (a) to (c)} + \text{non-tax \& capital rev.}}{\text{GG total tax rev.} + \text{non-tax \& capital rev.}} \tag{2.9}$$

$$RD2 = \frac{\text{SCG o.t.r. (a) to (c)} + \text{sh.t.r. (d.1) to (d.2)} + \text{n.-t. \& c.r.}}{\text{GG total tax rev.} + \text{non-tax \& capital rev.}} \tag{2.10}$$

[20] Due to the complexity of this area, possible limitations imposed by central legislation on the levying of user charges are not taken into account here.

[21] See, e.g., Wasylenko (1987) and Ebel and Yilmaz (2003).

[22] This is also in accordance with the OECD taxonomy which does not take into account the degree of discretion over the use of shared or ceded tax receipts. Of course, this might be different in federal or quasi-federal states where sub-central governments participate in decision-making upon the allocation of grants.

Considering all tax revenues of sub-central government irrespective of the degree of discretion, we obtain the conventional indicator of revenue decentralisation presented in section 2.2.2 (*RD3*):

$$RD3 = \frac{\text{SCG total tax rev. (a) to (e)} + \text{non-tax \& capital rev.}}{\text{GG total tax rev.} + \text{non-tax \& capital rev.}} \tag{2.11}$$

Further possible extensions of the OECD approach imply the differentiation of autonomous taxes in view of considering the degree of discretion to choose the tax instruments (compulsory vs. voluntary taxes), the limits imposed on setting tax rates or tax bases, or the distinction between own taxes and taxes levied as a surcharge on national taxes (piggybacked taxes).[23] Since any attempt to qualify the different types of autonomous taxes or other similar revenue sources by means of rankings bears serious problems of arbitrariness, we refrain from going into further detail here. Particularly the shares of autonomous own tax revenue of sub-central governments in total tax revenue of consolidated general government (indicator *TD1*) and respectively of own revenue of sub-central governments in total revenue of consolidated general government (indicator *RD1*) provide fairly good approximations of the degree of decentralisation. Since these two indicators are expected to best reflect real decision-making powers, the investigation below will focus on them.

## 2.4 A Current Overview of OECD Countries

In the following, we compare the degree of fiscal decentralisation of 23 OECD countries, employing both conventional and corrected measures. The focus lies on developed economies with long-standing democratic traditions where long time series are available.

### 2.4.1 Public Expenditures

To begin with, the degree of expenditure decentralisation is calculated using data reported by the Government Finance Statistics of the International Monetary Fund.[24] Figures 2.1 to 2.2 present direct and self-financed expenditure figures. Following the GFS classification, social security payments are considered first as a part of consolidated central government. Since they have own budgets and operate autonomously, these corporations have to be considered as a distinct centralised level of government which provides services on a nationwide scale.[25]

[23] See also OECD (1999) for a discussion.

[24] This represents the most complete international data set, containing information on sub-central levels of government with own budgets, collected over a long period of time over a large number of countries, consistent with the definitions and methods.

[25] Note that extra-budgetary accounts are included in consolidated central government, too.

Fig. 2.1: Degree of expenditure decentralisation (including social security), 1996-2001

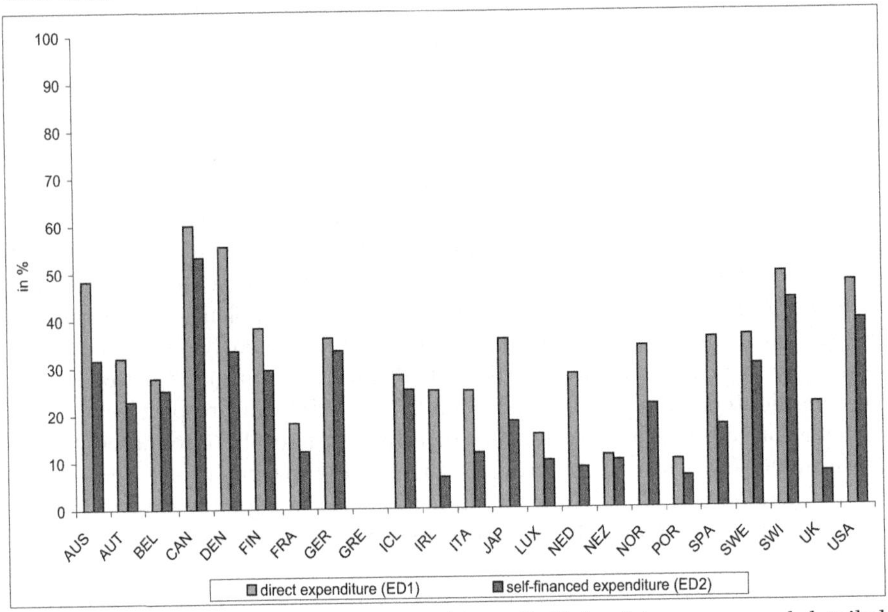


Note: Six-year-average. See Table B.4 in Appendix B for data sources and detailed figures.

The figures indicate large disparities between the different indicators. As expected, the subnational share of public spending is lower for self-financed expenditure (*ED2*) than for direct expenditure (*ED1*), since grants received from central government are deducted. When including social security, Canada is shown to be the most decentralised country in terms of both direct and self-financed expenditure, with a share of 60% and 53.2%, respectively. Other federal countries like Australia, Switzerland, or the USA, but also unitary countries like the Scandinavian countries, or Japan and Spain have also high degrees of decentralisation, particularly with respect to direct expenditure. Accordingly, Denmark is the second most decentralised country, with a direct expenditure share of 55.6%, whereas the lowest degrees of decentralisation are reported for Portugal and New Zealand.[26] In order to focus only on government functions which could reasonably be decentralised according to the theory of fiscal federalism, social security has been removed from the public sector. In this case, Switzerland proves to be the most decentralised country, with a share of 78.2% of consolidated direct expenditure, being followed by Germany, Canada, Spain and Japan.

[26] Though no current figures are available, Greece is expected to have a very low degree of decentralisation, too.

Fig. 2.2: Degree of expenditure decentralisation (excluding social security), 1996-2001

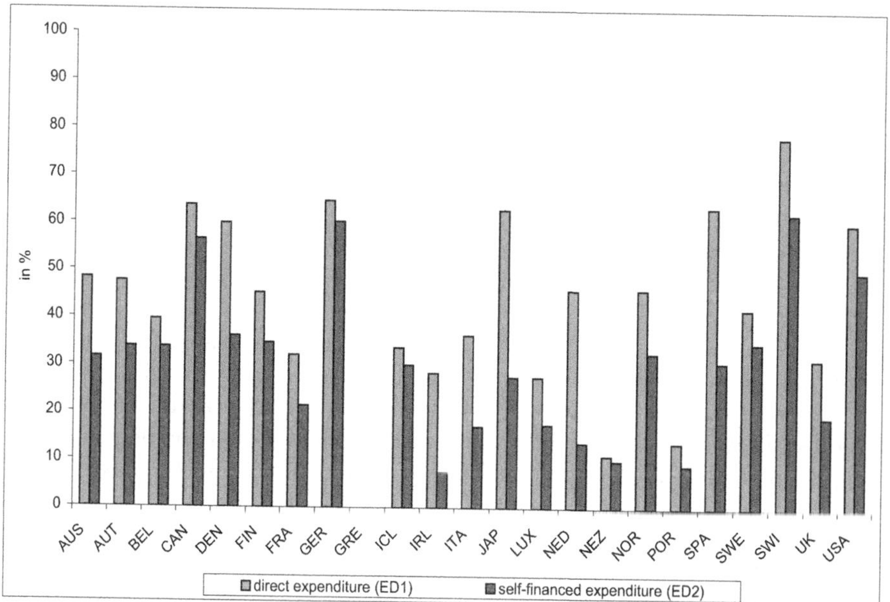


Note: Six-year-average. See Table B.4 in Appendix B for data sources and detailed figures.

### 2.4.2 Fiscal Autonomy and Revenue Decentralisation

Using the most recent data issued by the Revenue Statistics, we can now provide an update of the OECD (1999) classification of tax raising autonomy of sub-central governments. For this purpose, each sub-central tax has been evaluated on an annual basis during the period of investigation in terms of decision-making authority. Since we focus on developed economies with long-standing democratic traditions, certain countries reported in the OECD survey are not considered here, instead including some new countries.[27] Going beyond the OECD approach which only provides a classification of the different taxes, the present study derives current figures on both revenue autonomy of sub-central governments and the degree of tax and revenue decentralisation, applying the different measurement concepts described in section 2.3.2.

For reasons of consistency and comparability, the degree of tax autonomy is only derived according to the provisions fixed in legislation, and, particularly, the extent of participation of sub-central governments in decision-making. Therefore, actual implementation is not taken into account, focusing only on

[27] The new countries included here are Australia, Canada, France, Greece, Ireland, Italy, Luxembourg, and the United States.

the "potential" degree of fiscal autonomy.[28] As far as possible, the different tiers of subnational government are dealt with separately. In doing so, one must take into account that, especially in federal countries, local government taxes are regulated by regional or state legislation, without implication of the central government. Therefore, own local taxes and taxes shared with regional or state governments have to be classified in accordance with the degree of control exercised by the superior level of government.

To begin with, Table 2.2 presents most recent figures for the classification of different sub-central government taxes according to the scheme proposed by the OECD. The first three columns indicate a very high degree of fiscal autonomy in most OECD countries, sub-central governments controlling nearly all tax revenue accruing to them.[29] This is especially the case for state or local governments in federal states like Australia,[30] Canada, Switzerland, or the USA, as well as for local governments in unitary states like the Scandinavian countries, Netherlands, or the UK. In contrast to this, state and, to a lesser extent, local governments in Austria and Germany barely enjoy true fiscal autonomy. Only when taking into consideration the degree of participation in decision-making on legislation and allocation of shared taxes, a certain degree of autonomy can be ascribed to these countries. This provides some quantitative evidence for the widespread view in public finance literature which describes both countries as centralised federal states. Local governments in Greece, Ireland and Portugal are also found to rely heavily on non-autonomous revenue.

In order to compare the degree of subnational fiscal autonomy across countries, Figure 2.3 illustrates the two indicators of tax autonomy for consolidated sub-central levels of government. According to indicator *TA1*, sub-central governments in Austria and Germany have the lowest degree of real tax autonomy among the OECD countries considered here, roughly comparable to that of Greek local governments.

Setting tax revenues of sub-central government in relation to tax revenue of consolidated general government, Figure 2.4 portrays the different measures of tax decentralisation for the OECD countries. In terms of real fiscal autonomy (indicator *TD1*), Greece, Ireland, Austria, Portugal, and the United Kingdom exhibit the lowest degrees of decentralisation with values below 5%. Within this context, note that the relative scope of sub-central government activity

28 For this reason, our classification of certain taxes differs from that of the OECD survey. Just to give an example, in Norway, local governments choose de facto the same maximum local income tax rate, although, in principle, variation is allowed. Whereas the OECD study therefore classifies this tax as a shared tax, the revenue-split of which is determined unilaterally by the central government (d.4), we consider this tax as "potentially" autonomous (b).

29 However, note that for certain countries the data allows no distinction between the different tiers of sub-central government.

30 On the other hand, Australian states themselves are highly centralised, granting no real fiscal autonomy to their municipalities.

Table 2.2: Taxes of sub-central levels of government according to the degree of autonomy, 2001

| Country | Lev. gov. | (a) | (b) | (c) | (d.1) | (d.2) | (d.3) | (d.4) | (e) |
|---|---|---|---|---|---|---|---|---|---|
| AUS | Regional | 100.0 | | | | | | | |
| | Local | | | | | | | | 100.0 |
| AUT | Regional | | 2.4 | | | 97.6 | | | |
| | Local | 5.2 | 11.2 | | | 83.6 | | | |
| BEL | Reg./Loc.[a] | 3.7 | 51.3 | | | 44.4 | 0.3 | 0.3 | |
| CAN | Regional | 60.0 | 38.7 | | 1.3 | | | | |
| | Local | 7.9 | 87.3 | | | | 4.8 | | |
| DEN | Local | | 94.4 | | | | 3.5 | | 2.1 |
| FIN | Reg./Loc.[a] | 0.0 | 83.0 | | | | 17.0 | | |
| FRA | Reg./Loc.[a] | | 99.0 | | | | 0.2 | | 0.8 |
| GER | Regional | | | | | 100.0 | | | |
| | Local | 1.0 | 55.3 | | | 43.6 | | | |
| GRE | Local | | 13.9 | | | | 41.9 | | 44.2 |
| ICL | Local | 7.2 | 92.8 | | | | | | |
| IRL | Local | | 55.1 | | | | | | 44.9 |
| ITA | Reg./Loc.[a] | | 90.6 | | | | 3.3 | | 6.1 |
| JAP | Local | 0.1 | 91.1 | | | | | | 8.8 |
| LUX | Local | 0.2 | 99.4 | | | | 0.4 | | |
| NED | Regional | | 100.0 | | | | | | |
| | Local | 3.3 | 96.7 | | | | | | |
| NEZ | Reg./Loc.[a] | 98.8 | | | | | | | 1.2 |
| NOR | Local | | 98.2 | | | | 1.8 | | |
| POR | Reg./Loc.[a] | 6.7 | 29.9 | | | | 13.9 | | 49.5 |
| SPA | Reg./Loc.[a] | 51.3 | 35.0 | | | 5.6 | 8.1 | | |
| SWE | Reg./Loc.[a] | 0.0 | 100.0 | | | | | | |
| SWI | Regional | 88.4 | | | 5.5 | 6.1 | | | |
| | Local | | 100.0 | | | | | | |
| UK | Local | | 100.0 | | | | | | |
| USA | Regional | 100.0 | | | | | | | |
| | Local | 71.4 | 28.6 | | | | | | |

Note: Tax revenue by degree of autonomy, as per cent of total tax revenue of sub-central government. In case of multiple regional or local tiers of government, these are consolidated at each corresponding level of government. [a]Due to problems of data identification, local and regional levels of government are consolidated. See Table B.1 in Appendix B for an overview of the government structures. Data source: OECD, Revenue Statistics, 2003. Source for tax classification: see Tables 2.1 and 2.3.

Fig. 2.3: Degree of tax autonomy of sub-central government, 1996-2001

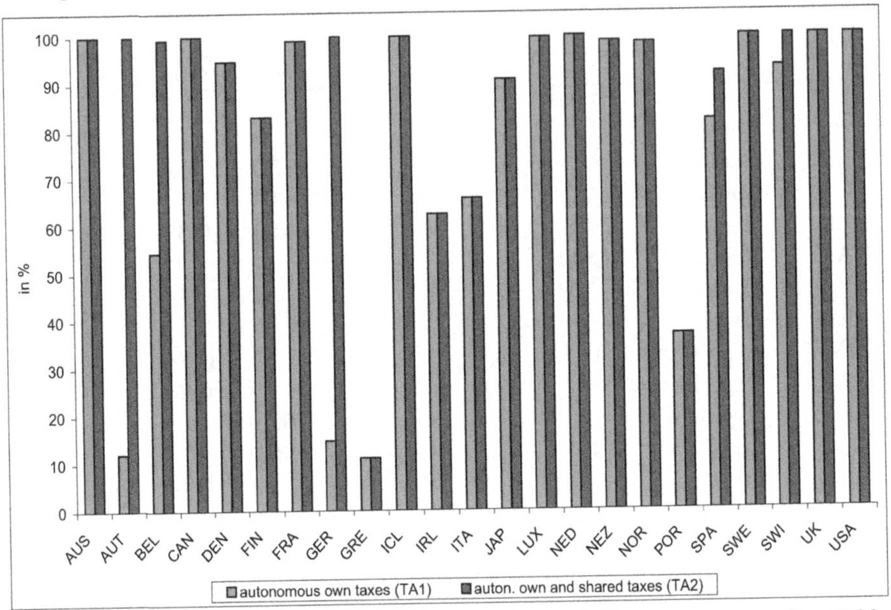


Note: Local and regional governments are consolidated. Six-year-average. See Table 2.3 for data sources and detailed figures.

plays an important role. Although local governments in certain countries like Netherlands, New Zealand, or the UK have maximum levels of fiscal autonomy, their share in total public revenues is rather small. As expected, federal states like Switzerland (53.9%), Canada (52.4%), and the USA (36.3%) belong to the most decentralised countries. However, unitary countries like Sweden (43.7%), Denmark (31.8%), and Japan (36.7%) also exhibit very high degrees of tax decentralisation, thus contradicting, at least in terms of budgets, the presumption that single-tiered or unitary systems are more centralised than multi-tiered or federal systems. With a share of 0.2% of total tax revenue, Greece is the most centralised country in terms of tax autonomy.

The situation changes considerably for countries like Austria, Belgium, or Germany, when shared taxes co-determined by sub-central levels of government are further taken into account (indicator *TD2*). Considerable differences between the conventional measure of decentralisation using all tax revenues accruing to sub-central governments (indicator *TD3*) and the measure accounting for real fiscal autonomy (indicator *TD1*) are also found for Finland, Greece, Ireland, Italy, Japan, Portugal, and Spain. This picture clearly illustrates that unadjusted revenue shares reflect the degree of fiscal decentralisation correctly only to the extent to which sub-central governments have entire control upon their revenue, as is the case, e.g., in the USA, Canada, or Sweden. For most countries, however, and particularly Austria, Belgium, Germany, or Portugal, the degree of real fiscal decentralisation is clearly overestimated by the indicators commonly used in empirical studies. For instance, accounting for tax autonomy, the degree of tax decentralisation of Germany amounts to only 7.3%, as compared to 49.6% when considering all sub-central government tax revenues.

Fig. 2.4: Degree of tax decentralisation, 1996-2001

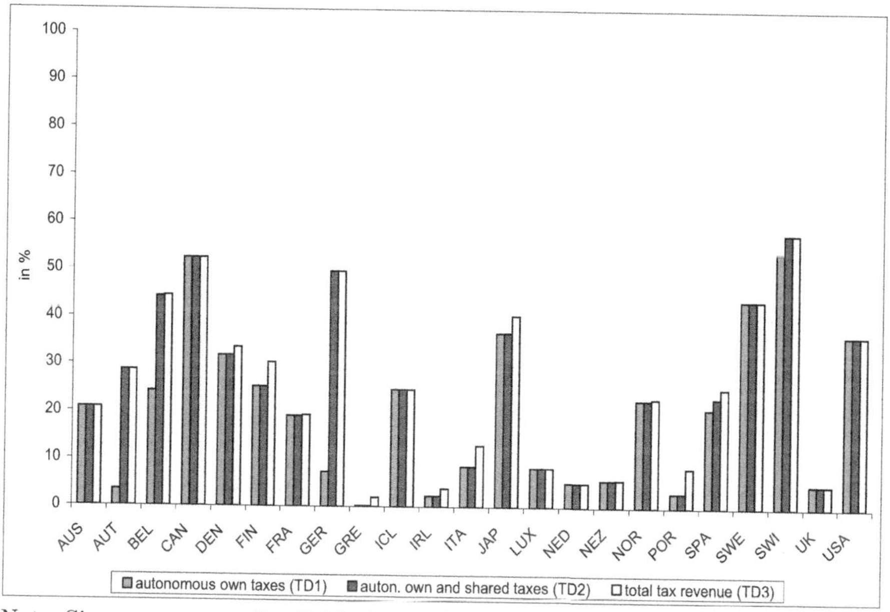


Note: Six year average. See Table B.9 in Appendix B for data sources and detailed figures.

With respect to total own revenue of sub-central governments, Figure 2.5 indicates quite similar patterns. Note, however, that with few exceptions the degree of decentralisation is generally higher for total revenue as compared to tax revenue. Particularly Australia, Austria, Germany, Ireland, the Netherlands, and the USA reflect significant reliance of local governments on non tax revenue such as user charges or surpluses of public enterprises. In general, the degree of decentralisation is found to be lower for revenue than for expenditure when comparing the unadjusted indicators, indicating positive net vertical transfers to sub-central levels of government. In most cases, total own revenue figures (*RD3*) prove to be a good approximation of self-financed expenditure (*ED2*), since the latter indicate the level of government financing for the provision of public services.

Fig. 2.5: Degree of revenue decentralisation, 1996-2001

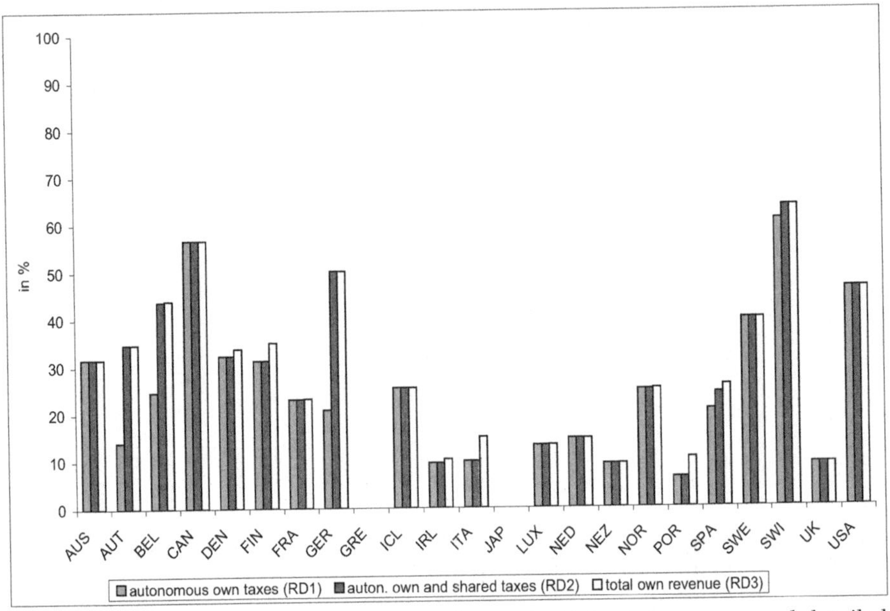


Note: Six-year-average. See Table B.11 in Appendix B for data sources and detailed figures.

These approaches to quantifying tax-raising autonomy still suffer, however, from certain limitations related to deviations between practice and legal provisions, and to problems of insufficiently disaggregated data. Concerning the latter aspect, for certain countries the data available allow no distinction between regional and local governments, or between different tiers within the same level of government.[31] Also, the 4-digit tax classification of the Revenue Statistics is often not detailed enough. The classification of some minor taxes according to the degree of autonomy might therefore be partly erroneous. Another major problem is related to the horizontal aggregation of data across jurisdictions belonging to the same level of government, but which are vested with different competencies.[32] This is particularly the case in the regions with special status in France, Italy, and Spain, or in the Portuguese islands of Madeira and Azores, and Scotland, Wales and Northern Ireland in the United Kingdom, which enjoy a certain degree of home rule. Furthermore, especially in federal states, where the competencies of local governments are determined by state legislation or constitution (e.g., USA, Canada, Switzer-

[31] The OECD (1999) survey reports figures for different local and regional levels of government, however, only for 1995.

[32] This is the case referred to as asymmetric fiscal decentralisation in section 2.2. See, also, IMF (2001) with respect to problems of horizontal aggregation.

land, Australia), there are considerable inter-state differences in the degree of tax autonomy granted to local governments. A more correct measure should therefore disaggregate tax revenue data by jurisdictions. However, due to the lack of appropriate data, this is not feasible in the present analysis. Finally, as already pointed to in section 2.2, the general question still arises whether countries with an intermediate level of government are to be considered as more decentralised than countries without such a level, even if the degree of fiscal decentralisation might be the same.

Despite these limitations, the indicators accounting for real fiscal autonomy presented above (*TD1* and *RD1*) definitely contribute to the correct measurement of fiscal decentralisation.[33]

## 2.5 Fiscal Decentralisation Trends in OECD Countries

In the following, the development of the vertical government structure of OECD countries is analysed in order to detect common decentralisation trends. Using annual data reported by the IMF and the OECD, both conventional measures of decentralisation and the indicators accounting for decision-making competencies are employed.

### 2.5.1 Public Expenditures

Two most prominent examples of increased fiscal decentralisation during the last three decades are certainly Belgium and Spain.[34] In Belgium, the process of decentralisation started in 1970 with the creation of regions and communities and their subsequent endowment with expenditure and tax-raising competencies in the 1980s, and culminated in the formation of a federal state in 1994. After the end of the Franco regime, local autonomy has been re-established in Spain and legislative powers and taxes have been transferred particularly to the newly created autonomous regions. Yet, the process of devolution is still open in both countries. Similarly, in Canada increasing separatism has led to the strengthening of autonomy for Québec. Apart from these examples, devolution of expenditure and tax-raising powers, particularly to regional governments, can be observed in France, Italy, Denmark, Portugal and Greece. Most recently, in the United Kingdom Scottish and Welsh parliaments have been created and endowed with some limited legislative and administrative

[33] Accordingly, in the present sample, the coefficient of correlation between the degree of tax autonomy (*TA1*) and the corresponding degree of tax decentralisation including only autonomous own taxes (*TD1*) is 0.50, as compared to 0.14 when considering the common measure of tax decentralisation (*TD3*).

[34] A broad overview of the most significant institutional changes with respect to both expenditure and tax-raising competencies is provided in Tables B.2 and B.3 in Appendix B. See, also, OECD (1997) for a description of recent changes in responsibilities across levels of government.

autonomy. And even in federal countries like Germany or Austria decentralisation of responsibilities is currently gaining importance in the political debate.

To begin with, Figure 2.6 compares the degree of fiscal decentralisation in terms of public expenditures at the beginning of the 1970s and the end of the 1990s, considering period-averaged figures. Drawing on the Government Finance Statistics of the International Monetary Fund for the period 1970 to 2001,[35] consolidated sub-central government expenditure is set in relation to consolidated general government expenditure, applying the conventional concepts described above.

Fig. 2.6: Trends in expenditure decentralisation (including social security), 1970-2001

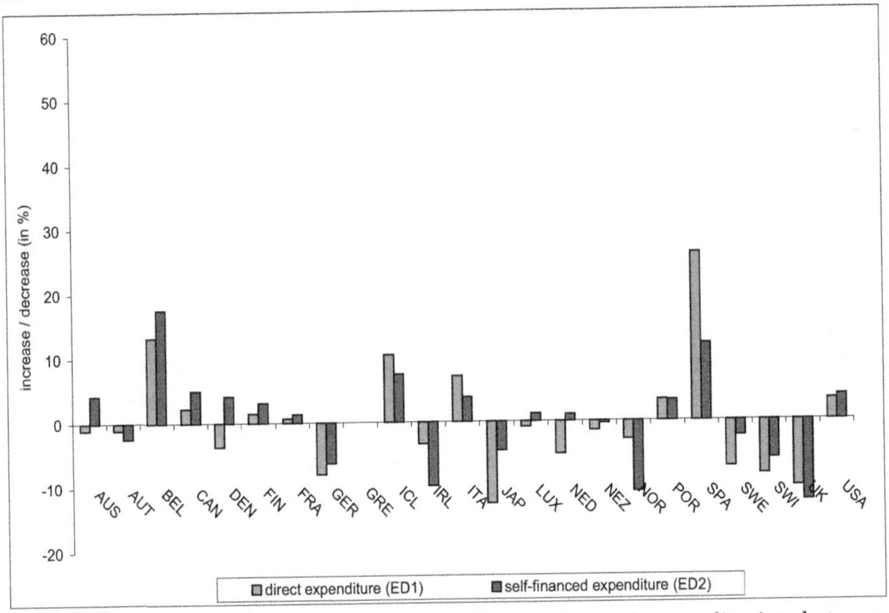


Note: Increase or decrease in the degree of expenditure decentralisation between 1970-1975 and 1996-2001, six-year-averages. See Table B.4 in Appendix B for data sources and detailed figures.

At first glance, the expenditure figures indicate no uniform pattern of development across OECD countries. As a result of the important constitutional changes, the subnational share of expenditure increased especially in

35 The time periods available for the individual countries are of different length. The OECD National Accounts also provide long time series, which, however, suffer from certain difficulties of calculation and missing current data.

Fig. 2.7: Trends in expenditure decentralisation (excluding social security), 1970-2001

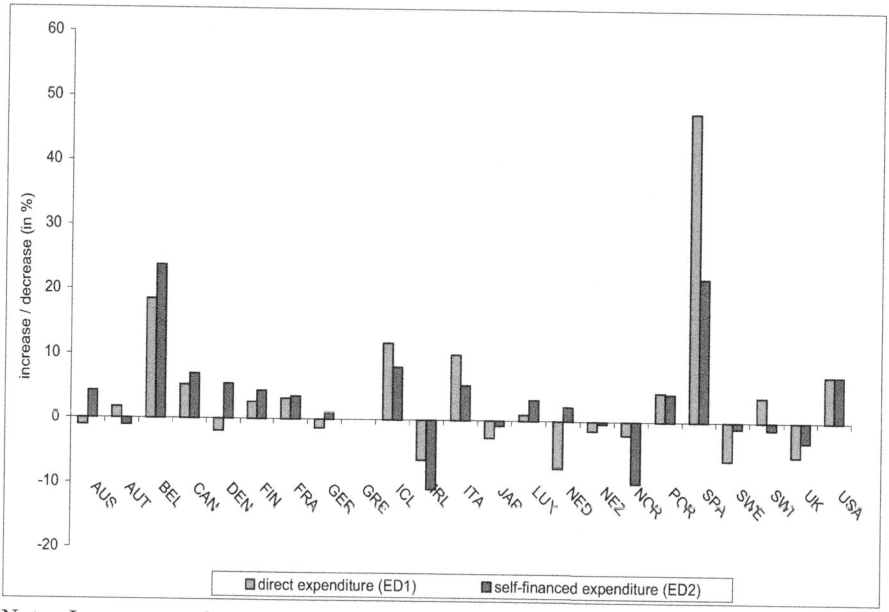


Note: Increase or decrease in the degree of expenditure decentralisation between 1970-1975 and 1996-2001, six-year-averages. See Table B.4 in Appendix B for data sources and detailed figures.

Belgium[36] and Spain, and also to a lesser extent in Canada, Finland, France, Iceland, Italy, Portugal, and the USA. In contrast to this, in many countries, among others Germany, Ireland, Norway, the United Kingdom, and even Switzerland, the development went in the opposite direction. Only with respect to self-financed expenditure, there is a decentralisation trend during the period of investigation in a majority of OECD countries. Accordingly, the median degree of decentralisation rose slightly from 21.3% during 1970/1975 to 22.3% during 1996/2001. Furthermore, European Union countries are found to be on average more centralised than other OECD countries.

The picture changes to some extent when taking a closer look at the composition of central government expenditure. When excluding social security, Figure 2.7 reveals on average a more pronounced process of decentralisation both in EU- and Non-EU-countries with respect to direct expenditure, 12 out

[36] Note that the GFS classification considers Belgian regions and communities as central government units. Therefore, previous studies using these data considerably underestimate the degree of fiscal decentralisation in Belgium, particularly from 1989 onwards. We use instead national statistics which distinguish the different levels of subnational government.

of 22 countries having higher decentralisation levels at the end of the 1990s. A strong process of decentralisation of direct spending is notably found for Spain. These quantitative figures seem to reflect quite well the devolution of competencies and the strengthening of political autonomy of sub-central governments observed during the last decades. The partly contradicting pieces of evidence in case of excluding social security also indicate that the observed tendency to decentralise certain government activities apparently interfered with the significant rise of the welfare state in most OECD countries.

### 2.5.2 Fiscal Autonomy and Revenue Decentralisation

According to the different patterns of development for direct and self-financed expenditure, central government grants to lower levels of government seemingly tend to be substituted by own revenues. Data on the share of revenue from formally own sources in total revenue of sub-central government reported by the IMF[37] confirm this. For regional, as well as for local governments we find evidence for increasing reliance on revenue from own sources – irrespective of the degree of control upon their allocation. Against the general trend, the relative importance of intergovernmental grants has increased for local governments in Germany, Ireland, Norway, and, particularly, the United Kingdom. The figures also indicate that local governments in Australia, Austria, Greece, Iceland, New Zealand, Norway and Switzerland, and "Länder" governments in Germany rely on average only to a minor extent on grants from other levels of government.

However, as discussed in section 2.2.2, no clear conclusions can be drawn from these figures, since budgetary data not adjusted for decision-making structures provide no clear information whether indeed fiscal powers have been transferred to lower levels of government in the course of time. Therefore, we employ the indicators presented in section 2.3 in order to account for decision-making autonomy. The analysis covers the period 1965-2001 for which data from OECD Revenue Statistics are available. Based on 23 comprehensive surveys of national financial laws and constitutions for the period of investigation, revenue data and the classification of autonomy are adjusted for each sub-central government tax on an annual basis for changes occurring in the legal provisions regarding the assignment of tax-raising powers.[38]

Table 2.3 shows that the degree of tax autonomy of sub-central governments barely changed over time. According to indicator *TA1*, a considerable increase in fiscal autonomy took place in France, especially owing to the laws granting tax-raising powers to regions, départements and municipalities at

[37] See Table B.5 in Appendix B for own revenue figures by level of sub-central government.

[38] The overview presented in Tables B.2 and B.3 in Appendix B provides only a very broad description of the most important trends in tax-raising autonomy. For the classification of taxes we have compiled more detailed annual information on the legislative competencies of sub-central governments.

the beginning of the 1980s. With transition to democracy, sub-central governments in Greece, Portugal, and Spain were assigned some taxes formerly allocated at the central level and obtained more legislative powers over already existing local taxes. In contrast to this, sub-central government reliance on autonomous taxes has significantly declined in Ireland.

However, note that the measure of fiscal autonomy is quite sensitive to changes in the assignment of taxes and tax competencies and to business cycles. Therefore, great leaps should be treated with caution. As illustrated by the cases of Belgium or Italy, consolidated data on different tiers of sub-central government may be misleading, too. The creation and endowment of regional governments with competencies and own revenues in both countries reduced the consolidated degree of tax autonomy.[39] On the other hand, this implied an increase in the degree of tax decentralisation, which will be seen later. These problems are therefore solved when focusing instead on the degree of decentralisation which accounts for the scope of sub-central government activity.

The development of the degree of tax and revenue decentralisation during the period 1965-2001 is depicted in Figures 2.8 and 2.9 using the three different indicators elaborated in section 2.3.[40] Though considerably differing in the level of decentralisation measured, the indicators mostly confirm the trend towards an increasing role of sub-central governments in a majority of OECD countries. [41] This is also true, albeit to a lesser extent, when considering only EU member countries. Even though there is no uniform pattern of development across OECD countries, the median degree of tax decentralisation rose considerably from 12.1% during 1965/1970 to 20.8% during 1996/2001. Though not entirely comparable, the trends for total revenue of sub-central governments including other revenue from own sources (*RD1-RD3*) are quite similar to those reported for tax revenue. An empirical verification for different decentralisation measures corroborate those findings, providing evidence for a statistically significant positive linear trend.[42]

Focusing on the indicator which best represents tax decentralisation (*TD1*), we notice a significant process of fiscal decentralisation in Belgium (from 6.7% to 24.2%), France (from 1.1% to 19.2%), and Spain (from 5.1% to 20.8%). Apart from these extreme cases, decentralisation trends are additionally reported in Iceland, Italy, Japan, Portugal, and Sweden. On the other hand, sub-central government has been pushed back in Ireland, New Zealand,

---

39 This is especially due to the assignment of shares in national tax receipts.

40 Note that data on subnational total revenue are missing for Greece and Japan, and are only available from 1975 on for the other countries. The entire time series on the two most appropriate measures of tax and revenue decentralisation, *TD1* and *RD1*, are reported in the Tables B.8 and B.10 in Appendix B.

41 Earlier OECD tax revenue statistics even report a decentralisation trend since the 1950s, see OECD (1981).

42 The regression results for different indicators of decentralisation are provided in Table B.7 in Appendix B.

Table 2.3: Degree of tax autonomy of sub-central government, 1965-2001

| Country | Lev. gov. | Auton. own taxes (TA1) | | Auton. own & shared taxes (TA2) | |
|---|---|---|---|---|---|
| | | 1965-1970 | 1996-2001 | 1965-1970 | 1996-2001 |
| AUS | Regional | 100.0 | 100.0 | 100.0 | 100.0 |
| | Local | 0.0 | 0.0 | 0.0 | 0.0 |
| AUT | Regional | 1.9[a] | 2.5 | 100.0 | 100.0 |
| | Local | 16.9[a] | 18.7 | 100.0 | 100.0 |
| BEL | Reg./Loc.[c] | 93.7 | 54.5 | 93.7 | 99.4 |
| CAN | Regional | 100.0 | 98.9 | 100.0 | 100.0 |
| | Local | 100.0 | 95.0 | 100.0 | 95.0 |
| DEN | Local | 96.7[a] | 94.8 | 96.7[a] | 94.8 |
| FIN | Reg./Loc.[c] | 89.7 | 83.1 | 89.7 | 83.1 |
| FRA | Reg./Loc.[c] | 12.1[b] | 99.1 | 12.1[b] | 99.1 |
| GER | Regional | 0.0 | 0.0 | 100.0 | 100.0 |
| | Local | 55.6[a] | 57.5 | 100.0 | 100.0 |
| GRE | Local | 6.4[a] | 11.1 | 6.4[a] | 11.1 |
| ICL | Local | 100.0 | 100.0 | 100.0 | 100.0 |
| IRL | Local | 100.0 | 62.5 | 100.0 | 62.5 |
| ITA | Reg./Loc.[c] | 95.9 | 65.8 | 95.9 | 65.8 |
| JAP | Local | 87.5 | 90.8 | 87.5 | 90.8 |
| LUX | Local | 100.0 | 99.7 | 100.0 | 99.7 |
| NED | Regional | | 100.0 | | 100.0 |
| | Local | 100.0 | 100.0 | 100.0 | 100.0 |
| NEZ | Reg./Loc.[c] | 100.0 | 98.8 | 100.0 | 98.8 |
| NOR | Local | 100.0 | 98.5 | 100.0 | 98.5 |
| POR | Reg./Loc.[c] | 0.0 | 36.9 | 0.0 | 36.9 |
| SPA | Reg./Loc.[c] | 65.4[a] | 82.1 | 65.4[a] | 92.0 |
| SWE | Regional | 100.0 | 100.0 | 100.0 | 100.0 |
| | Local | 100.0 | 100.0 | 100.0 | 100.0 |
| SWI | Regional | 92.8 | 88.8 | 100.0 | 100.0 |
| | Local | 100.0 | 100.0 | 100.0 | 100.0 |
| UK | Local | 100.0 | 100.0 | 100.0 | 100.0 |
| USA | Regional | 100.0 | 100.0 | 100.0 | 100.0 |
| | Local | 100.0 | 100.0 | 100.0 | 100.0 |

Note: Tax revenue by degree of autonomy, as per cent of total tax revenue of sub-central government. In case of various regional or local tiers of government, these are consolidated at each corresponding level of government; six-year-average. [a] 1973-75; [b] 1970; [c] due to problems of identification, local and regional level of government are consolidated. Data source: OECD, Revenue Statistics. Source for tax classification: OECD (1997, 1999, 2002b), Committee of the Regions (1999, 2000, 2001), European Commission (2002), Döhler (2002), Engel and van Ginderachter (1992), Fossatti and Panella (1999), Norton (1994), Ter-Minassian (1997), Rahmann et al. (1994), different country studies provided by the Council of Europe, and national fiscal constitutions and laws. Own calculations.

Norway, and the United Kingdom. This quantitative evidence seems to reflect very well the institutional changes which took place in these countries.

With minor exceptions, this pattern of development is generally confirmed when adding revenue from shared taxes upon the allocation of which sub-central governments have significant control (*TD2*), or when considering total tax receipts irrespective of decision-making structures (*TD3*). However, the magnitude of the changes varies considerably depending on the indicator employed.

Fig. 2.8: Trends in tax decentralisation, 1965-2001

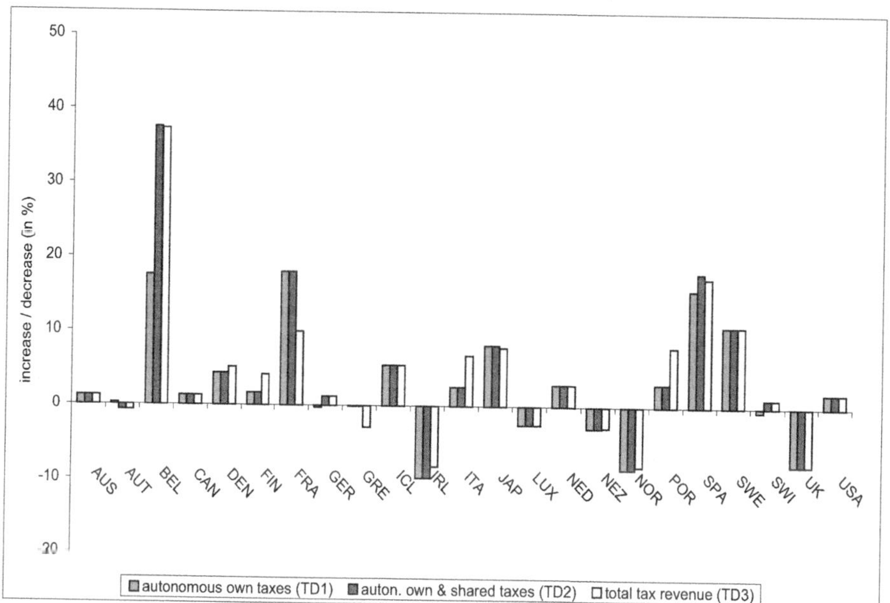


Note: Increase or decrease in the degree of tax decentralisation between 1965-1970 and 1996-2001, six-year-averages. See Table B.9 in Appendix B for data sources and detailed figures.

With regard to Germany, these figures confirm the results of Blankart's (2000) analysis, which identifies a process of "hidden centralisation" in Germany. Accordingly, the degree of tax decentralisation dropped from 40% in 1950 to 7% in 1995.[43] At the same time the trend in Switzerland went in the

[43] The constitutional reforms in 1955 and 1969 transferred certain taxes from the Länder to the federal government and extended the scope of concurrent legislation. However, as will be shown in chapter 5, no significant changes occurred in the allocation of legislative powers. Since OECD data for Germany are only available from 1973 on, we cannot verify quantitatively the long-term centralisation trend indicated by Blankart.

Fig. 2.9: Trends in revenue decentralisation, 1975-2001

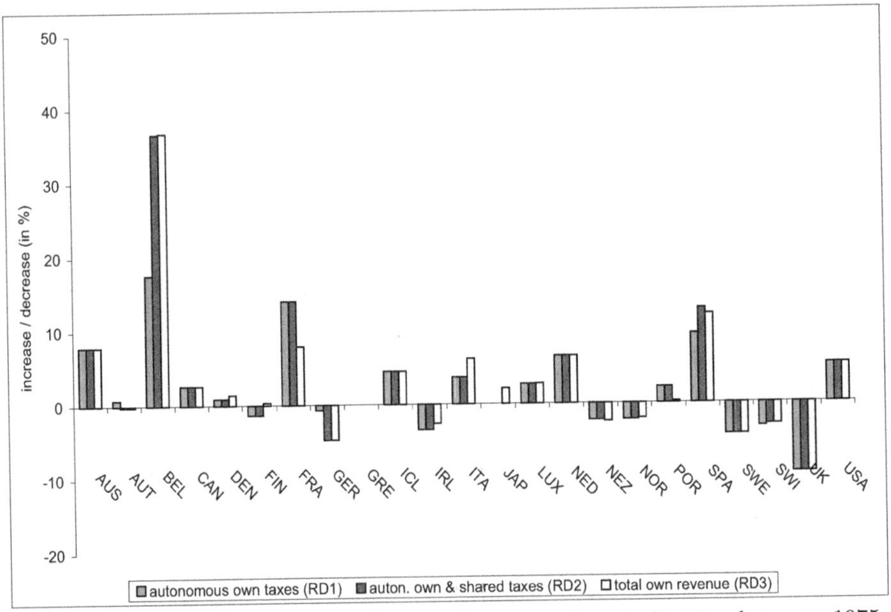


Note: Increase or decrease in the degree of revenue decentralisation between 1975-1980 and 1996-2001, six-year-averages. See Table B.11 in Appendix B for data sources and detailed figures.

opposite direction, the degree of tax decentralisation increasing to 53%. Note that Blankart's figures for 1995 correspond to our own calculations reported in the third column of Table B.9 in Appendix B.

Even if these measures of fiscal decentralisation account for decision-making competencies, they still provide no remedy to all limitations of aggregate fiscal measures described in section 2.2.2. Tax bases of central and sub-central governments typically have different elasticities. Therefore, business cycles automatically cause fluctuations in the tax revenue indicators, even though the assignment of competencies remains unchanged. For example, the subnational share of total tax revenue might fall when local governments rely heavily on taxing relatively mobile bases.[44] Yet, this could not be interpreted as increasing fiscal centralisation. By comparing period-averaged figures, some of these problems can be solved.

On the other hand, the transfer of tax-raising powers to sub-central levels of government may not be reflected in a corresponding increase in the aggregate indicator, when, for instance, revenues of central government rise simultaneously. Also, the shift from the positive to the regulatory state observed since

[44] See OECD (2003).

the late 1970s[45] which implies increasing recourse of central governments to rules, norms, and minimum quality standards, is not captured by fiscal data.

However, in comparison to conventional measures, indicators accounting for decision-making structures have the definite advantage of providing a better distinction between real fiscal decentralisation and sheer revenue effects in most cases. For example, even if the attribution of tax receipts to levels of government remains unchanged, the extension of legislative competencies upon these taxes is reflected by an increase in these indicators of decentralisation. Therefore, besides providing a better approximation for the actual level of fiscal decentralisation, the corrected indicator also reflects more accurately changes in the vertical government structure.

## 2.6 Discussion and Conclusions

This chapter has given an analysis of the problems encountered in measuring the degree of fiscal decentralisation and has provided an overview of recent international trends. The new contribution consists both in deriving alternative measures of decentralisation, and in providing more recent figures and a comprehensive analysis of the long-term development of vertical government structures in OECD countries.

Based on an analytical framework provided by the OECD for the classification of local taxes according to the degree of discretion of sub-central governments, the degree of fiscal decentralisation is measured by the share of sub-central government revenue from those taxes or other resources which are significantly controlled by them in total tax or other revenue of consolidated general government. Using annual data for over 30 years reported by the Revenue Statistics and taking account of changes in the assignment of tax-raising powers to sub-central governments on an annual basis, new time series are provided for 23 OECD countries, including also countries not considered in the OECD study.

The general discussion and the comparison of figures based on different measurement concepts indicate that common fiscal indicators tend to considerably overestimate the extent of fiscal decentralisation or fiscal autonomy in most countries. Especially federal countries like Germany or Austria, where sub-central governments have only limited autonomy upon taxation, are shown to be more centralised than unitary countries like Denmark or France. Only when sub-central governments have considerable control over their financial resources, common indicators are reasonable proxies of public sector decentralisation.

With respect to the development over time, both conventional and improved indicators provide strong evidence for increasing fiscal decentralisation in a majority of OECD countries during the last three decades. Particularly

[45] See Majone (1997).

sub-central governments in Spain, Belgium, France, and Italy increasingly rely on own autonomous revenues. However, no uniform pattern could be determined, several countries also exhibit tendencies to centralise government activity. Also, with few important exceptions, vertical government structures seem to change only gradually in the course of time, displaying significant inertia. Therefore, even longer periods of investigation would be necessary to detect significant long-term trends.

To conclude, the conventional indicators using expenditure and revenue shares are shown to often misrepresent the actual level of fiscal decentralisation, therefore unsuitable for cross-country comparisons. On the other hand, even though differing considerably in magnitude, both conventional and adjusted fiscal indicators seem to perform well in describing long-term trends in the public sector. Despite several shortcomings related to aggregation and to the use of budgetary data, when adjusted for decision-making structures, expenditure and revenue shares still have the definite advantage of being operational. The new data set provided in this chapter therefore contributes to improving empirical studies on fiscal decentralisation.

Also, as suggested in this chapter, the analysis of fiscal decentralisation could analogously be extended to classify sub-central expenditure or borrowing according to the degree of autonomy. Generally speaking, it seems reasonable to use a set of different indicators instead of a single measure in order to represent the different aspects of decentralisation. However, the measure of decentralisation to be selected in empirical studies ultimately depends on the specific purpose of the investigation.

# 3

# Costs, Preferences, and Institutions: The Determinants of Fiscal Decentralisation

## 3.1 Introduction

The purpose of this chapter is to verify empirically the general factors determining cross-national differences in the degree of public sector decentralisation.

General reference for the analysis of vertical government structures is the theory of fiscal federalism in the tradition of Musgrave (1959) and Oates (1972).[1] According to the "Decentralisation Theorem", the efficient allocation of government functions between different layers of government is determined by the trade-off between the benefits of decentralised provision of public goods, which allows for differentiation according to local preferences and conditions, and the costs of missing coordination in case of interjurisdictional spillovers and potential economies of scale. Consequently, national public goods, like defence, as well as income redistribution and macroeconomic stabilisation are more efficiently provided by the central government, whereas local public goods with geographically limited benefits should typically be in the competency of local governments.

Hence, the optimal degree of decentralisation of the public sector depends both on the degree of interjurisdictional heterogeneity and the characteristics of the public goods supplied. The welfare-maximising view, however, fails to explain enduring deviations from the optimum in the real world. This is, for example, illustrated by the persistence of different levels of decentralisation among countries with similar economic and preference structures, or by significant changes in vertical government structures in the course of time, in spite of unchanged economic and preference structures. First, the theoretical considerations hinge on the crucial assumptions of missing coordination between local governments, and of policy uniformity in the case of centralisation, which

[1] See, also, Olson (1969), and Inman and Rubinfeld (1997), among others.

in general are both theoretically and empirically dismissed.[2] Another reason may be related to the problems of preference revelation and excludability described in the literature on public goods. But the most important limitation consists in neglecting the role of elected policy makers and of decision-making processes in democracies.

The importance of decision-making rules is already emphasised by Oates (1972: 18), who pointed out that "[...]it is the extent to which the decisions themselves reflect local interests that matters for the economist, and constitutional structure assumes importance only to the degree that it affects the responsiveness of the provision of local services to local preferences." Institutions have long time been viewed as "veils" which were supposed not to affect policy outcomes, the literature usually assuming that policies are in line with the preferences of the median voter. As shown by recent theoretical and empirical work, the median voter model does not always hold, institutional rules actually playing an important role. This suggests the explicit consideration of the collective decision-making process and of the institutional set-up in explaining the degree of fiscal decentralisation.

The Leviathan theory in the tradition of Brennan and Buchanan (1980) argues that decentralisation leads to efficiency enhancing fiscal competition and constrains revenue-maximising activities of governments.[3] Yet, in spite of decentralisation, local governments may cooperate in order to establish political cartels, the result being inefficiently high public spending and taxation. Without considering the extreme case of revenue-maximising Leviathans, more recent theoretical contributions of Besley and Coate (2003), Lockwood (2002, 2004), and Redoano and Scharf (2004), among others, show that preferences and technologies, as well as political decision-making processes and the underlying institutional rules determine the choice between centralisation or decentralisation.

These political-economic considerations, however, have only partly been addressed in empirical studies. Most of the empirical work deals with the determinants of the degree of decentralisation as derived from the traditional theory of fiscal federalism, mostly using cross-sectional analyses of industrial and developing countries, or of subnational governments.[4] In general, the results support the "Decentralisation Theorem" which illustrates that particularly heterogeneous countries or jurisdictions are more decentralised. The role of collective decision-making and of institutional rules has instead been analysed mostly with respect to the level of public spending and revenue

[2] Some recent contributions, e.g., Lockwood (2002) and Schwager (1999b), depart from the uniformity assumption. In practice, centralised systems usually differentiate the levels of public goods according to local tastes. On the other hand, constitutions often contain specific provisions aimed at ensuring a certain degree of uniformity of socio-economic and legal conditions, and at preventing preferential treatment of single jurisdictions.

[3] See also Edwards and Keen (1996).

[4] Table B.12 in Appendix B provides an overview of the different studies.

and, particularly, for the subnational level. Collusion among sub-central governments, which is represented by the share of federal grants in sub-central government revenue in different studies, is generally shown to increase the size of consolidated government and of each separate level of government.[5] Other studies report a negative effect of bicameralism[6] and of budget referendums and citizen initiatives[7] on the level of public spending and revenue.

With respect to the vertical government structure, democracies and federal countries are generally found to be more decentralised. At the subnational level, Schaltegger and Feld (2001) and Matsusaka (1995, 2000) detect a positive impact of budget referendums and citizen initiatives on the degree of fiscal decentralisation of Swiss cantons and US states, respectively. This is explained by the direct control exercised by citizens on the government budget and the higher demand for local instead of state public services. Corresponding cross-national evidence for the effect of direct democracy at the national level is, yet, largely missing. Based on a comparative analysis, Blankart (2000) suggests that referendums at the federal level contributed to higher decentralisation in Switzerland as compared to Germany. Vaubel (1996) analyses the impact of decision-making institutions in a cross-section of industrial and developing countries. He shows that particularly independence of constitutional courts from central government, and, to a lesser extent, involvement of subnational entities and citizens in constitutional amendment concerning subnational competencies are associated with increased decentralisation.

Given this background, this chapter takes a comprehensive empirical approach which integrates costs, preferences, and institutions in order to verify the contribution of the fiscal federalism literature to the explanation of cross-country differences in the degree of decentralisation. More specifically, we investigate whether participation of elected or appointed subnational representatives in decision-making processes concerning the assignment of government

[5] See Shadbegian (1999) for US states, and Grossman and West (1994) for Canadian provinces. Other studies verify the inverse relationship between decentralisation and government size postulated by the Leviathan theory, providing mixed results. See, among others, Oates (1972) for a cross-country study, and Oates (1985), Nelson (1987) and Marlow (1988) for US states.

[6] Bradbury and Crain (2002) analyse the influence of different bases of representation of bicameral chambers. They show for US states that decreased constituent homogeneity across bicameral chambers tends to reduce redistributive spending and to increase spending on public goods instead. The reason is that bicameral differences restrict the ability of coalitions to manipulate fiscal policy for redistributive purposes. Bradbury and Crain (2001) provide evidence for a positive relationship between legislative size and spending across countries, the effect being stronger in unicameral legislatures than in bicameral legislatures.

[7] See Feld and Kirchgässner (2001) and Feld and Matsusaka (2003) for Swiss cantons, and Matsusaka (1995) for US states. Note, however, that Matsusaka (2000) finds a positive correlation between public spending and initiatives in US states before the Second World War. Frey and Stutzer (2003) provide an overview of this empirical literature.

functions and revenues and the budgetary policy of the central government leads to excessive centralisation, as compared to direct involvement of the citizens.

For this purpose, a detailed analysis of decision-making institutions is carried out for a sample of OECD countries from 1965 to the present. Based upon this, the cross-sectional time-series regression analysis relates the degree of expenditure and tax decentralisation to institutional indicators, at the same time controlling for heterogeneity of preferences and conditions, economies of scale, and other determinants of the vertical government structure and of the demand for public services. In doing so, the quantitative approach taken in this chapter addresses the issue of institutional endogeneity and explicitly accounts for institutional changes over time. Since commonly used measures tend to misrepresent the degree of fiscal decentralisation, a corrected measure is used instead which accounts for tax-raising powers of sub-central government. This allows us to conduct a more appropriate test of the collusion and the common pool hypotheses laid down in the literature.

This chapter is organised as follows. We begin with a summary of the main theoretical results of recent political-economic work on fiscal federalism. Section 3.3 provides a descriptive-comparative analysis of decision-making institutions of OECD countries. In the next two sections, the investigation approach is discussed and the empirical analysis is carried out. Finally, section 3.6 draws the conclusions.

## 3.2 Decision-Making Institutions and Government Decentralisation

Since the degree of fiscal decentralisation is commonly associated with the share of sub-central government in total public output, decision-making institutions are expected to affect the degree of decentralisation in two ways. The first aspect involves the decision on the formal assignment of functional responsibilities, revenues and legislative powers across levels of government. Given this decision, the second aspect concerns the concrete policy choice of each government unit.[8]

The validity of the "Decentralisation Theorem" crucially hinges on the extent to which local preferences or demands for decentralisation are actually transferred into corresponding policy outcomes. Within this context, institutions generally act as a link between voter tastes and policy outcomes and influence the choice of the decision-makers and the nature of their interactions. In democracies political decision-making powers are either assigned directly to the citizens or delegated to elected representatives of the local communities. One may generally distinguish between three or four important veto

[8] These considerations follow the constitutional economics approach, see, e.g., Buchanan (1967), which assumes that at the first stage the constitution is designed, and at the second stage policies are chosen.

players at the national level: central government, national legislature, and, if existing, an upper chamber of parliament consisting of elected or designated subnational representatives, and, finally, voters. In case of delegated decision-making, the representation of voter preferences ultimately depends on the way the delegates are chosen and on the rules of collective decision-making.

Contrary to the predictions of the traditional median voter model, more recent work has shown that decisions taken by elected politicians significantly diverge from the preferences of the median voter in their districts.[9] According to Buchanan and Tullock (1962) and Weingast et al. (1981), collusive behaviour in political choice institutions is stronger when representatives are selected on a geographic basis than if they are selected at large from across the nation. Representatives elected in geographically based constituencies view the tax base as a common pool, and, consequently, engage in vote-trading by approving projects which do not correspond to their preferences in exchange for financial support of projects which benefit their own constituencies. Particularly universalistic legislatures where decisions are taken cooperatively in contrast to legislatures dominated by minimum winning coalitions tend to favour collusive behaviour. This happens particularly in the area of distributive policies where benefits are geographically concentrated, while costs can be spread across all constituencies through generalised taxation. While internalising the benefits of expenditures, the constituencies underestimate the costs imposed on the economy. Geographical representation thus leads in the end to the formation of policy cartels and inefficient over-spending. According to the "Law of 1/n" excessive spending is expected to increase with the number of legislative districts.

Analogously, the same common pool problem arises with respect to the assignment of functions and revenues in multi-level government structures. The Leviathan theory in general assumes that decentralisation is associated with increased fiscal competition, thus constraining revenue-maximising behaviour of sub-central governments. However, according to the collusion hypothesis of Brennan and Buchanan (1980), lower level governments may cooperate and form tax and expenditure cartels in order to oppose competitive pressures of fiscal decentralisation and to reap higher rents.[10] As argued by Mueller (1996), the danger is that geographically elected representatives become lobbyists for local interests instead of representatives of the citizen preferences.

Due to the intrinsic instability related to their public good character, the implementation of political cartels requires the support of a higher authority. Being typically less exposed to fiscal competition, the central government is in the best position to enforce collusive agreements between subnational

[9] This is also increasingly supported by empirical evidence, see, e.g., Pommerehne (1978), Peltzman (1992) or, more recently, Gerber and Lewis (2004). The significant impact of initiatives and referendums on policy outcomes reported in the empirical literature is generally interpreted as evidence that legislatures do not implement median voter preferences.

[10] See also Wrede (2004) for a more recent contribution.

governments. Therefore, tax collusion may imply the transfer of taxing powers to the central government, which then imposes a uniform tax and shares the revenues with the lower levels of government either through vertical grants or other explicit rules of tax sharing. Fiscal equalisation payments between subnational governments represent a further option. Despite centralisation of public funds, lower level governments may retain full spending autonomy. Even without considering the extreme case of Leviathans, as a result of the common pool problem, participation of representatives of subnational entities in central decision-making is expected to lead to over-centralisation, particularly with respect to taxing powers.

Blankart (2000) provides an application for Germany, suggesting that increasing government centralisation resulted from tax and expenditure cartels formed by the Länder governments. Within this context, the *Kompetenzkompetenz* of the federal government, i.e. the constitutional power to take over subcentral government legislation, is assumed to have significantly contributed to enforce cartelisation. In contrast to this, by allocating the ultimate taxing power to the voters, referendums are expected to prevent cartelisation and logrolling of elected legislators. The possible conduct of referendums, and particularly citizen initiatives force greater agreement between voter preferences and policy outcomes. The over-spending problem becomes less likely, since referendums make vote-trading across jurisdictions more difficult. Furthermore, citizens are supposed to internalise the total social costs of public funds, and not only a part of them.[11] Apart from the behaviour of elected legislators, the fact that referendums deal with very specific issues, as compared to general elections where multi-dimensional issues are decided at once, is expected to further intensify the correspondence between preferences of the median voters and actual policy outcomes.[12]

The results of empirical studies at the subnational level mentioned in the introduction to this chapter mostly support these views. The empirical evidence does, however, not allow one to say with confidence whether the observed discrepancy between voter preferences and policy outcomes is due to vote-trading, as described above, or to other reasons, like, for example, missing information of the legislators.[13] Also, as indicated by the analysis of Matsusaka (2000), provisions for popular initiatives and, to a lesser extent, for referendums might only lead to policies closer to the preferences of the voters. Whether voters are in favour of cutting or increasing public spending is not a priori clear and would depend on different cultural and social aspects.[14]

These general considerations are confirmed by recent theoretical work which integrates the traditional cost-benefit approach of the "Decentralisation

[11] See also Besley and Case (2002).

[12] According to Besley and Coate (2000) citizen initiatives allow an "unbundling" of issues as compared to representative democracies.

[13] See Matsusaka (1995) with respect to this.

[14] This view is also supported by Pujol and Weber (2003) who provide evidence that German speaking cantons are more fiscally conservative than other cantons.

Theorem" with different rules for decision-making on the vertical allocation of functions and financial resources. In general, the choice of centralisation or decentralisation is assumed to be prior to the legislative bargaining process. Crémer and Palfrey (1996) show that federal states, where the decision on centralisation has to be approved in a referendum by a majority of regions, are more centralised than unitary states, where the majority of votes at the national scale is decisive.[15] Provided that heterogeneity is not too high, this is explained by the aggregation of preferences at the regional level. Extending this analysis to allow for efficiency gains and even for local differentiation in centralised provision of public goods, Lockwood (2004) reaches a different conclusion. He shows that in case of strong inter-regional preference heterogeneity, i.e. when the distribution of project benefits across regional medians is negatively single-peaked, regional referendums in federal states lead to less centralisation than national referendums in unitary states, and vice versa for a positively single-peaked distribution of project benefits. The intuition for this result is that in federal referendums the median voters' preferences in each region are decisive, dissenting regional voters not being taken into account, whereas in unitary referendums the national median, and thus the majority of the electorate overall is decisive. Provided that inter-regional preferences are not uniformly distributed, regional and national medians differ.

Finally, Redoano and Scharf (2004) compare decisions on policy centralisation taken either directly by the citizens in each region or by elected regional representatives. They demonstrate that in case of strong preference heterogeneity, the conduct of regional referendums is associated with less centralisation, as compared to bargaining between elected regional policy makers in representative democracies. The reason is that in a representative democracy voters in a pro-centralisation jurisdiction can induce another jurisdiction to cooperate and centralise policies by electing a representative which commits to the policy preferred by the other jurisdiction. Owing to vote-trading between regional representatives, centralisation finally occurs and the policy preferred by the reluctant region is chosen. In contrast to this, in a referendum democracy the median voter of each region decides independently upon centralisation, the heterogeneity of preferences therefore preventing an agreement.

Related work focuses instead on the efficiency issues of legislative bargaining of locally elected representatives in different systems of centralised decision-making. Besley and Coate (2003) and Gradstein (2000), among others,[16] show that apart from heterogeneity and spillovers, the benefits of centralisation or decentralisation depend upon the involvement of local jurisdic-

[15] Note that in line with the median voter theorem, regional and national referendums are supposed there to yield similar results to decisions taken by regional, and national representatives, respectively.

[16] See also Persson and Tabellini (1996a, 1996b), Alesina et al. (2001a), and Wrede (2004) for related studies.

tions in national legislation. Without participation of subnational entities with equal rights in centralised decision-making,[17] especially smaller jurisdictions run the risk of being dominated by the national majority or powerful jurisdictions. From this viewpoint, centralised decision-making proves to be more attractive in countries with constitutionally guaranteed fair representation of minorities or of the constituent jurisdictions.[18] To some extent, these analyses confirm Oates' insights demonstrating that centralisation is the most efficient arrangement when spillovers are high and heterogeneity is low. Cooperative or unanimous central decision-making therefore has the advantage of protecting the rights of the minorities, and, moreover, the status quo. Yet, on the other hand, it creates the common pool problem and incentives to interjurisdictional vote-trading as mentioned above, thus increasing the inefficiency of centralisation.[19]

To conclude, two empirically testable implications arise when combining the different theoretical considerations described above. First, provided that preference heterogeneity is high, we expect direct participation of the citizens of the subnational entities (regional referendums) in central decision-making on the vertical assignment of government functions and revenues to lead to less centralisation, as compared to decisions made by delegated representatives. This is due to the fact that collusive behaviour interferes with the inter-regional differences in preferences which might support decentralisation. Accordingly, involvement of subnational representatives in other areas of ordinary national legislation might also produce increased central government spending. Necessary preconditions for cartelisation are, thus, geographically based representation, the provision of mechanisms of cooperative decision-making, and the power of the central government to stabilise collusive arrangements. Second, the open issue is, to what extent and in which direction does direct democracy at the national level (national referendum) influence

[17] In the above mentioned literature, legislatures providing appropriate representation of subnational entities are referred to as cooperative or egalitarian legislatures, as compared to non-egalitarian legislatures where decisions are made by a minimum winning coalition.

[18] Seabright (1996), Schwager (1999a), and Zantman (2002) also show that decentralisation improves the control over policy makers and prevents a non-benevolent central government from giving preference to certain jurisdictions. These considerations may have influenced constitutional design in several federal states, and even the decision-making rules in the European Union. For example, Section 99 of the Australian Constitution explicitly forbids preferential treatment of any state by the Commonwealth.

[19] Besley and Coate (2003) show that due to the common pool problem, centralisation is strictly inferior to decentralisation even when both spillovers and heterogeneity are low. The problems involved by unanimity rules are best illustrated by the complex outcomes of decision-making processes in the Council of the European Union. There, the agreement to some major projects was often obtained in exchange for the allocation of additional resources or projects to the reluctant countries.

the level of central government spending and taxation, and, thus, indirectly the degree of fiscal decentralisation, too.

## 3.3 An Institutional Overview of OECD Countries

The analysis of the determinants of fiscal decentralisation draws on the 23 OECD countries considered before, thus including only comparable nations with long-standing well functioning democratic institutions. In view of the empirical analysis, this section provides a detailed description and quantification of the mechanisms of representation and participation of subnational entities in centralised decision-making and of the institutions of direct democracy at the national level. Due to the large institutional heterogeneity across countries, the different institutional details are summarised by means of qualitative indicators.

### 3.3.1 Participation of Subnational Entities in Central Decision-Making

To begin with, we compare the extent to which subnational entities participate in decision-making on the assignment of government functions and financial resources across levels of government and on other issues of centralised legislation. Within this context, as argued above, both the form of participation and the rules for decision-making and legislation have to be taken into account. The form of participation at the national level determines the extent to which local preferences are translated into policy outcomes. One may distinguish between *direct participation*, which involves the electorate or elected institutions of the component entities, and *indirect participation*, when decisions are taken by delegated representatives of the entities to an upper chamber of the national parliament.[20] Conditioning on the form of representation of local preferences, the rules for decision-making ultimately determine the decision-making power of the subnational entities and, thus, influence the policy choice itself.

#### Representation in the Upper Chamber

Table 3.1 first presents an overview of the different forms of representation of subnational entities in the upper chamber of the national parliament in the 23 OECD countries considered here. The quantification relies particularly on information collected from constitutional and legal documents of the individual countries and covers the period 1965-2003, taking institutional changes into account.[21]

[20] This classification partly draws on Council of Europe (1997).

[21] See, also, the description of the data sources in Appendix C.

Table 3.1: Representation of subnat. entities at the national level, 2003

| | Fed. state[a] | Subnational representatives in upper chamber of parliament | Index subnat. represen. Meth. select. (0-1) | Sym- metry (0-1) | Over- repr. (0-1) | Comp. index (0-2) |
|---|---|---|---|---|---|---|
| AUS | 1901 | direct election in the states (equal number repres. per state) | 0.60 | 1.00 | 0.82 | *1.51* |
| AUT | 1918 1945 | indir. election by Länder parl. (prop. to populat., min. number of representatives per Land) | 0.80 | 0.25 | 0.25 | *1.05* |
| BEL | 1994 | election on linguistic basis: 56% dir. elected (prop. repres.), 30% indir. elected by legislatures of linguist. communities (French-Flemish parity), rest coopted[b] | 0.49 | 0.71 | 0.13 | *0.91* |
| CAN | 1867 | appointed by PM/governor-gen. on provincial basis (asymmetr.) | 0.40 | 0.17 | 0.87 | *0.92* |
| FRA | | indir. election by elect. colleges representing all subnat. entities | 0.20 | 0.00 | 0.00 | *0.20* |
| GER | 1871 1949 | appointed by Länder governm. (prop. to popul., min. number and uniform vote per Land) | 1.00 | 0.50 | 0.81 | *1.66* |
| ITA | | direct election on regional basis (prop. to popul., min. number representatives per region) | 0.20 | 0.02 | 0.36 | *0.39* |
| NED | | indir. election by elect. college of provinces | 0.20 | 0.00 | 0.00 | *0.20* |
| SPA | | 80% dir. elected in provinces (equal number repres.), 20% indir. elected by regional parl. (min. (number repres. per region) | 0.32 | 0.13 | 0.66 | *0.71* |
| SWE | | formerly bicameral: indir. election by elect. college | | | | |
| SWI | 1848 | direct election in the cantons (equal number per canton) | 0.60 | 1.00 | 0.88 | *1.54* |
| USA | 1787 | dir. election in the states (equal number per state); before 1914: indir. election by state parl. | 0.60 | 1.00 | 0.91 | *1.56* |

Note: [a] year of coming into force. [b] before 1994, 28% of the representatives were indirectly elected by the provincial councils, the rest by proportional representation and cooptation. The figures for symmetry of representation and degree of overrepresentation are averages for the period 1965-2003 (GER: after 1991). See Table B.13 in Appendix B for the construction of the indices.

In federal systems of government, powers are typically divided among the federal government and the state or regional governments, whereas in unitary states control of the government is given to the central government which can regulate certain powers to local governments. Typical characteristics of most federal states are the historical formation through the association of formerly sovereign states and the equal or disproportionately strong representation of the component units in the upper chamber of a bicameral national parliament. However, this characterisation does not always hold. Belgium, for example, was gradually transformed from a unitary state into a federal state between 1970 and 1994.[22] Moreover, among federal states the form and the extent of geographical representation in the upper chamber varies considerably. Apart from the federal states, different forms of representation of subnational entities in the upper chamber also exist in regionalised unitary countries like Italy and since 1978 also in Spain, and even in strictly unitary countries like France or the Netherlands.

Following Tsebelis and Money (1997) and Lijphart (1984), subnational representation in the upper chamber may be classified along two dimensions: the method of selection of the representatives and the degree of representation of the component sub units. The composite index of subnational representation presented in the last column of Table 3.1 combines these two aspects.[23] The method of selection (column 5) determines the way geographically based preferences are aggregated and the extent to which incentives for collusive behaviour among subnational representatives may be created. We assume that representatives directly elected in the regions are less inclined to take common attitudes and engage in logrolling than representatives appointed by the regional governments or assemblies which are subject to their instructions.[24] The reason for this is the stronger re-election restriction imposed on them by the voters of their constituency. The degree of representation of the individual sub-units is described in terms of the number of representatives of the smallest unit as compared to both the largest unit (symmetry of representation, column 6) and its own population share (degree of overrepresentation, column 7).[25] The stronger the control of subnational governments on the representatives delegated to the upper chamber, and the more equal the representation of the component subnational units, the more likely vote-trading and the common pool problem will occur.

Subnational representatives are either elected directly by the people of the constituent units (Australia, Switzerland, USA, and, partly, Italy) or in-

[22] On the other hand, the United Kingdom or Italy, which were also created by the unification of sovereign states, are unitary countries. Note, also, that in Germany most of the present Länder have been newly created after World War II.

[23] See Table B.13 in Appendix B for details on the construction of the indices.

[24] The strongest form of interest aggregation represents Germany, where each Land has only a uniform vote in the upper chamber.

[25] See Lijpahrt (1984) for an alternative aggregate measure covering all constituent units.

directly by electoral colleges (Netherlands, France) or regional parliaments (Austria), or they are appointed by the central government (Canada) or the regional governments (Germany). Mixed forms are found in Belgium and in Spain, where in the former since 1994 representation is based on linguistic rather than on geographic criteria.

In line with the theoretical expectations, the figures in column (7) indicate that most federal countries tend to considerably overrepresent the smaller component units, their share of seats in the legislature exceeding their share of population. Interestingly enough, formally non-federal countries Italy and Spain have higher degrees of overrepresentation than Austria and Belgium, where the number of representatives is more or less proportional to the population. As can be seen in column (6), Australia, Switzerland, and the USA grant equal representation regardless of the units' population. On the contrary, representation of Canadian provinces is strongly asymmetric. According to the composite index, Germany has the highest extent of subnational representation at the national level, being followed by the USA, Switzerland and Australia.[26]

## Forms of Participation

Besides formal representation in the upper chamber, the influence of the subnational entities on the policy choices at the national level depends on their relative power of decision-making. The political-economic literature shows that apart from the distribution of veto rights, the allocation of agenda control and agenda-setting powers plays an important role.[27] The higher the required majority of subnational representatives or entities to pass legislation, the stronger is the power of each unit to block decisions. Quasi-unanimity in decision-making therefore tends to preserve the status quo. However, as discussed before, the resulting implications are divergent for direct and indirect forms of participation.

Taking the form of participation and decision-making power into account, indices representing the degree of direct and indirect participation of subnational entities in central decision-making on different issues are presented in Figures 3.1 and 3.2 for the countries involved.[28] The power of veto increases with the majority required in the lower chamber to overrule a (suspensive)

---

[26] Note that, though having a comparatively low degree of representation in the upper chamber, subnational entities in Belgium and Spain are also represented by regionalist parties in both chambers of parliament.

[27] See, e.g., Baron and Ferejohn (1989). Moser (1999) provides an overview of this literature.

[28] See Table B.14 in Appendix B for details on the construction of the indices. A further aspect which could be taken into account is the existence of interchamber conference committees which are expected to facilitate logrolling. See Tsebelis and Money (1997) with respect to this.

veto in the upper chamber and with the required majority of subnational entities or representatives to agree legislation.

The indicator developed here differs from the related approach of Vaubel (1996) by treating direct and indirect participation separately, and in accounting for both the form of representation and the power to veto and to initiate legislation at the national level. Furthermore, we distinguish between decision-making on the assignment of spending and taxing powers to levels of government, and consider also other issues of centralised policy-making, such as constitutional amendments not directly concerning the subnational entities, and financial and non-financial national legislation. This allows us to test directly the theoretical considerations discussed in the previous section.

Fig. 3.1: Indirect participation of subnational entities in central decision-making, 2003

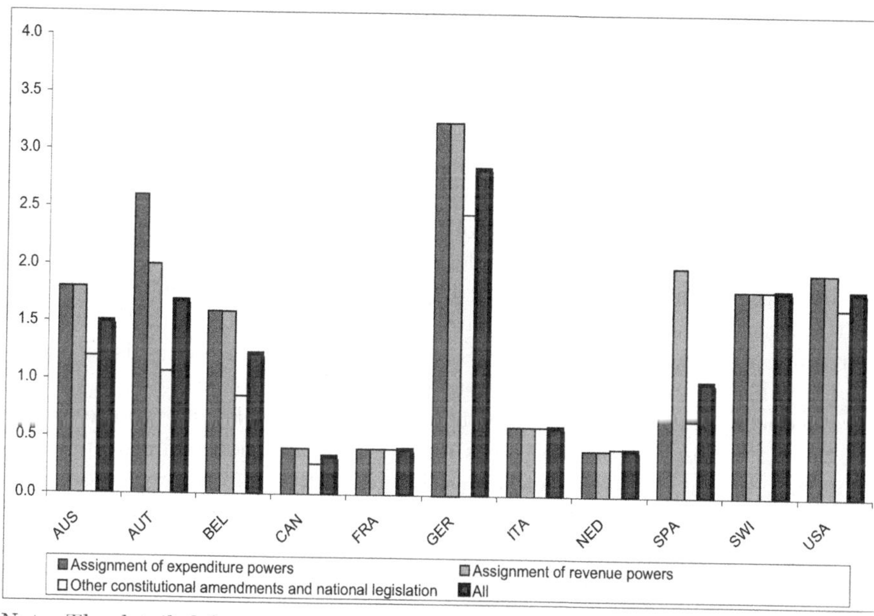


Note: The detailed figures are presented in Table B.15 in Appendix B.

The assignment of spending and taxing powers to levels of government is stipulated by the constitution in most federal countries, and by ordinary legislation in the national parliament in most unitary countries. The reallocation of competencies requires the approval of the absolute majority in the upper chamber consisting of regional representatives in Australia and Switzerland, and of a two thirds majority in Austria, Germany, and the USA. However, in Austria and in the regionalised states such as Spain and Italy, only the assignment of regional government functions is explicitly laid down in the constitution. Even if the lower chamber of parliament ultimately decides on the allocation of financial resources, direct negotiations are previously taking place between sub-central governments and the central government in Austria and, since 1987, also in Spain. In the case of Spain, assignment and transfer of government functions is laid down in the constitution, as well as in ordinary laws with constitutional character and in specific regional statutes negotiated separately with each region. Therefore, inter-regional asymmetries concerning the distribution of competencies exist. Belgium represents a further special case. The expenditure competencies of the French and Flemish communities and of the regions are laid down in the constitution and in special ordinary legislation respectively. The financial resources of both the regions and the two communities are also determined by special ordinary law. The allocation of expenditure and revenue powers requires since 1970 and 1989 the consent of the majority of each linguistic group and of a total majority of two thirds in each house of parliament.

Accordingly, the figures indicate for Germany and, to a lesser extent, for Austria the highest degree of indirect participation in decision-making concerning the assignment of expenditure and revenue powers. Collusive behaviour and centralisation of taxing powers might therefore be more pronounced in these countries. This seems to be confirmed by the recent federalism reform debates in both countries which from the outset exclude the transfer of taxing powers to lower level governments. Note that a high degree of participation in the assignment of revenue is also reported for Spain. On the other hand, despite being a federal country, subnational representatives in the upper chamber are shown to play a minor role in Canada. This is due to the fact that the Canadian Senate partly resembles the British House of Lords in consisting of representatives appointed by the prime minister almost for life, who do not exercise their veto power in practice.

Except for other constitutional amendments which likewise require the approval of the absolute or two thirds majority of both houses in most federal countries, subnational representatives are generally less involved in ordinary national legislation and, particularly, in the adoption of financial laws. Switzerland represents an exception on this matter. Considering all issues of central decision-making, Germany, and to a lesser extent Switzerland and the USA report the highest degree of indirect participation.[29]

In addition to representation in the national parliament, a few countries also provide for direct participation of subnational entities in central decision-making. Strictly speaking, provisions for national referendums requiring a double majority of citizens and regions correspond to the separate conduct

[29] Note also that subnational entities furthermore participate indirectly in the election of the head of state in Italy, Switzerland, and the USA. In the case of the latter, apart from disproportional representation of the states in the electoral college, in the absence of an absolute majority the constitution stipulates that the House of Representatives elects the President, with each state having one vote. These aspects are, however, not taken into account here.

Fig. 3.2: Direct participation of subnational entities in central decision-making, 2003

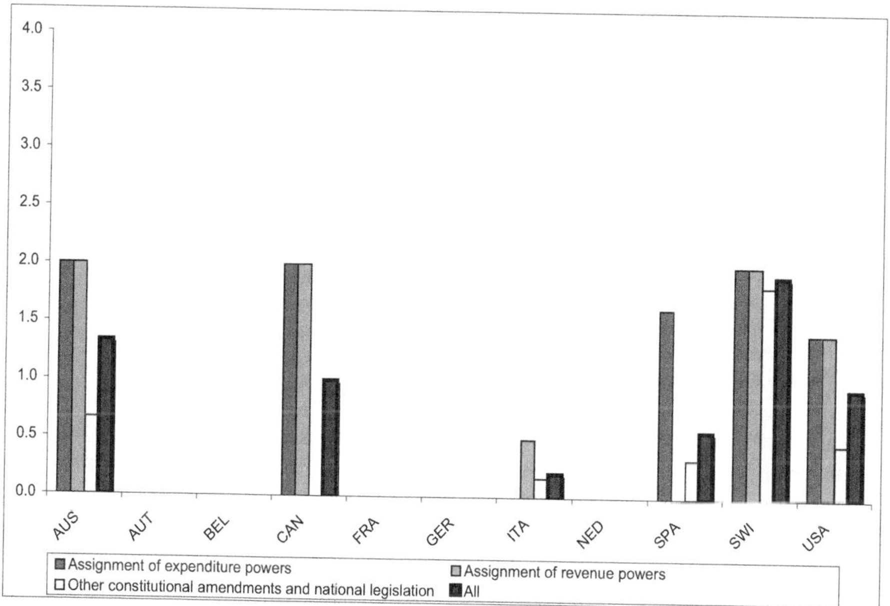


Note: The detailed figures are presented in Table B.16 in Appendix B.

of regional referendums. Moreover, we assume that representation of local preferences is higher and, thus, the probability of vote-trading lower, when decisions at the national level have to be approved directly by the citizens of the individual jurisdictions instead of the jurisdictional legislatures.

Apart from the upper chamber, reallocation of spending and taxing powers and other constitutional amendments must be approved by the majority of the national electorate and the majority of states and cantons (double majority) in Australia and Switzerland, whereas in the USA they require the agreement of the legislatures of three-quarters of the states. In Canada all issues concerning the provinces have to be approved by a qualified majority of the provincial legislatures, providing the possibility of opting out for disagreeing provinces. In Spain, depending on the autonomy statute, the transfer of expenditure competencies to the autonomous communities often requires the consent of both the legislature and the voters of the region concerned. At the level of national legislation, direct participation is even more restrained, Switzerland being the only country to provide for regional referendums on certain financial and non-financial bills and to allow regional legislatures to introduce a bill in the national parliament. Consequently, the highest degree of direct participation over all issues is reported for Switzerland, Australia, Canada, followed by the USA.

## Further Institutional Aspects

Apart from participation in central decision-making, further institutional aspects may permit the expansion of central government powers, particularly in federal countries. The first aspect involves the legislative *Kompetenzkompetenz* of the central government mentioned by Blankart (2000) which helps ensure tax and expenditure cartels. In Germany this is typically associated with concurrent legislative powers giving the central government the power to exhaust all aspects of a specific matter, the subnational entities retaining the power to legislate only as long as that matter has not been exhausted by the central government. The power of the central government to appropriate certain functions and revenues of subnational government is explicitly stipulated in Art. 72(1) and 105(2) of the German Basic Law.[30] Despite precedent negotiations between all levels of government, in Austria taxing powers and the distribution of revenues are ultimately determined by federal legislation. With respect to taxing powers, only Australia, Canada, Switzerland, USA and, to a lesser extent, Italy since the constitutional reform of 2001, provide for parallel tax finding powers of central and sub-central government. In all other countries the central government retains the ultimate tax-raising competency.

Increased centralisation might additionally be stimulated by constitutional provisions empowering the central government to legislate in all areas not explicitly assigned to sub-central government. The "necessary and proper clause" in the US Constitution (Art. I, Sec. 8(18)), for example, gives the Congress powers inferred from the constitution, but not stated exactly. Accordingly, the federal government may pass laws that have universal applicability in order to implement its remaining powers. Section 91(29) of the Canadian Constitution Act of 1867 and Art. 149(3) of the Spanish Constitution provide for similar residual competencies of the central government.

A further aspect concerns the extent to which the central government is legally committed to pursuing uniformity and to reducing interjurisdictional disparities. For example, in Germany concurrent legislation is weighted in favour of the federal government with the aim to ensure uniform living conditions and economic and legal unity and to remove inter-regional distortive effects (Art. 72(2) of the Basic Law). Similar, though weaker uniformity and equality requirements also exist in other federal or quasi-federal countries Canada (Sec. 36 of the Constitution Act of 1982), and Spain (Art. 138 of the Constitution).

Finally, Vaubel (1996) points to the important role of constitutional or supreme courts which rule power conflicts between federal and sub-central government. There is some evidence that particularly judicial reinterpretation of constitutional provisions regarding the uniformity of certain legal or socio-economic conditions tends to favour the expansion of central government powers over time. For example, since the 1980s the US Supreme Court

[30] See also chapter 5 for more details.

increasingly strengthened federal powers with regard to the regulation of interstate commerce and social legislation.[31] The same occurs in the European Union where decisions of the Court of Justice concerning the functioning of the Common Market and harmonisation of legislation tend to support the expansion of the competencies of the Commission. On the other hand, in Spain most competency conflicts were decided in favour of the autonomous communities, and, recently, in Germany the powers of the Länder in the field of education were strengthened by the constitutional court.

### 3.3.2 Direct Democracy at the National Level

Apart from subnational entities, the extent to which the national electorate takes part directly in spending and tax decisions of the central government is expected to affect the degree of fiscal decentralisation. In the following, we provide an overview of the main instruments of direct democracy at the national level in OECD countries. Previous work focused instead on referendums and citizen initiatives at the local or regional level of government.[32] The approach taken in this chapter consists in adapting the indicators of direct democracy rights developed by Stutzer (1999) and Frey and Stutzer (2000) in order to address the greater complexity and diversity of institutions across countries.

Usually, the different legal instruments of direct democracy are classified according to the issues involved (constitutional or legislative) and the form of initiation (referendums or popular initiatives).[33] Referendums are commonly defined as a vote on a measure adopted by the parliament, whereas the initiative allows citizens to propose an amendment which may be adopted in a popular vote. By removing agenda control from the legislature, initiatives exert a stronger control over policy-making. In case of legislative referendums one may furthermore differentiate between financial issues which are related to spending and tax policy and non-financial issues.

Following this classification, the extent of direct democratic control is quantified for each of the six instruments according to three major parameters. First, there is the range of specific objects which can be submitted to referendum or popular initiative. Second, we discriminate between referendums that are required (mandatory) and those that are not (facultative). In

[31] See Elazar (1994).

[32] The only exception is Vaubel (1996) who constructed an index of direct popular participation in constitutional amendments concerning subnational competencies.

[33] See Hug and Tsebelis (2002) for an overview. More detailed classifications also consider, e.g., the number of veto players and who is able to frame the question of the popular vote. According to the initiator, Mueller (1996) distinguishes between constitutionally mandated referendum, government-initiated referendum, citizen-initiated veto and citizen initiative. One might also further differentiate between positive referendums aimed at changing the status quo, and negative referendums which stop a bill that intends to change the status quo.

Fig. 3.3: Direct democracy at the national level (referendums), 2003

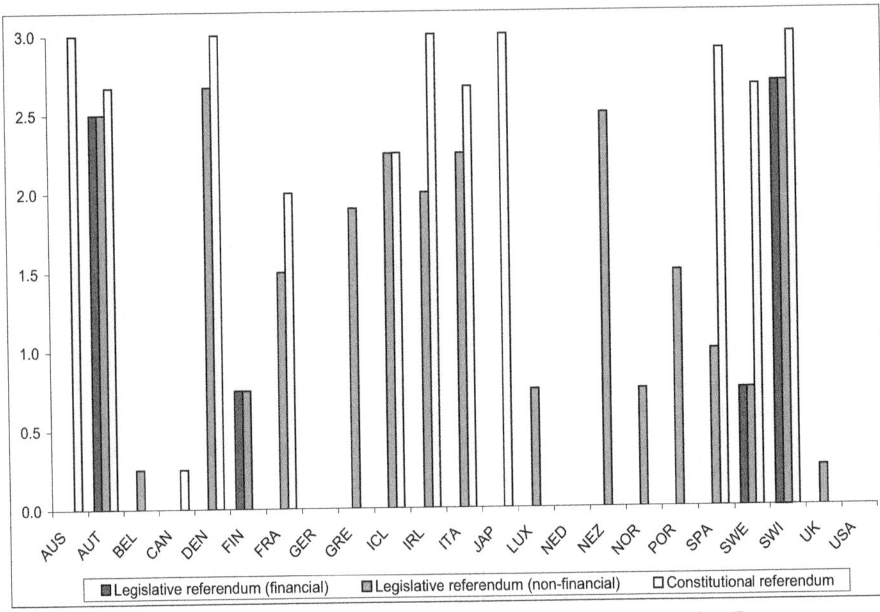


Note: The detailed figures are presented in Table B.18 in Appendix B.

the case of the latter, only a predetermined number of signatures from citizens, or a particular quorum of members of the national parliament or of regional parliaments can request a referendum. The lower the legal threshold to initiate a referendum, the higher is the extent of direct democracy. Most empirical evidence confirms the fact that the effects of citizen initiatives are largest with relatively easy ballot access in terms of low signature requirements. And, finally, we consider whether the different legal instruments have a binding legal effect on policy-making, that is, whether the results are decisive or only consultative.[34] Consequently, a mandatory decisive referendum on any policy issue represents the strongest form of direct democratic control.

The extent of direct democracy at the national level is quantified for the 23 OECD countries according to the legal and constitutional provisions. Figures 3.3 and 3.4 present the figures on referendums and popular initiatives for the latest available year.

As expected, the figures indicate the highest degree of direct democracy for Switzerland, both in terms of legal provisions and referendum practice. This is particularly true for popular initiatives on legislative and constitutional matters. Moreover, as already described, a double majority of the citizens and

[34] See Table B.17 in Appendix B for the construction of the indices. Despite not being able to account for the entire institutional diversity, we expect these three aspects to represent the most important features of direct democracy.

Fig. 3.4: Direct democracy at the national level (initiatives), 2003

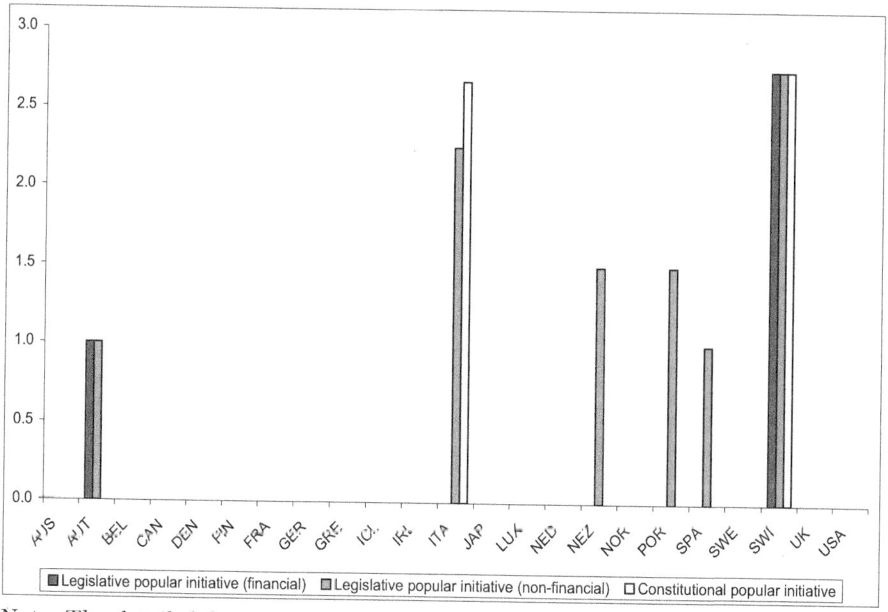


Note: The detailed figures are presented in Table B.19 in Appendix B.

the cantons is required in many cases. Except for Switzerland, only Austria and Italy provide for citizen initiatives on financial and constitutional matters respectively. Countries like Denmark or Ireland, for example, which quite often hold referendums on constitutional amendments concerning the European Union, are not allowing for citizen initiatives at the national level.

In general, referendums on constitutional matters are typically more widespread among OECD countries than referendums on legislative matters or popular initiatives. Again, financial referendums are only provided for in very few countries, particularly in Switzerland and Austria, whereas most constitutions explicitly rule out a popular vote on strictly budgetary matters.

On aggregate, Figure 3.5 indicates that apart from Switzerland, referendums are rarely used in a regular and systematic way at the national level. Nonetheless, important direct democratic elements are also legally enshrined in a few other countries like Italy and Austria. Note, however, that in the case of the latter, as in cases of other countries, legal provisions and practice also significantly fall apart.[35] On the other hand, national referendums are explicitly ruled out in Germany, the Netherlands, the USA, or are rarely conducted in a few exceptional cases such as Belgium, Canada, and the United Kingdom.

35 Though the coefficient of correlation is very high (0.784), there is no perfect correspondence between the composite index of direct democracy and the period-averaged number of national referendums among OECD countries.

Fig. 3.5: Direct democracy at the national level (all instruments), 2003

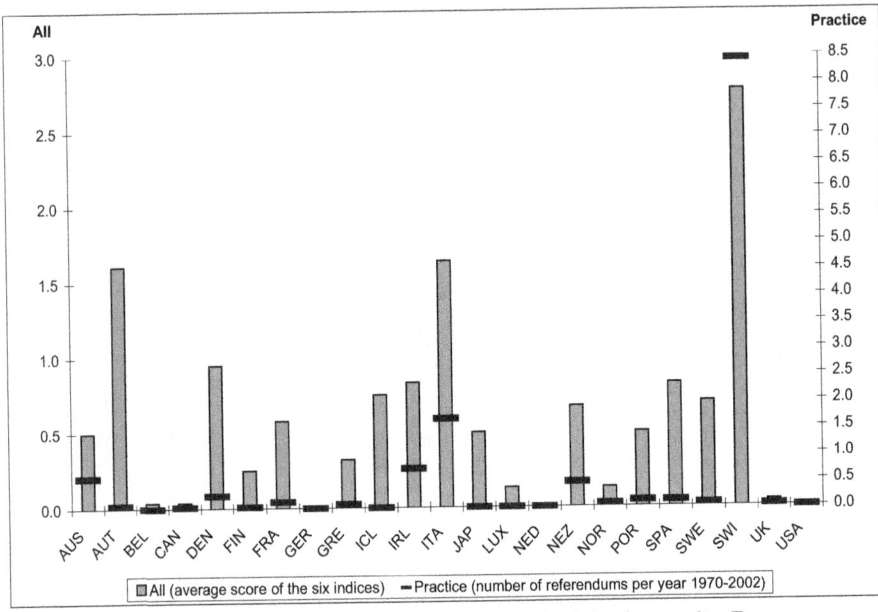


Note: The detailed figures are presented in Table B.19 in Appendix B.

In contrast to this, particularly in the USA, and increasingly in Germany, too, direct democracy is intensively practiced at the regional or local level.

These results thus confirm the general view that referendums are more common at the regional and local levels than at the national level. More recently, an overall tendency towards greater direct participation of citizens in local and, to a lesser extent, in national policy-making, has been noticed across all OECD countries. Accordingly, during the last 30 years, elements of direct democracy have been introduced at the national level in a couple of countries including Finland, Greece, Italy, New Zealand, Portugal, Spain, and Sweden. In general, legal provisions for direct democracy seem to change more frequently than mechanisms of participation of subnational entities in decision-making which rather reflect long-standing considerations.

## 3.4 Quantitative Analysis

The determinant influence of decision-making institutions on the degree of fiscal decentralisation described in section 3.2 is tested empirically for the OECD countries. In line with the theoretical considerations, we expect direct involvement of the citizens in central decision-making to be associated with less centralisation as compared to delegation of decision-making to elected or appointed subnational representatives. In the following section, the empirical model is presented and the explanatory variables are described.

### 3.4.1 Empirical Model

The quantitative analysis covers the panel of 23 OECD countries presented above for the period 1965-2001.[36] The inclusion of comparable industrial nations with longstanding well functioning democratic institutions enables us to control for the positive correlation between democracy and public sector decentralisation revealed by the study of Panizza (1999) and for other features, like the degree of economic and social development, and the existence of common cultural and political traditions. Accordingly, Greece, Spain, and Portugal are included in the sample just after transition to democracy.

The empirical model relates the degree of fiscal decentralisation to decision-making institutions, and to other factors which determine both the vertical assignment of government functions and revenues according to the traditional cost-benefit approach, and the demand for public services provided either by the local or the central government. Whereas the vertical assignment of competencies depends on the costs and benefits of decentralised provision and the institutional rules, the budgetary shares of the different expenditure categories and the extent of public or private supply depend on the relative demand for certain public goods.

Formally, the estimation equation is described by

$$Decentr_{it} = \beta_0 + \beta_1 \cdot Cost_{it} + \beta_2 \cdot Prefer_{it} + \beta_3 \cdot Diverse_{it} + \beta_4 \cdot Instit_{it} + u_{it},$$

where $Decentr_{it}$ is the degree of fiscal decentralisation of country $i$ in period $t$, as represented by the share of sub-central government expenditure in consolidated general government expenditure.[37] Considering only expenditures carried out directly by sub-central government, intergovernmental transfers are attributed to the recipient levels of government. $Instit_{it}$ is a vector of different decision-making rules, explicitly taking variation over time into account. In line with the "Decentralisation Theorem", we furthermore control for the cost of decentralisation in terms of foregone economies of scale and spillovers ($Cost_{it}$), and the extent of interjurisdictional heterogeneity of preferences and conditions ($Prefer_{it}$). Finally, $Diverse_{it}$ denotes a set of further variables controlling for the demand for certain public services and decentralisation. A more detailed discussion of the variables is presented below.

Differently from other related studies, we refrain from considering the role of history. Since the vertical government structure exhibits considerable inertia over time, the inclusion of the past degree of decentralisation in the

[36] The period considered depends on the data available for the different measures of decentralisation. Note that due to gaps in the data the panel is unbalanced.

[37] See Appendix C and D for a description of all variables and the data used in the regression analysis.

estimation equation would explain most of the variation in the contemporaneous degree of decentralisation, thus obscuring the individual factors actually shaping government structures.

The empirical model is estimated by ordinary least squares regressions on cross-sectional time-series. The pooling of time series and cross-sections permits large-sample analysis that draws on temporal and cross-national variation. As compared to using only country means, pooled regressions have the advantage of using additional information which can make the estimates more precise. On the other hand, the time dimension in the data is not adequately exploited and simultaneity problems may arise due to the omission of potential explanatory variables. It could be more appropriate to include country fixed effects to absorb all country-specific factors which are constant over time. However, fixed effects models leave the explanation of time-invariant cross-country differences to the intercepts and therefore allow no analysis of the effect of specific institutions which barely change over time. Also, it may be difficult to control for institutional endogeneity and, thus, for sources of unobserved heterogeneity with country fixed effects when other country-specific characteristics do not change over time, either.

Therefore, we prefer to estimate ordinary least squares regressions with robust standard errors. Nonetheless, the results of the analysis should be treated with a certain caution, since panel data are only of limited value when some variables, like institutions, vary across countries, but rarely within countries over time.

A final specification has to be made with respect to the degree of fiscal decentralisation. To investigate the resulting implications of the common pool problem and of collusive behaviour of sub-central governments associated with participation in centralised decision-making, one has to focus alternatively on government revenue. Since the Leviathan theory assumes intergovernmental transfers to reflect collusive behaviour, previous empirical work used the share of grants received from central government in total revenue of sub-central government to test the collusion hypothesis.

Taking a different approach, we verify the direct implications of this theory by analysing the effect of subnational participation in central decision-making on the degree of tax decentralisation. Since the collusion hypothesis predicts the formation of tax cartels to prevent fiscal competition, we expect participation of delegated subnational representatives in central decision-making to be associated with lower tax autonomy of sub-central government and, thus, with a lower degree of tax decentralisation. The difficulty consists, however, in the fact that public finance statistics report tax revenues at the level of government which ultimately receives them, irrespective of whether it has discretion upon them. Therefore, it would be difficult to clearly identify whether collusive behaviour led to centralised tax legislation. Taking account of the tax-raising autonomy of sub-central governments, we use the indicator of tax decentralisation constructed in chapter 2, which relates autonomous own tax revenue of sub-central government to total tax revenue of consolidated general government (*TD1*). Consequently, yields from shared taxes or from taxes determined by central government legislation are excluded from sub-central government revenues.

### 3.4.2 Institutions

#### Institutional Variables

The empirical analysis focuses on the role of institutions providing for representation and decision-making of subnational entities and citizens. Generally speaking, the direct effect of specific institutions on policy outcomes may be better tested by using dummy variables instead of indices which suffer from a certain degree of arbitrariness. However, due to the complexity and diversity of institutional rules, this is a very difficult task in cross-country comparisons. Despite several shortcomings, the indicators developed in section 3.3 have the advantage of aggregating a multitude of institutional aspects into one measure and as a result removing potential multicollinearity problems in the empirical analysis and increasing the degrees of freedom. The figures indicate considerable institutional variation across OECD countries and, though to a lesser extent, even across time in certain cases. Note again that institutional changes in the course of time are explicitly taken into account in the regression analysis.

The first set of institutions considered in the quantitative analysis contains rules which determine the form of participation of subnational entities in central decision-making. These may affect the decision on the vertical assignment of government functions and revenues, as well as the level of central government spending and taxation. Analogously to previous empirical studies, we begin with considering first the role of *federal* constitutions. However, this dummy variable captures only differences between federal and non-federal countries, and not within either group. The institutional analysis has shown that representation of subnational entities at the national level differs considerably among federal states and even exists in some formally unitary countries. Accordingly, one cannot necessarily conclude that federal constitutions per se lead to stronger fiscal decentralisation, as commonly expected.

Therefore, second, the index of *subnational representation* constructed in section 3.3.1 is used instead. To account for both, form of representation and decision-making power, we also employ alternatively the indices of *direct* and *indirect subnational participation* in central decision-making. Note that the effects of each form of participation are analysed separately. This allows us to test explicitly the implications of regional referendums on the assignment of competencies at the national level described in Redoano and Scharf (2004) and Lockwood (2004), and to draw on a larger sub-sample consisting of 11 countries with subnational representation, as compared to the 6 to 7 federal states. According to the theoretical literature, direct participation of the citizens of the subnational entities is expected to prevent collusive behaviour inherent in cooperative decision-making at the national level, and, thus, excessive centralisation. Finally, in order to test the effect of instruments assumed to enforce political cartels among sub-central governments, a dummy variable is included which considers whether the central government disposes over the ultimate competency in terms of tax legislation (*central tax competency*).

The second set of institutions to be considered is directly related to the fiscal policy of the central government, and, thus, may indirectly affect the degree of fiscal decentralisation, too. The effect of citizen participation in decision-making with respect to central government spending and revenue is tested by the inclusion of the indices of *direct democracy* presented before. To account for the discrepancy between legal provisions and practice, the average number of national referendums is used alternatively.

Apart from subnational or direct citizen participation in decision-making, further institutions which might exert an influence on the level of central government spending and taxation, are taken into account. A large empirical literature has recently shown that presidential regimes are associated with smaller governments and majoritarian electoral rules with less welfare spending and lower taxes.[38] Majoritarian electoral systems are characterised by stronger geographically based representation. In line with the previous theoretical discussion, they are thus assumed to favour spending programs that can be geographically targeted to powerful minorities. The plurality rule reduces the minimal coalition of voters needed to win the election. In contrast to this, proportional representation induces politicians to fully internalise the policy benefits for a larger group of voters, and, therefore, to put emphasis on universal expenditure programs, such as social transfers. Moreover, proportional electoral systems produce fragmented coalition governments, which in turn lead to more moderate policies with less pronounced partisan cycles. Analogously, weaker political accountability and the confidence vote requirement in parliamentary regimes also encourage more stable legislative majorities, resulting in higher taxes and higher spending, as compared to presidential systems.

In terms of the vertical government structure one might therefore expect the share of central government expenditure or revenue in total public sector expenditure or revenue to be lower in presidential regimes and under majoritarian electoral rules, all other things being equal. On the other hand, reduction of the number of veto players in presidential systems and first-past-the-post nature of plurality systems are assumed to insulate the executive power and permit certain groups to impose their authority.[39] Presidential systems therefore provide worse protection and representation of minorities in general, at the same time increasing the likelihood of uneven distribution of public goods. Apart from this, the missing confidence requirement in the leg-

---

38 See particularly Persson and Tabellini (1999, 2001), Persson (2002, 2003), Persson et al. (2003), and Milesi-Ferretti et al. (2002).

39 See Aghion et al. (2004).

islature favours a stronger central government. As a consequence, presidential regimes may be associated with higher centralisation, too.

To control for these effects, a dummy variable is introduced which classifies as *presidential regimes* where the executive is not accountable to the legislature through a vote of confidence. The multitude of dimensions of electoral rules is instead represented by a continuous measure for the degree of disproportionality of the *electoral system*.[40]

## Endogeneity Issues

The common assumption in most empirical studies is that institutions are exogenous. Particularly institutional rules laid out in the constitution are rather difficult to modify. This view is also supported by the institutional overview provided in the present study, which detected only few institutional changes during the last 38 years in OECD countries. In particular, rules of subnational representation and participation in central decision-making appeared to exhibit considerable inertia over time, Spain and Belgium being the only exceptions. Therefore, one can exclude, at least in the short run, possible reverse causation going from policy outcomes, the decision on decision-making rules generally preceding the decision on the vertical assignment of competencies or on the budgetary policy.

This long-time inertia does, however, not necessarily justify treating institutions as fully exogenous. Serious problems arise in estimating the impact of institutions on fiscal decentralisation when institutions are in reality endogenous, i.e. they are determined by other observed or unobserved factors.[41] As noted by Poterba (1996), observed correlations between institutions and policy outcomes could be spurious, when they simply reflect the influence of an omitted third variable on both, namely voter preferences for certain policies. For example, if citizen initiatives are associated with more fiscal decentralisation, this might be due to the fact that voters support rules which prevent collusive behaviour of legislators and over-centralisation. One may also imagine that heterogeneous regions join a federation provided that they have disproportionately large representation in the upper chamber of parliament and participate with equal rights in central decision-making. Since heterogeneity induces at the same time a higher degree of decentralisation in line with the traditional fiscal federalism theory, it may interfere with the centralising effect of cooperative decision-making mechanisms.

[40] The empirical literature typically uses dummy variables or differentiates between majoritarian, mixed-proportional and proportional representation.

[41] See, e.g., Besley and Case (2002), or, Persson and Tabellini (2001) for a discussion of institutional endogeneity issues. Aghion et al. (2004) provide evidence for a causal relationship between institutions and different socio-cultural and historical factors, such as ethno-linguistic fractionalisation and legal and colonial origin.

One must not exclude the possibility that politicians choose institutions strategically to affect future policy outcomes.[42] This is particularly the case when institutions are set up by ordinary laws which can be easily changed by the government majority in parliament. Nonetheless, except for few examples, fundamental institutions rarely change in functioning democracies. Therefore, even if institutions are assumed to partly reflect deeper cultural or societal aspects, they also have important direct effects on policy outcomes due to their inertia. The more difficult it is to change the institutions, the more valuable the cross-country variation is in identifying the effect of these institutions on the degree of fiscal decentralisation.

Not considering these endogeneity issues, one runs the risk of omitted-variable bias in estimating the effect of institutions. One possibility to address endogeneity consists in instrumenting one institution using another. However, this approach may not be reasonable, since one has to assume then that the institution used as an instrument is not itself correlated with the unobservables. Therefore, in order to take into account that institutions and fiscal decentralisation may be determined simultaneously by other right hand side factors, we include institutions in our regressions and at the same time control for costs and benefits of decentralisation and voter tastes for decentralisation. For ordinary least squares to yield an unbiased estimate of the effect of institutions, we have then to assume in the usual way that institutions are uncorrelated with the error term. This is the approach taken by previous studies on the effect of institutions on public spending, too, which account, for example, for the political affiliation of executive or legislative power, or for cultural influences.[43] Strictly speaking, both interjurisdictional heterogeneity of preferences and general tastes for centralised or decentralised provision of public goods have to be taken into account.

### 3.4.3 Costs and Preferences

According to the "Decentralisation Theorem" missing coordination in decentralised provision of public goods leads to costs in terms of foregone economies of scale and interjurisdictional spillovers. On the other hand, decentralisation allows to tailor public services to local preferences and conditions.

Following the empirical literature, the present analysis captures potential economies of scale and spillovers of public goods by the size of the country in terms of *population* and *area*, and by the spatial allocation of the population, as depicted by the degree of *urbanisation*. The higher the size and the geographic concentration of the population, the more likely economies of

[42] Certain changes in electoral rules which occurred in France and Italy, or frequent alterations of the delimitation of electoral constituencies seem to support this view.

[43] See Poterba (1995), Dafflon and Pujol (2001), Pujol and Weber (2003), and Feld and Matsusaka (2003), among others.

scale in the consumption of public goods could be exploited at lower levels of government, thus increasing the benefits of decentralisation. In addition to this, the costs of centralised information, administration, and decision-making are likely to increase with the size of the country, whereas spillovers of public goods tend to decrease with geographic area. It is also commonly assumed that the diversity of preferences increases with the size of the country, thus supporting decentralisation.[44] Apart from this, the degree of urbanisation is also included to control for potential differences between urban and rural areas in benefits of spending and costs of raising revenues. Some authors argue that more urbanised areas are associated with higher per capita costs of local public goods, and thus, with higher public spending of sub-central governments, which, *ceteris paribus*, would imply a higher degree of fiscal decentralisation.[45]

Measurement of interjurisdictional preference heterogeneity is confronted with several problems. First of all, preference heterogeneity has multiple dimensions which cannot be summarised by simple aggregate measures. The extent of preference diversity is expected to differ depending on the public goods concerned. For example, local preferences for certain national public goods like defence or welfare might be more homogeneous than preferences for typical local public goods like school education or local infrastructure. Therefore a disaggregated approach to testing the implications of the "Decentralisation Theorem" for individual public services might be more appropriate. Comparing inter-regional differences in voting behaviour in national referendums on specific objects could provide a direct measure of preference heterogeneity.[46] Alternatively, Strumpf and Oberholzer-Gee (2002) represent intra-state heterogeneity of preferences of US states based on estimates of local tastes for the liquor control policy.

However, a disaggregated approach cannot be easily replicated in cross-country analyses in view of the difficulty of defining strictly comparable issues submitted to voting. Also, as shown before, national referendums are missing or considerably restrained in quite a lot of countries. The alternative therefore consists in using proxies for aggregate preference heterogeneity based on inter-regional cultural or economic differences. Previous studies on fiscal decentralisation approximate interjurisdictional diversity of preferences by means of the

---

44 See, e.g., Alesina and Spolaore (1997), and, also, Greenberg (1956) with respect to linguistic diversity. This claim, however, lacks clear empirical evidence. For example, small countries like Belgium or Switzerland are more heterogeneous than certain large countries like France, Australia, or even the USA.

45 For example, based on an empirical study for Germany, Brecht (1932) claims that higher population density is associated with higher public expenditure. However, the German literature doubts the theoretical foundation and the empirical evidence.

46 This is the approach taken by Dafflon and Pujol (2001) who measure fiscal preferences of Swiss cantons drawing on the voters' behaviour in federal fiscal referendums.

degree of ethno-linguistic fractionalisation.[47] This is calculated as one minus the Herfindahl index of ethno-linguistic group shares, and measures the likelihood that two randomly selected individuals belong to different ethnic or linguistic groups.

Two problems have to be taken into account when using these fractionalisation measures. By focusing only on the number and the relative size of ethnic or linguistic groups, the geographical distribution of the different ethnic or cultural groups is not accurately represented. Since the geographical grouping of people with similar preferences constitutes the crucial precondition for the validity of the "Decentralisation Theorem", one has to implicitly assume that the ethnic or linguistic structure is perfectly correlated with the spatial allocation of the population.[48] Moreover, these indicators also ignore the extent of inter-cultural differences, assuming equal distances. Greenberg (1956) and Fearon (2003) propose alternative fractionalisation measures which account for the resemblance or "cultural distance" between the different ethno-linguistic groups. However, note that these classifications are only based on purely philological considerations.[49]

Another problem of common fractionalisation measures is related to the fact that preferences are determined by a multitude of ethno-linguistic, cultural, social or economic factors, and it is not clear which aspect is likely to dominate for a particular political issue or in a certain country at a certain time.[50] However, as the history of secessionist movements shows, linguistic cleavages seem to exert the strongest force.[51] Therefore, despite being highly

---

47 See, e.g., Panizza (1999), and Garrett and Rodden (2003). Fearon (2003) and Alesina et al. (2003) provide more recent data and a general discussion of the measurement of ethno-linguistic, religious and cultural diversity.

48 For instance, some studies report high degrees of fractionalisation for certain countries like Australia, Netherlands or the USA. However, the different groups considered there often represent recently immigrated people which have no deeply rooted local traditions, and which are dispersed throughout the country, instead of being geographically concentrated. Lijphart (1984) proposes as alternative indicator the population-weighted average degree of fragmentation of the component sub-units of the country. Considerable differences between this measure and the common index of fragmentation at the national level noticed for certain countries seem to demonstrate that Tiebout stratification indeed leads to the formation of relatively homogeneous sub-units.

49 Esteban and Ray (1994) present a similar measure of polarisation. Alternatively, inter-cultural differences might be better represented by surveys on regional identification and attachment to the nation, like those conducted by Euro-Barometer.

50 See, e.g., Laitin and Posner (2001) for a detailed critique of common fractionalisation measures. They propose a more disaggregated approach. They also point to problems associated with the endogeneity of ethnic or linguistic distinctions to other political and economic variables. However, over sufficiently long time horizons these structures are expected to be exogenous.

51 This is illustrated, e.g., by the cases of Belgium, Spain, Quebec, USSR, Yugoslavia, or of the canton Jura in Switzerland. The empirical analysis of Pujol

imperfect proxies, we rely on data provided by the Ethnologue project on linguistic *fractionalisation* to capture preference heterogeneity, since better quantitative measures which account for all aspects mentioned above are not yet available. Though not removing all difficulties, these data have the definite advantage of considering only indigenous languages and dialects in each country, thus, e.g., excluding languages of recent immigrants. Since it is not necessarily clear to which extent linguistic differences actually reflect different preferences for public goods, we refrain from considering the degree of resemblance of the different language groups.

In addition to the measure of linguistic fractionalisation, which is constant over time, the degree of *regional disparity* of per capita income is used as an indicator of time-variant inter-regional heterogeneity of preferences and endowments. We expect higher inter-regional income disparity to be associated with higher decentralisation. On the other hand, however, the demand for stronger central government support or inter-regional risk-sharing may also increase with income disparity.[52] The empirical studies of Pommerehne (1977) and Vaubel (1996) provide no conclusive results with respect to the effect of regional income disparity.

We also control for the influence of other potential determinants of government decentralisation, such as historical, social, cultural and economic conditions. First, we consider the country's *legal origin* by including a dummy variable for legal systems based on English common law. Civil law is commonly regarded as an instrument of the State in expanding its power, whereas the common law tradition puts more emphasis on private and property rights of the individuals. Religion, or, more precisely, the percentage of *Catholic* population, is also included as a proxy for general preferences for centralisation and a strong central government.[53] Cultural theories classify the Catholic doctrine as more hierarchical and interventionist than the Protestantism, which instead stresses individual responsibility. Strong preferences for uniformity and solidarity are expected to be associated with support for a strong central government and for inter-regional and interpersonal income redistribution.

---

and Weber (2003) also shows that language plays an important role in explaining fiscal preferences of Swiss cantons.

52 Note that, in general, regional indicators involve certain difficulties. First, in several countries regional boundaries often change for political or administrative reasons, thus questioning the exogenity and integrity of administrative divisions, and, at the same time, affecting the measurement of inter-regional disparity. Certain EU countries, such as Ireland, Greece or Finland, created development regions without vesting them with real fiscal powers, in order to allocate EU structural funds payments. See also chapter 4 with respect to this. This aspect is directly related to another problem, that of comparing countries with autonomous regional governments, with countries where regions merely represent administrative units of central government or statistical areas.

53 Since nearly all of the countries considered here are predominately Catholic or Protestant, we refrain from considering other religious affiliations.

La Porta et al. (1999) indeed provide some empirical evidence that Catholic and civil law countries are more interventionist than Protestant and common law countries. However, even if these aspects are transferred into the political sphere, it is not necessarily clear whether a more interventionist state might be more centralised, too.

Following the empirical literature, we also consider the voter ideology in order to capture preferences for certain institutions or policy outcomes. This is done by focusing on the parties composing the central government, since political power is basically exercised through the cabinet. As a proxy for government ideology we use the fraction of seats held by leftist parties in total seats of the government coalition in the legislature (*left government*). According to the partisan theory, politicians base their decisions on the preferences of their parties and of the voters who support them rather than on the preferences of all voters.[54] This theory predicts that left-dominated governments favour higher public spending. The empirical literature, however, provides quite inconclusive evidence with respect to the partisan cycle hypothesis[55] and neglects for the most part the resulting implications for the vertical government structure. Some political scientists argue that progressive governments are more concerned with equity considerations and therefore favour state control and stronger centralisation.[56]

Further standard control variables capturing varying demands for certain public goods are included, too. According to the "laws" of Wagner (1876) and Popitz (1927), economic development and growing prosperity are associated with the expansion and centralisation of the public sector. For example, demand for income redistribution and the establishment of generous welfare systems are expected to be positively related to higher income per capita. This also corresponds to the Meltzer-Richard hypothesis according to which an increase in the mean income relative to the income of the decisive median voter increases the size of government.[57] On the other hand, empirical evidence shows that high-income countries are likely to be more decentralised, a typical characteristic of underdevelopment being the relative unimportance of local government. This is explained by higher real costs of decentralised structures at lower stages of economic development due to scarcity of quali-

---

54 See, e.g., Hibbs (1977) and Castles (1982). See also Lijphart (1984) on the issue dimensions of partisan conflict. Poole and Rosenthal (1996) provide some evidence from the United States that legislators' ideology matters.

55 Cameron (1978), and Hicks and Swank (1992), among others, show that left governments are associated with higher public spending and revenues. On the other hand, Blais et al. (1993) find only small differences between spending patterns of left and right governments.

56 See, e.g., Steunenberg and Mol (1997).

57 See Meltzer and Richard (1981). This aspect could have been tested by the use of income inequality measures. However, due to the lack of internationally comparable consistent time series and general measurement problems, we refrain from doing so here.

fied government personnel, and to costs of political coordination and creation of local government institutions.[58] Apart from this, increasing wealth is expected to raise the diversity of preferences, too, thus fostering demands for fiscal decentralisation. In order to test for these effects, we include the natural log of real *income* (GDP) *per capita*.

Since there may exist certain life-cycle patterns to demand for public services, such as schools or old age homes, the demographic structure is represented by the *dependency ratio*, the proportion of population aged below 15 or above 64. Since the degree of decentralisation also reflects the budgetary share of different government activities, we finally control for temporary expenditure and revenue effects. The inclusion of a dummy variable taking the value of 1 for years of national *elections* captures possible electoral cycles mentioned in the literature. Central government expenditure are expected to increase in the run-up to national elections and decrease the year after, and vice versa with respect to tax revenues.[59] The degree of expenditure (revenue) decentralisation might therefore be lower (higher) in election years. Different elasticities of expenditure and revenue of the different levels of government with respect to business cycles are finally accounted for by including the *growth rate* of real per capita income.

## 3.5 Results

The degree of fiscal decentralisation is first regressed on the non-institutional determinants presented above, and, afterwards, on alternative institutional indicators. The results of the regression analysis for direct government expenditure are presented in Table 3.2. In view of the pooled cross-sectional time-series data structure, we estimate robust standard errors which account for both heteroscedasticity and an unspecified autocorrelation structure within units according to Newey and West (1987).[60] The F-tests indicate that all model coefficients are jointly significant, and the goodness of fit of the regression is very high. Checks for collinearity and outliers have been carried out. The territorial change in Germany is accounted for by the inclusion of a dummy variable for the period after reunification.

---

58 See, e.g., Oates (1972) and Wheare (1963). However, as Kee (1977) found out, this more likely reflects fundamental differences between industrial and developing countries, the relationship between income and decentralisation disappearing when considering only high-income countries.

59 Persson and Tabellini (2001, 2003), e.g., provide some evidence that electoral cycles depend on the electoral rules and the political regime.

60 The alternative estimation of robust standard errors using the White/Huber-sandwich-estimator (see White, 1980) adjusted for within-country clustering of errors leads to less precise estimates, without significantly changing the results. However, according to Davidson and MacKinnon (1993), the reliability of the White variance matrix estimator is questionable in case of small samples or cross-sections.

With respect to the variables approximating economies of scale and spillovers, only the geographic size has the expected positive effect on fiscal decentralisation. Contrary to previous studies, the estimates report a negative significant effect of urbanisation, and, though mostly insignificant, of population size. One possible explanation might be that these variables capture both demand and supply side aspects, the demand for certain public services provided by the central government possibly dominating vis-à-vis the economies of scale aspect. For example, urban agglomeration is typically associated with higher interjurisdictional spillovers and stronger demand for social transfer programs, both involving an increased role of the central government.

The estimates for both linguistic and economic heterogeneity are clearly in line with the "Decentralisation Theorem".[61] In general, countries with civil law traditions and predominantly catholic population are shown to be associated with more centralisation. We have also checked whether increased factor mobility may support centralisation. According to Bolton and Roland (1996), under certain conditions, perfect mobility removes the diversity of fiscal policies across jurisdictions. Apart from this, high interjurisdictional mobility is typically associated with increased spillovers and reflects a low diversity of preferences. Indeed, the additional inclusion of a measure of inter-regional individual *mobility* yields a negative effect on the degree of fiscal decentralisation (not shown), however, without considerably contributing to the goodness of fit of the regression.[62]

With respect to the role of economic development, the results confirm previous studies in providing evidence that higher income countries are more decentralised. The demographic composition also plays a certain role. As the percentage of population below 15 or above 64 increases, either the demand for central government services increases or the demand for local services decreases, thus reducing the degree of decentralisation. Electoral and business cycles seem to play a minor role, partly indicating that the share of subcentral government expenditure is lower in years of national elections and strong economic growth. According to these findings, the income elasticity of demand for centrally provided services seems to exceed that for subnational services. Finally, we provide some evidence that party ideology matters for policy outcomes. Contrary to the expectations, central governments dominated by leftist parties are correlated with a higher degree of expenditure decentralisation. The results are consistent with those of Schaltegger and Feld (2001) and with recent developments in a number of countries which indicate that

---

61 Note that the use of alternative indices of ethno-linguistic fractionalisation presented in the literature yielded similar results.

62 The results of regressions using alternative specifications not shown here are reported in Tables B.21 and B.22 in Appendix B.

leftist cabinets tend to support government decentralisation[63] and to commit to restrictive fiscal policy.

As can be seen, the inclusion of institutions considerably improves the goodness of fit of the regressions. With minor exceptions, the effects of the other variables remain unchanged. Due to multicollinearity, institutions of decision-making are included separately. To check for endogeneity, Hausman tests have been carried out by first regressing institutions on other variables which represent preferences and costs, and, afterwards, including the derived residuals in the initial regressions. The tests indicate strict exogeneity. Note again that institutional changes in the course of time are explicitly taken into account by the indicators employed here.

Table 3.2: OLS estimates of fiscal decentralisation, direct expenditure (incl. social security), 23 OECD countries, 1970-2001

| | Dep. var.: Degree of expen. decentralisation (indic. ED1) | | | | | | |
|---|---|---|---|---|---|---|---|
| | (1) | (2) | (3) | (4) | (5) | (6) | (7) |
| *Population* | -.012** | -.005 | -.003 | -.008 | .000 | -.006 | -.006 |
| | (.006) | (.006) | (.005) | (.005) | (.005) | (.005) | (.006) |
| *Area* | .027*** | .034*** | .024*** | .028*** | .015*** | .026*** | .026*** |
| | (.006) | (.006) | (.006) | (.006) | (.006) | (.005) | (.006) |
| *Urbanisation* | -.276*** | -.311*** | -.238*** | -.314*** | -.252*** | -.241*** | -.242*** |
| | (.065) | (.077) | (.065) | (.072) | (.069) | (.071) | (.079) |
| *Fractionalisation* | .159*** | .147*** | .140*** | .120*** | .040 | .070 | .070 |
| | (.043) | (.040) | (.040) | (.037) | (.041) | (.043) | (.050) |
| *Regional disparity* | .330*** | .232** | .149 | .169* | .231** | .230*** | .231*** |
| | (.094) | (.094) | (.093) | (.097) | (.092) | (.089) | (.086) |
| *Per capita income* | .170*** | .181*** | .118*** | .145*** | .151*** | .144*** | .144*** |
| | (.027) | (.031) | (.033) | (.029) | (.029) | (.028) | (.029) |
| *Catholic* | -.160*** | -.158*** | -.189*** | -.181*** | -.166*** | -.151*** | -.151*** |
| | (.036) | (.026) | (.033) | (.028) | (.030) | (.030) | (.038) |
| *Legal origin* | .097*** | .076*** | .035 | .059** | .033 | .040 | .040 |
| | (.024) | (.026) | (.025) | (.024) | (.024) | (.026) | (.026) |
| *Dependency ratio* | -1.058*** | -.731* | -.788** | -.792** | -.566 | -.704* | -.707* |
| | (.364) | (.443) | (.385) | (.396) | (.376) | (.396) | (.394) |
| *Growth rate* | -.190 | -.197 | -.092 | -.129 | -.039 | -.079 | -.078 |
| | (.163) | (.139) | (.131) | (.132) | (.134) | (.136) | (.138) |
| *Election* | -.006 | -.005 | -.007* | -.008* | -.008** | -.008* | -.008* |
| | (.005) | (.004) | (.004) | (.004) | (.004) | (.004) | (.004) |

[63] This has been the case in France and Spain under socialist governments at the beginning of the 1980s, or, more recently, in the United Kingdom under the Labour government.

Table 3.2 (cont.): OLS estimates of fiscal decentralisation, direct expenditure

| | Dep. var.: Degree of expen. decentralisation (indic. ED1) | | | | | | |
|---|---|---|---|---|---|---|---|
| | (1) | (2) | (3) | (4) | (5) | (6) | (7) |
| *Left government* | .052*** | .036** | .028* | .028* | .026* | .030** | .030** |
| | (.169) | (.016) | (.015) | (.015) | (.014) | (.015) | (.015) |
| *Presidential regime* | | -.102*** | -.081*** | -.094*** | -.080*** | -.091*** | -.091*** |
| | | .025 | (.025) | (.024) | (.025) | (.024) | (.025) |
| *Electoral system* | | | | | | | .009 |
| | | | | | | | (.235) |
| *Direct democracy* | | .011 | .002 | -.002 | -.015 | -.020 | -.020 |
| | | (.014) | (.012) | (.013) | (.012) | (.015) | (.015) |
| *Federal* | | | .098*** | | | | |
| | | | (.018) | | | | |
| *Subnat. represent.* | | | | .061*** | | | |
| | | | | (.013) | | | |
| *Subnat. particip.*[a] | | | | | .074*** | .072*** | .072*** |
| *(direct)* | | | | | (.011) | (.018) | (.020) |
| *Subnat. particip.*[a] | | | | | .014* | .023** | .023* |
| *(indirect)* | | | | | (.008) | (.010) | (.012) |
| No. obs. | 482 | 482 | 482 | 482 | 482 | 482 | 482 |
| adj. $R^2$ | .682 | .737 | .782 | .768 | .799 | .779 | .779 |

Note: Newey-West heteroscedasticity and autocorrelation consistent standard errors are in parentheses. ***, **, and * indicate significance at the 1%, 5% and 10% level, respectively. All regressions include a dummy variable for Germany after reunification whose coefficient is not reported. [a] The following alternative indices have been used: decision-making on assignment of expenditure powers (5), and on all policy areas (6)-(7).

As expected, presidential regimes which are typically associated with stronger central governments and weaker representation of minorities have a highly significant negative effect on government decentralisation. In contrast to this, the degree of disproportionality of the electoral system seems to play no clear role.[64] We have also tested the hypothesis according to which the common-pool problem in fiscal policy might be more pronounced under broad-based coalition governments, where the number of veto players is higher.[65] Coalition governments may therefore lead to over-spending at the national level and, *ceteris paribus*, to a lower degree of decentralisation. The

64 The alternative use of a dummy variable for electoral systems based on *majority rule* yielded no significant effect either, see Table B.21 in Appendix B.

65 Roubini and Sachs (1989) show that fragmented coalition governments are associated with higher budget deficits in industrial countries. On the other hand, the analysis of Schaltegger and Feld (2004) for Swiss cantons provides no clear evidence for such a relationship.

inclusion of a measure of political *fragmentation* of the central *government* (not shown) yielded, however, no significant effect.

The decentralising effect of referendums found by Schaltegger and Feld (2001) and Matsusaka (1995, 2000) for subnational governments cannot be confirmed at the national level. The coefficients are insignificant and the signs are contradictory. First of all, this is not surprising when considering that the conduct of referendums is more restricted at the national level as compared to the local level, certain highly decentralised countries like the USA or Canada do not provide for national referendums at all. Also, as shown in section 3.3.2, with the exception of Switzerland, financial issues are usually excluded from consultation at the national level. Indeed, a decentralising effect is supported when considering alternatively only legal provisions for financial referendums and initiatives or the referendum practice in terms of the average number of national referendums (see Table B.21 in Appendix B.).[66] An alternative explanation for the inconclusive effect of national referendums may be provided by the Meltzer-Richard hypothesis according to which more unequal income distribution will create a majority in favour of increased redistribution.[67] The decisive national median voter – who is distinct from the regional median voters – may consequently support more centralisation aimed to increase redistribution. As concluded by Matsusaka (2000), too, the spending reducing impact of initiatives is not certain. Initiatives only serve to adjust policy outcomes to citizens' preferences, yet, citizens may prefer higher central government spending.[68]

With respect to the participation of subnational entities in central decision-making, the estimates confirm the standard result of previous studies according to which countries with a federal constitution are more decentralised than unitary countries. The index of subnational representation which also accounts for regional representation in unitary countries, has also a highly significant positive effect on government decentralisation, which is consistent with the analysis of Vaubel (1996).

The evidence also supports a significant positive relationship between participation of subnational entities in central decision-making and the degree of decentralisation. Particularly participation in the assignment of spending

---

66 The last result seems to partly contradict Besley and Case (2002) who argue that the actual conduct of initiatives need not be a good indicator of their influence, since the effect of an initiative can be felt even if it is not actually called. This might be certainly true with respect to citizen initiatives at subnational levels, or when referendums are frequently held. Hence, the referendum intensity does not only reflect the restrictions imposed upon organisation, but also deeply rooted traditions of "citizen participation". For example, in Austria, despite extensive legal provisions, referendums are barely conducted at the national level.

67 See Meltzer and Richard (1981).

68 This is also partly in line with Matsusaka (1995) who pointed out that voters are not hostile to public spending per se, the evidence showing that voters wanted more local public services than actually delivered.

powers performs better than the federalism dummy in explaining variation in the degree of expenditure decentralisation. The effect is generally stronger for direct than for indirect forms of participation, which provides first circumstantial evidence for the collusion hypothesis, according to which centralised decision-making by elected subnational representatives favours cartelisation and centralisation. However, note that the coefficient of linguistic fractionalisation becomes insignificant especially when taking account of direct subnational participation in central decision-making.[69] This possibly indicates that particularly in heterogeneous countries certain decisions at the national level have to be approved additionally by the voters or legislatures of the regions in order to prevent excessive centralisation.

The results with respect to expenditure decentralisation are also confirmed, with few exceptions, when focusing alternatively on self-financed expenditure.[70] In order to provide a more appropriate test of the implications of the common-pool problem for public revenues, the analysis focuses next on the degree of tax decentralisation. Tables 3.3 and 3.4 each confront the results for total tax revenues of sub-central government as reported in financial statistics (columns 1-4), and for autonomous own tax revenues accounting for tax-raising powers (columns 5-8), drawing on the tax decentralisation figures calculated in chapter 2. Note, again, that in case of the latter, changes in tax-raising powers of sub-central government in the course of time are taken into account.

The estimates for the corrected decentralisation measure (*TD1*) clearly confirm the expectations according to which the more decision-making is delegated to representatives of sub-central entities, the more centralised are the taxing powers. In contrast to this, direct participation of the regional electorate or of regional legislatures in decisions concerning the assignment of taxing powers or other policy areas has a significant positive effect on the share of autonomous own tax revenues of sub-central government in total tax revenue of consolidated general government.

Furthermore, as expected, countries where the central government possesses the ultimate competency in tax legislation are found to be more centralised.[71] These results therefore support the predictions of Redoano and Scharf (2004) and the collusion hypothesis. On the other hand, the estimates now contradict the analysis of Vaubel (1996), indicating that stronger subnational representation at the national level has a negative, though statistically insignificant, effect on tax decentralisation. Also, in terms of tax autonomy, the estimates provide no clear support for the hypothesis that federal coun-

---

[69] The coefficients of correlation with fractionalisation are indeed higher for direct than for indirect forms of participation.

[70] See Table B.20 in Appendix B. Among the most important exceptions are a positive, but insignificant effect of the dependency ratio, and the statistically stronger effects of population size, electoral system and direct democracy.

[71] Note that only in Australia, Canada, Sweden, Switzerland, and the USA the central government possesses no ultimate tax competency.

Table 3.3: OLS estimates of fiscal decentralisation (institutions 1), tax revenue, 23 OECD countries, 1965-2001

| | Dep. var.: Degree of tax decentralisation | | | | | | | |
|---|---|---|---|---|---|---|---|---|
| | Total tax revenue (TD3) | | | | Auton. own tax revenue (TD1) | | | |
| | (1) | (2) | (3) | (4) | (5) | (6) | (7) | (8) |
| *Population* | -.011 | -.002 | .003 | -.006 | -.022*** | -.018*** | -.018*** | -.018*** |
| | (.007) | (.007) | (.006) | (.007) | (.006) | (.006) | (.006) | (.006) |
| *Area* | .040*** | .048*** | .029*** | .035*** | .040*** | .044*** | .043*** | .045*** |
| | (.007) | (.007) | (.007) | (.007) | (.006) | (.006) | (.006) | (.006) |
| *Urbanisat.* | -.431*** | -.499*** | -.349*** | -.512*** | -.475*** | -.480*** | -.469*** | -.480*** |
| | (.083) | (.091) | (.075) | (.083) | (.068) | (.081) | (.080) | (.082) |
| *Fractional.* | .284*** | .270*** | .219*** | .204*** | .442*** | .427*** | .423*** | .428*** |
| | (.059) | (.051) | (.045) | (.051) | (.056) | (.053) | (.054) | (.054) |
| *Reg. dispar.* | .267** | .135 | -.013 | .008 | .049 | -.009 | -.019 | -.006 |
| | (.125) | (.115) | (.106) | (.118) | (.091) | (.088) | (.089) | (.091) |
| *P.c. income* | .280*** | .301*** | .204*** | .249*** | .233*** | .236*** | .229*** | .237*** |
| | (.027) | (.036) | (.027) | (.029) | (.027) | (.029) | (.029) | (.028) |
| *Catholic* | -.114*** | -.108*** | -.137*** | -.137*** | -.215*** | -.212*** | -.214*** | -.212*** |
| | (.031) | (.026) | (.026) | (.024) | (.034) | (.032) | (.033) | (.032) |
| *Legal origin* | .010 | -.016 | -.095*** | -.051** | .056** | .045* | .039 | .045* |
| | (.031) | (.032) | (.020) | (.023) | (.026) | (.026) | (.026) | (.026) |
| *Depen. ratio* | .805 | 1.257** | 1.265*** | 1.346*** | .956** | 1.126*** | 1.127*** | 1.125*** |
| | (.534) | (.539) | (.407) | (.462) | (.419) | (.431) | (.431) | (.434) |
| *Growth rate* | -.544** | -.580*** | -.234 | -.355** | -.429** | -.416** | -.392** | -.420** |
| | (.233) | (.212) | (.154) | (.170) | (.205) | (.190) | (.177) | (.183) |
| *Election* | -.002 | -.002 | -.007* | -.009* | -.003 | -.002 | -.003 | -.002 |
| | (.006) | (.005) | (.004) | (.005) | (.004) | (.005) | (.004) | (.004) |
| *Left govern.* | .020 | .009 | -.009 | -.006 | -.012 | -.018 | -.020 | -.018 |
| | (.019) | (.018) | (.017) | (.017) | (.016) | (.016) | (.016) | (.016) |
| *Pres. regime* | | -.119*** | -.085*** | -.110*** | | -.059*** | -.057*** | -.059*** |
| | | (.025) | (.019) | (.021) | | (.020) | (.021) | (.020) |
| *Dir. democr.* | | .003 | -.019 | -.029* | | .010 | .009 | .011 |
| | | (.019) | (.013) | (.015) | | (.015) | (.016) | (.017) |
| *Federal* | | | .198*** | | | | .014 | |
| | | | (.020) | | | | (.026) | |
| *Subnat. repr.* | | | | .123*** | | | | -.002 |
| | | | | (.020) | | | | (.019) |
| No. obs. | 549 | 549 | 549 | 549 | 549 | 549 | 549 | 549 |
| adj. $R^2$ | .621 | .663 | .781 | .740 | .739 | .753 | .753 | .753 |

Note: Newey-West heteroscedasticity and autocorrelation consistent standard errors are in parentheses. ***, **, and * indicate significance at the 1%, 5% and 10% level, respectively. All regressions include a dummy variable for Germany after reunification whose coefficient is not reported.

Table 3.4: OLS estimates of fiscal decentralisation (institutions 2), tax revenue, 23 OECD countries, 1965-2001

| | Dep. var.: Degree of tax decentralisation | | | | | | | |
|---|---|---|---|---|---|---|---|---|
| | Total tax revenue (TD3) | | | | Auton. own tax revenue (TD1) | | | |
| | (1) | (2) | (3) | (4) | (5) | (6) | (7) | (8) |
| *Population* | -.007 | -.009 | -.018*** | -.005 | -.001 | -.002 | -.005 | -.010* |
| | (.006) | (.006) | (.007) | (.007) | (.005) | (.005) | (.005) | (.006) |
| *Area* | .031*** | .037*** | .028*** | .028*** | .026*** | .030*** | .028*** | .024*** |
| | (.008) | (.007) | (.007) | (.008) | (.007) | (.005) | (.006) | (.006) |
| *Urbanisat.* | -.467*** | -.452*** | -.522*** | -.335*** | -.309*** | -.301*** | -.324*** | -.306*** |
| | (.094) | (.091) | (.097) | (.099) | (.074) | (.070) | (.074) | (.074) |
| *Fractional.* | .215*** | .201*** | .239*** | .083 | .216*** | .195*** | .207*** | .228*** |
| | (.076) | (.070) | (.074) | (.070) | (.067) | (.055) | (.057) | (.059) |
| *Reg. dispar.* | .103 | .107 | .226* | .180 | -.018 | .073 | .111 | .039 |
| | (.112) | (.120) | (.122) | (.121) | (.084) | (.084) | (.089) | (.088) |
| *P.c. income* | .244*** | .245*** | .239*** | .243*** | .222*** | .236*** | .234*** | .174*** |
| | (.030) | (.030) | (.030) | (.032) | (.026) | (.024) | (.025) | (.026) |
| *Catholic* | -.137*** | -.118*** | -.175*** | -.056** | -.143*** | -.127*** | -.145*** | -.157*** |
| | (.030) | (.028) | (.038) | (.027) | (.029) | (.026) | (.031) | (.031) |
| *Legal origin* | -.051** | -.053** | -.059*** | -.088*** | -.047** | -.040** | -.042** | -.033 |
| | (.025) | (.023) | (.021) | (.028) | (.020) | (.019) | (.018) | (.022) |
| *Depen. ratio* | 1.529*** | 1.352*** | 1.075** | 1.102** | 1.390*** | 1.337*** | 1.249*** | .962** |
| | (.446) | (.469) | (.466) | (.512) | (.392) | (.358) | (.361) | (.382) |
| *Growth rate* | -.361** | -.350** | -.234 | -.378** | -.302** | -.292** | -.255** | -.201 |
| | (.170) | (.171) | (.161) | (.176) | (.144) | (.129) | (.127) | (.147) |
| *Election* | -.007 | -.007 | -.005 | -.005 | -.003 | -.002 | -.002 | -.006 |
| | (.005) | (.005) | (.005) | (.005) | (.004) | (.004) | (.004) | (.004) |
| *Left govern.* | -.007 | -.004 | -.009 | .003 | -.003 | -.008 | -.010 | -.024 |
| | (.018) | (.018) | (.018) | (.018) | (.017) | (.014) | (.015) | (.016) |
| *Pres. regime* | -.100*** | -.109*** | -.122*** | -.105*** | -.048*** | -.050*** | -.054*** | -.044** |
| | (.022) | (.022) | (.023) | (.025) | (.018) | (.017) | (.017) | (.021) |
| *Elect. syst.* | | | 1.061*** | | | | .338 | |
| | | | (.277) | | | | (.213) | |
| *Dir. democr.* | -.036** | -.043** | -.044*** | -.014 | -.015 | -.035*** | -.035*** | -.008 |
| | (.016) | (.018) | (.016) | (.016) | (.014) | (.013) | (.013) | (.012) |
| *Subn. part.*[a] | .047* | .067** | .047 | | .119*** | .191*** | .185*** | |
| *(direct)* | (.025) | (.029) | (.028) | | (.023) | (.021) | (.021) | |
| *Subn. part.*[a] | .064*** | .063*** | .092*** | | -.033*** | -.065*** | -.055*** | |
| *(indirect)* | (.010) | (.013) | (.015) | | (.009) | (.008) | (.011) | |
| *Cen. tax c.* | | | | -.187*** | | | | -.199*** |
| | | | | (.041) | | | | (.032) |
| No. obs. | 549 | 549 | 549 | 549 | 549 | 549 | 549 | 549 |
| adj. $R^2$ | .746 | .737 | .757 | .708 | .805 | .848 | .849 | .807 |

Note: [a] the following alternative indices have been used: decision-making on the assignment of revenue powers (1) and (5), and on all policy areas (2)-(3) and (6)-(7). See Table 3.3 for further details.

tries are more decentralised than unitary countries. However, in order to take a closer look at the upper chamber of parliament, dummy variables for different types of regional representation have been used alternatively. As expected, general regional representation in the upper chamber irrespective of its form is found to be associated with a higher level of tax decentralisation, whereas upper chambers consisting of representatives delegated by regional governments are strongly correlated with higher centralisation.[72]

Interestingly enough, certain differences are reported when comparing the estimates for the expenditure and the revenue side of the public sector. For example, the centralising effects of business cycles and national referendums are stronger for tax revenues. Also, the signs of the dependency ratio and legal origin are reversed and become partly ambiguous, whereas electoral cycles and government ideology lose significance. However, with regard to the revenue side of the public sector, other determining factors are possibly omitted, such as the mobility of different tax bases or economies of scale in tax collection, which are assumed to determine the assignment of taxing powers to different levels of government. In general, the goodness of fit of the regressions is higher when considering only autonomous tax revenues.

The divergent results therefore indicate the importance of correct measurement of fiscal decentralisation in quantitative analyses. In order to control for the presence of common patterns of "spatial" correlation across countries, additional regressions have been run including year dummies (not shown). The previous results are mainly confirmed. However, this methodological approach seems rather suited to studies in the subnational context, since subnational entities are more likely to be exposed to common exogenous influences. For cross-country analysis this is, at most, relevant for groups of countries, such as EU countries, which are strongly integrated with each other. Finally, with few exceptions, the robustness of the results is also confirmed by alternative OLS regressions on three year averages.[73]

## 3.6 Discussion and Conclusions

This chapter has aimed at verifying empirically the contribution of the traditional fiscal federalism literature and of new political economic approaches to explaining cross-national differences in the degree of fiscal decentralisation. Based upon a detailed examination of decision-making institutions for 23 OECD countries from 1965 to 2003, a regression analysis is carried out to determine the effect of specific institutions and other factors on the degree of fiscal decentralisation. The comparative-descriptive analysis indeed reveals a large variety of institutional rules, even among formally federal countries. The results of the cross-sectional time-series regression analysis are mostly in

[72] The results are reported in Table B.22 in Appendix B.
[73] See Tables B.23 and B.23 in Appendix B.

line with the "Decentralisation Theorem", indicating that large linguistically and economically heterogeneous countries are more decentralised. Overall, factors depicting general preferences and the demand for certain public services supplied by local or central government significantly contribute to explaining cross-national differences in decentralisation.

The analysis also indicates that institutions actually influence policy outcomes. For example, presidential regimes are found to be associated with increased centralisation. With total subnational tax revenues (indicator *TD3*) or with expenditures (indicator *ED1*) as dependent variable, participation of sub-central governments in central decision-making leads to more decentralisation. However, when accounting for tax-raising powers of sub-central governments instead (indicator *TD1*), it turns out that particularly participation of representatives delegated by sub-central governments and legislatures in central decision-making is associated with less subnational fiscal autonomy and more centralisation. In contrast to this, direct involvement of the citizens through regional referendums leads to more decentralisation of tax-raising powers. On the other hand, contrary to previous analyses at the subnational level, direct democracy at the national level mostly tends to favour increased centralisation.

The new contribution of this analysis is therefore twofold. First, these estimates support the collusion hypothesis and the theoretical predictions of Lockwood (2004) and Redoano and Scharf (2004). Bargaining at the national level provides sub-central governments with more financial resources from the common pool to spend, while at the same time independent tax-raising autonomy is restricted. And second, the analysis shows how important it is to use in empirical studies the indicator of decentralisation *TD1*, which accounts for subnational decision-making autonomy instead of received expenditure and revenue shares.

The empirical analysis certainly suffers from certain limitations. First, one should be cautious in drawing final conclusions with respect to the role of institutions, since the analysis draws on a small cross-section of countries, only half of which provide for subnational representation at the national level. A second difficulty consists in representing institutional rules by means of indicators. And, finally, problems related to institutional endogeneity and omitted-variable bias cannot be completely ruled out. Possible extensions may involve the consideration of a larger sample of democratic countries, the correct measurement of the degree of decentralisation with respect to public expenditures, and the conduct of a disaggregated analysis of the determinants of decentralisation for different government functions. Notwithstanding this, the main contribution of the present study to the positive theory of fiscal federalism consists in providing cross-national evidence that cost-benefit aspects as well as institutional rules determine the observed degree of public sector decentralisation. Furthermore, the analysis presents a detailed approach to the quantification of institutions and points at the sensitivity of empirical results to the correct measurement of fiscal decentralisation.

# 4

# Economic Integration and Fiscal Decentralisation

## 4.1 Introduction

Drawing on the previous analysis of the determinants of vertical government structures, this chapter investigates the specific causal relationship between those two trends described in the introduction, addressing the question whether economic and political integration of countries fosters the decentralisation of the public sector.

While explaining cross-country differences in the vertical government structure, the theory of fiscal federalism fails to give an adequate explanation of the recent process of decentralisation. According to the welfare-maximising view, shifts in the degree of fiscal decentralisation are either due to changes in the vertical allocation of functions – e.g. due to changing local preferences and conditions, or costs of public good provision – or to changes in the relative demand for certain public goods. For example, international conflicts raise the demand for security and military protection, thus increasing the role of the central government provided that defence is a national public good. Changing population and social patterns, economic and technological development, and increasing mobility of individuals and firms can necessitate changes in the optimal assignment of government functions and in the boundaries of political jurisdictions.

Inspired by the spread of political separatism and the emergence of new countries throughout the world, recent literature (Alesina and Spolaore, 1997, Bolton and Roland, 1997) explores the economic determinants of the creation and disintegration of countries.[1] In contrast to the traditional theory of fiscal federalism which assumes fixed borders, the size of the country is shown to be determined endogenously by the trade-off between the benefits of size

[1] A survey of this literature is found in Bolton et al. (1996), Drazen (2002), Persson and Tabellini (2000), and Ruta (2005). See, also, Alesina and Spolaore (2003) for a more recent contribution, and Bookman (1992) for a general discussion of the determinants of secession.

and the costs of heterogeneity of preferences. In the tradition of the "Decentralisation Theorem", a region's decision of leaving the nation-state or, respectively, demanding more fiscal autonomy thus depends on the benefits of providing public goods and taxes in accordance with local preferences, and the costs of reduced coordination with the rest of the nation in terms of foregone economies of scale in the provision of public goods and technological and fiscal spillovers.

It turns out that by impeding the internalisation of externalities associated with secession, majority decisions in democracies result in the emergence of an inefficiently large number of countries. Within this context, by increasing the market size and reducing political and economic transaction costs, economic integration lowers the benefits of country size, thus enhancing the incentives to separation.[2] The intensification of the separatist movement in Québec after creation of NAFTA, and increasing demands for regional autonomy in certain EU countries seem to support these theories.

However, changes of national borders represent an extreme case. The direct implications of integration for the vertical government structure are mostly neglected by the literature on secessions. Bolton and Roland (1997) show that regional autonomy is less costly than secession, since it mainly avoids the efficiency losses involved. By lowering the relative costs of local provision of public goods, integration is thus expected to enhance public sector decentralisation.

According to the New Economic Geography literature in the tradition of Krugman (1991a), integration generates agglomeration and specialisation effects at the regional level, thus increasing the scope for economies of scale in production. Local governments could exploit these benefits by demanding more autonomy in the provision of local public goods and taxes in order to compete for mobile factors. Political integration, too, might contribute to public sector decentralisation, since the costs of supplying certain public goods now in the competency of the supranational level are reduced. On the other hand, by increasing the economic risk, economic integration is also expected to enhance the demand for inter-regional risk-sharing or other policies carried out by the central government, such as income redistribution. Therefore, the ultimate result of integration hinges on the trade-off between increased local growth prospects and higher economic risk.

So far, there is only little empirical evidence with regard to the impact of integration on the vertical government structure. As shown in chapter 3, in general, most of the work deals with the determinants of public sector decentralisation as derived from the theory of fiscal federalism. Alesina and Wacziarg (1998) provide some evidence for a negative relationship between the size of the country and the degree of economic openness, thus confirming the hypothesis that larger countries benefit less from economic integration. This is also supported by Alesina et al. (2000) who find a positive effect of both

[2] See Alesina and Spolaore (1997), Alesina et al. (2000), Etro (2003), and Casella and Feinstein (2002).

openness and country size on economic development, the growth inducing impact of the market size being determined by the degree of openness.[3]

With regard to the vertical government structure, the results of a few – particularly politico-scientific – studies seem to support a positive relationship between integration and centralisation. Rodrik (1998), for instance, finds a positive significant effect of economic openness on the size of the public sector which he attributes to higher public expenditure for redistribution and macroeconomic stabilisation due to increasing exposure to exogenous shocks.[4] Since these functions are in general in the competency of the central government, one would therefore expect a centralising effect of economic integration.

Using a panel of industrial and developing countries, Garrett and Rodden (2003) show that indeed integration is associated with public sector centralisation. This is broadly explained by growing demand for inter-regional risk-sharing and central government transfers aimed at preventing the secession of rich regions. Hiscox (2003) focuses instead on the effects of globalisation on inter-regional income distribution and demands for political decentralisation, showing that the importance of primary commodity exports has a significant positive effect on the extension of local electoral control over state and municipal governments. In a cross-section analysis for OECD countries Verdier and Breen (2001) provide evidence for a positive relationship between financial openness and fiscal centralisation, whereas the interaction with European integration, as captured by the EU structural policy payments, has a negative sign. This is attributed to the insurance function of the EU structural policy which partly substitutes for national income redistribution. However, the advance of European integration and other possible determinants of the vertical government structure are not taken into account. Finally, van Houten (2003) finds no clear evidence for a stimulating effect of economic integration on the recent regional autonomy movements in EU countries.

Drawing on the theoretical framework provided by the literature on fiscal federalism and secessions, this chapter investigates the vertical government structure in terms of the impact of economic integration in general, and in particular, political integration in the European Union. For this purpose a theoretical model is set up, which relates the degree of fiscal decentralisation to economic integration, preference heterogeneity, and economies of scale. The hypothesis of a decentralising effect of integration is then tested empirically for the panel of OECD countries, also controlling for other possible factors. In contrast to the pooled regression analysis in chapter 3, the model is estimated with country fixed effects. In doing so, we focus on the impact of changes

---

3 See also Spolaore and Wacziarg (2002), as well as Wacziarg et al. (2002) for a survey of this work.

4 Cameron (1978) yields similar results in a related study. However, the result of Rodrik's analysis applies especially to countries with high terms-of-trade risk, and less to OECD countries. See also Schulze and Ursprung (1999) for a critical review of the empirical literature on the impact of integration on public expenditure.

in the degree of integration and in other factors on costs and benefits of decentralisation over time.

This chapter is organised as follows. In the following section a theoretical model relating integration and the vertical government structure is set up and the main hypotheses are derived. In section 4.3 various empirical considerations are discussed and some descriptive statistics and the investigation approach are presented. Finally, section 4.4 provides the results of the empirical analysis, and section 4.5 draws the conclusions.

## 4.2 Theoretical Framework

In the following, a theoretical framework is presented which relates public sector decentralisation to economic integration, economies of scale and preference heterogeneity, and the main hypotheses are set up. The aim is not so much to contribute to the theoretical discussion, but to formalise testable empirical implications of the theoretical considerations already made in the literature.

### 4.2.1 Basic Assumptions

The model presented here extends the theoretical framework provided by Alesina and Spolaore (1997), Alesina et al. (2000), and Etro (2003) in order to illustrate the relationship between economic integration and the degree of fiscal decentralisation. The welfare-maximising approach chosen draws on the "Decentralisation Theorem" by taking into account the cost/benefit ratio of decentralisation, which is assumed to be affected by economic integration.

In contrast to the literature on secessions which deals with the optimal size of countries, national borders are assumed to be fixed, and the analysis focuses instead on the effect of integration on the optimal vertical government structure. Marginal changes in national borders generally imply high separation costs, and therefore seldom occur in reality.[5] Young (1994) pointed out that secessions are very rare in advanced industrial countries and functioning democracies, since ethnic or cultural minorities are assured equal rights with the majority and effective representation in national institutions.

Generally speaking, demands for secession concern only particular regions, and are often solved through specific arrangements, such as home rule. Unlike this, decentralisation entails the devolution of fiscal powers to lower levels of government as a whole. Alesina and Spolaore (1997) and Etro (2003) investigate the effect of integration on the size of countries, and refrain from considering different levels of government, therefore assuming that public goods are provided uniformly by the central government according to the preferences of the national median. Panizza (1999) extends the model of Alesina and

[5] See also Drazen (2002: 726f.), concerning this.

Spolaore (1997) to analyse the determinants of the degree of public sector centralisation, however, without considering the aspect of integration.

To begin with, consider a federation of fixed population size $N$, which is equally divided among two regions $i = 1, 2$. Assuming that Tiebout stratification has already taken place and there is no more interjurisdictional mobility, all individuals are identical within a region and share identical preferences described by the parameter $\delta_i$, but differ between the regions. The individuals consume a national and a local public good, which are non-rival and not close substitutes. Think, e.g., of defence or income redistribution, and, respectively, local infrastructure or school education. The local public good $g^L$ is supplied in equal absolute quantity, yet of different type, in each region according to the local preferences.[6] By assuming that the local public good benefits exclusively the inhabitants of the respective region, we abstract from inter-regional spillovers. The national public good $g^C$ provided by the central government is of uniform type and located in the middle of an ideological spectrum of regional preferences. The preference parameter $\delta_i$ then measures the preference distance between the type of national public good preferred by the regional inhabitant and the type of good actually provided.[7] In the symmetric setting considered here, the regional preference distances are assumed to be of different signs but of equal magnitude: $\delta_1 = -\delta_2 = \delta$, with $0 \leq \delta < 1$.[8]

The utility of an individual located in region $i$ is then described by the following additive function

$$U_i = v^L(g^L, \alpha) + v^C\left(g^C, \delta, \beta(\omega, \gamma)\right) + y_i - t,$$

with $v^C_{g^C} > 0$, $v^L_{g^L} > 0$, and strict concavity. According to the fiscal federalism theory, increasing preference heterogeneity reduces both the absolute and the marginal utility from centrally provided public goods, therefore $v^C_\delta < 0$ and $v^C_{g^C,\delta} < 0$. $0 < \alpha, \beta \leq 1$ finally denote general preference parameters. In order to account for the possible centralising effects of integration mentioned in the literature,[9] preferences for the national public good are assumed to depend themselves on the degree of integration of the federation in the world econ-

[6] In principle, the amount of the local public good supplied in each region could differ. However, for the sake of simplicity we consider only symmetric allocations here. Interjurisdictional preference heterogeneity is therefore only related to the type of public goods. Think, e.g., of a local public good as an amenity, such as standards, education or administration in native language, quality of public services, or other ethno-linguistic, cultural or social aspects.

[7] See also Alesina et al. (1999), and Panizza (1999) for similar specifications of preference heterogeneity. In the median voter model this is referred to as the "median distance from the median".

[8] In case of more than two regions one could imagine that preferences are located on a circle, the national public good being located at the centre. $\delta = 1$ is excluded, since in case of missing minimum affinity of preferences there is no justification for the existence of the federation.

[9] See, e.g., Rodrik (1998), and Garrett and Rodden (2003).

omy, $\omega \in [0,1]$, and on other determinants combined in the parameter $\gamma$. The degree of economic integration $\omega$ is exogenous, and is determined by the magnitude of political and physical trade barriers. By increasing economic risk and income disparities, integration is assumed to enhance the insurance function of the central government, which mainly consists in income redistribution and macro-economic stabilisation.

Given the public budget constraint, the identical lump-sum tax $t$ is determined by the per capita costs of public goods provision

$$t = \kappa(g^C, g^L, N),$$

with $\kappa_{g^C} > 0$, $\kappa_{g^L} > 0$, and $\kappa_N < 0$. In case of pure public goods, the costs of providing the national public good can be shared with the entire federation, whereas the costs of the local public good are shared only among the region's inhabitants.

Finally, considering household-producers, we assume that regional output per capita $y_i$ is generated by the production function[10]

$$y_i = \psi(A_i, g^L, \omega).$$

Following the literature in the tradition of Barro (1990), output is linked apart from technology $A_i$ to the local public good which – in contrast to the national public good – serves as a production input, with $\psi_{g^L} > 0$ and strict concavity. Therefore, in addition to providing utility directly, the local public good is also assumed to generate income. Several studies[11] have shown that particularly public infrastructure enhances productivity in the private sector.

Inserting $t$ and $y_i$ we obtain

$$U_i(g^L, g^C) = v^L(g^L, \alpha) + v^C\left(g^C, \delta, \beta(\omega, \gamma)\right) + \psi(A_i, g^L, \omega) - \kappa(g^C, g^L, N). \tag{4.1}$$

According to the traditional trade theory, integration and international specialisation increase global output and factor productivity. Therefore, we assume that $\psi_\omega > 0$, and in this particular case, $\psi_{g^L,\omega} > 0$. The supposed relationship between integration and the marginal productivity of the local public good is based on the extent-of-the-market hypothesis.[12] In an integrated world national borders no longer delimit the size of the market. Expanded market

10 Note that in this setting inter-regional income differences are only due to different technological endowments. We also abstract from intra-regional aspects of income distribution.

11 See, e.g., Aschauer (1989), among others.

12 See, e.g., Alesina et al. (2000), and Wacziarg et al. (2002) for some recent contributions on the relationship between economies of scale and market size. Ades and Glaeser (1999) provide empirical support for a positive relationship between economic growth and the size of the market.

size facilitates economies of scale in the production, thus increasing the productivity of the local public input and fostering economic growth regardless of the size of the political jurisdiction. The benefit of country size for economic growth thus diminishes with economic integration. With increasing liberalisation and deregulation of markets, and the reduction of political and physical impediments to trade and factor movements, local and regional factors of location become more significant as compared to national economic conditions.

These considerations correspond to the findings of the literature on the creation and disintegration of countries mentioned above, according to which the optimal size of the country decreases with economic integration.[13] In general, the relative costs of separation or local autonomy depend on the degree of integration in the world economy, whereas the benefits associated with public good provision according to local preferences remain unaffected. Therefore, in the present model, preference heterogeneity costs $v_{\delta}^{C}$ are assumed to be independent of the degree of economic openness. With high trade barriers and restrained international factor mobility, separation or local autonomy implies higher economic and political transaction costs with the rest of the nation and the world. Apart from higher local taxes, in case of secession even the benefits of trade are lowered, since formerly domestic trade is then reduced. Young (1994) argues that the costs of secession crucially depend on whether economic and political cooperative relations would be re-established between the predecessor state and the seceding sub-unit. In case of open economies, however, the costs of local autonomy or independence in terms of higher taxes are partly compensated by higher benefits from trade.

### 4.2.2 The Optimal Degree of Decentralisation

Based on the model assumptions presented above, we next analyse the optimal allocation of the public goods among both levels of government. In order to illustrate the role of the vertical government structure, the utility function is transformed in terms of the sub-central government share in total public output provided in each region (degree of public sector decentralisation),

$$\theta = \frac{g^L}{g^C + g^L}.^{14}$$

Especially in view of the empirical verification, a continuous measure is used to describe the degree of public sector decentralisation. Defining total public

[13] See Alesina and Spolaore (1997), Alesina et al. (2000), or Casella and Feinstein (2002).

[14] With $\theta$ describing the degree of decentralisation from the viewpoint of a region, in this symmetric setting the degree of decentralisation of the federation $\bar{\theta}$ is then given by

$$\bar{\theta} = \frac{2g^L}{g^C + 2g^L} \equiv \frac{2\theta}{1 + \theta},$$

which is by definition higher than $\theta$.

output provided in each region as $g = g^C + g^L$, using $g^L = \theta g$, and respectively $g^C = (1-\theta)g$, we can reformulate the individual utility function as a function of $g$ and $\theta$:

$$\widetilde{U_i} = \upsilon^L\left(g\theta, \alpha\right) + \upsilon^C\left(g(1-\theta), \delta, \beta(\omega, \gamma)\right) + \psi\left(A_i, g\theta, \omega\right) - \kappa\left(g(1-\theta), g\theta, N\right), \tag{4.2}$$

with

$$\frac{\partial \upsilon^L}{\partial g} = \upsilon^L_{g^L}\theta > 0, \quad \frac{\partial \upsilon^L}{\partial \theta} = \upsilon^L_{g^L} g > 0,$$

and respectively,

$$\frac{\partial \upsilon^C}{\partial g} = \upsilon^C_{g^C}(1-\theta) > 0, \quad \frac{\partial \upsilon^C}{\partial \theta} = \upsilon^C_{g^C}(-g) < 0,$$

$$\frac{\partial^2 \upsilon^C}{\partial g \partial \delta} = \upsilon^C_{g^C,\delta}(1-\theta) < 0, \quad \frac{\partial^2 \upsilon^C}{\partial \theta \partial \delta} = \upsilon^C_{g^C,\delta}(-g) > 0,$$

provided that the marginal utility of the centrally provided public good decreases with increasing preference distance, $\upsilon^C_{g^C,\delta} < 0$, as defined above. Accordingly, the larger the share of public output provided by the central government, and the greater the heterogeneity of preferences, the lower is the utility from the national public good. Therefore, in contrast to the literature on secessions which implicitly assumes that heterogeneity is increasing with country size, in the present model heterogeneity costs are not related to the size of the country, but instead to the degree of decentralisation.

On the other hand, due to foregone economies of scale decentralised provision of public goods entails higher per capita cost, $\kappa_\theta > 0$. With increasing population size, however, the cost savings of centralisation are expected to decrease ($\kappa_{\theta,N} < 0$). This implies that cost advantages of centralisation are lower in larger countries, where economies of scale could be exploited at the subnational level, too. Note, also, that due to the productivity-enhancing effect of the local public good, income is increasing both in total public output and in the degree of decentralisation:

$$\frac{\partial \psi}{\partial g} = \psi_{g^L}\theta > 0, \quad \frac{\partial \psi}{\partial \theta} = \psi_{g^L} g > 0.$$

Accordingly, the income generating effect of integration is higher in case of decentralisation:

$$\frac{\partial^2 \psi}{\partial \theta \partial \omega} = \psi_{g^L,\omega} g > 0.$$

In order to obtain simple closed form solutions, the following log-linear specification is chosen:

$$U_i = ln(g^L)^\alpha + ln(g^C)^{\beta(1-\delta)} + lnA_i(g^L)^\omega - \left(\frac{g^C}{N} + \frac{g^L}{N/2}\right), \tag{4.3}$$

assuming that the unit costs of both public goods are equal to one. Inserting for $g^L$ and $g^C$, we finally obtain

$$\widetilde{U_i} = \alpha ln\theta g + \beta(1-\delta)ln(1-\theta)g + lnA_i + \omega ln\theta g - \frac{g(1+\theta)}{N}. \qquad (4.4)$$

A welfare-maximising social planner decides simultaneously both on total public output $g$ and the degree of decentralisation $\theta$, that is the allocation of public goods among the two levels of government, as to maximise the sum of individual utilities. In the present symmetric setting this corresponds to maximising the utility of an individual in region $i$. Differentiating the utility function with respect to both political instruments, we obtain the following optimal solution:

$$\theta^* = \frac{\alpha+\omega}{\alpha+\omega+2\beta(1-\delta)}, \quad g^* = \frac{N}{2}\left(\alpha+\omega+2\beta(1-\delta)\right). \qquad (4.5)$$

Accordingly, the optimal degree of decentralisation is always above zero even in case of homogeneous preferences ($\delta = 0$) and autarchy ($\omega = 0$), since the public goods are not close substitutes, and the local public good always generates direct utility ($\alpha > 0$). Also, as long as certain benefits could be derived from the national public good, that is $\beta > 0$, staying within the federation is always preferable to secession ($\theta < 1$).[15]

This corresponds to the conclusions derived by Bolton and Roland (1997). In case of secession, new administrative systems and institutional rules have to be set up, and income redistribution and formerly national public goods, such as defence, have to be provided at a lower scale and with higher per capita costs. Apart from higher taxes, the fiscal costs of secession also depend on the result of negotiations with the predecessor state concerning the division of the federal public debt or of federal institutions. As Alesina and Perotti (1998) point out, staying within the nation-state furthermore provides the advantage of inter-regional risk-sharing and redistribution in case of asymmetric economic shocks. Despite the significant removal of trade barriers in the world, sub-units of a country are still more deeply integrated with each other than with the rest of the world or even with sub-units of neighbour countries.[16] Even in an integrated world, high transaction costs can still persist due to cultural, linguistic or legal differences. Therefore, even in case of peaceful secession and the set-up of a free-trade area between the predecessor state and the seceding region, certain economic and political transaction costs would still persist due to different institutions and legal systems.

The comparative statics show that the optimal degree of decentralisation is increasing with preference heterogeneity, whereas the total amount of public goods supplied in each region is decreasing ($\theta^*_\delta > 0, g^*_\delta < 0$). As expected,

[15] Note, again, that $\delta = 1$ has been excluded right from the beginning.

[16] Based on bilateral trade flows, Helliwell (1996) shows that Quebec trades more with the rest of Canada than with US states of similar distance.

higher preferences for the local public good, and respectively, the national public good have opposite effects on decentralisation ($\theta^*_\alpha > 0$, $\theta^*_\beta < 0$), and total public output is increasing with population size ($g^*_N > 0$). Note that due to the even distribution of population, in this specific case economies of scale aspects have no influence on the degree of decentralisation.[17]

Since local and national public goods are complementary, economic integration raises the total supply of public goods ($g^*_\omega > 0$). In contrast to this, the effect on the vertical allocation of the public goods, and thus on the degree of public sector decentralisation is ambiguous, depending on the magnitude of the two opposite effects of integration:

$$\theta^*_\omega = \frac{2(1-\delta)\left(\beta - \beta_\omega(\alpha+\omega)\right)}{\left(\alpha+\omega+2\beta(1-\delta)\right)^2} \lessgtr 0$$

Strictly speaking, only if the marginal effect of integration on the preference for the national public good is relatively small, that is $\beta_\omega < \frac{\beta}{\alpha+\omega}$, integration exerts a decentralising impact, otherwise the opposite occurs. Note that due to the growth enhancing effect of the local public good, integration might foster fiscal decentralisation even in case of uniform preferences ($\delta = 0$). This possibly explains the process of decentralisation taking place in several homogeneous countries. To sum up, the benefits of decentralisation hinge on the trade-off between increased local growth prospects and higher economic vulnerability associated with progressing integration. The empirical investigation should therefore reveal which effect ultimately predominates.

### 4.2.3 Political Integration

The model presented above abstracts from an important aspect, also neglected by the literature on secessions, namely the possible effect of political integration on the vertical government structure of the countries involved. Particularly in the European context, the process of political integration may have stimulated the regional autonomy movements observed in several member countries.

On the one hand, political integration, that is the transfer of certain national competencies to a supranational authority, entails a centralising effect on the government structures. Decisions are made by a more remote body, while at the same time the role of the central government is reduced. On the other hand, demands for the transfer of fiscal powers to subnational levels of government within the integrating countries are likely to be intensified, too. This corresponds to the "Sandwich" hypothesis which postulates that national governments are expected to be further pushed back in the course of European integration.

[17] In case of different regional population sizes, optimal decentralisation is shown to depend on both total and regional population size. See the alternative model specifications in Appendix A.

As illustrates the case of the European Union, the benefits of secession or local autonomy are further increased, since the costs of providing certain public goods now in the competency of Brussels are shared on a larger scale between the member countries. Through the structural and cohesion funds, the European Union even begins to take on certain insurance functions of the national governments. Also, national policies and legislation are increasingly harmonised, fostering the integration of goods and factor markets and thus enhancing local growth prospects and competition for mobile factors. The activity of the European Union comprises all policies related to the Common Market, such as common trade and agriculture policies, regulation and market supervision, environment policy, and, most recently, monetary and foreign policies.

As a result, national factors of location are increasingly determined by the European Union, thus increasing the scope of lower level governments to shape the local factors of location. Regional and cultural identities are also expected to have increased as a reaction to increasing "Europeanisation". Last but not least, by tightening the control over their fiscal policy, the Stability and Growth Pact may force central governments to shift deficits to lower levels of government by providing them with additional tasks, but insufficient resources.[18]

One might object that the transfer of competencies for the provision of national public goods to a supranational authority automatically involves an increase in the degree of public sector decentralisation of the member countries. However, this is not necessarily true. First of all, this depends on whether regulatory or executive powers or both of them are concerned. Also, as the example of the regional policy illustrates, the European Union is increasingly involved in regional development and infrastructure projects, taking on tasks of sub-central government. And, finally, the scope of government activity is expected to change over time, with the central government possibly appropriating new functions.

In case of secession, however, the seceding regions would have to join the European Union, in order to benefit from political integration. This case is not yet provided for in the European treaties,[19] and seems rather unlikely when taking into account that admission of new member countries has to be decided unanimously. The predecessor state might withhold recognition of the seceding region, other EU member countries following its example. The rejection of the "Ibarretxe plan" of Basque independence[20] by the Spanish parliament

[18] This point is also made by Garrett and Rodden (2003: 97), though in a more general context.

[19] However, note that Art. 59 of the draft of the European Constitution currently provides a mechanism regulating the withdrawal of member countries from the union.

[20] This plan of the Basque government aimed at creating an independent Basque country, loosely associated with Spain and with own representation in the European Council.

seems to best illustrate this problem. Therefore, in case of exclusion from the political union, secession implies significantly higher costs in comparison to the case of economic integration discussed above. Even if admitted in the EU, with extended majority decision-making in the European Council, small secessionist regions might possibly exert less influence on European policy-making as compared to forming part of a larger member country.

Therefore, regional autonomy and decentralisation are supposed to be preferred to secession in the context of European integration in order to avoid these efficiency losses and to carry on sharing the costs for the provision of certain public goods with the rest of the nation. Despite the increasing role of the European level of government, income redistribution and fiscal equalisation, among other things, are still carried out by the national governments.

Apart from this, the role of regional and local governments within the member countries is further strengthened by certain European policies. Especially the European structural and cohesion funds introduced in 1975 and 1994, respectively, but also activities in fields such as health, education, or environment, increasingly require implementation and planning by subnational governments, thus augmenting the scope for direct implication of local decision-makers and lobbying groups. For example, in response to EU structural and cohesion policy, administrative regions were created and provided with some limited resources and functions in Finland, Greece, Ireland and Portugal.[21] The still growing number of regional offices opened in Brussels indicates that regional governments tend to bypass national governments and represent directly their interests at the European level. Marcou et al. (2000) suggest that the European Commission actively encouraged the process of regionalisation in the member countries, in order to reduce the control of the national governments over the structural funds.

Therefore, political integration may have been an important driving force in the process of decentralisation of the public sector in EU countries.

## 4.3 Empirical Analysis

Based on the theoretical framework presented above, we test the hypothesis according to which economic integration in general, and the political unification in Europe in particular, foster the decentralisation of the public sector. The empirical analysis starts with a discussion of some general empirical aspects. After that, a comparative-descriptive overview of the parallelism of fiscal decentralisation and integration is provided, and the investigation approach is described.

[21] See, e.g., Hooghe and Marks (2001) with respect to this. For example, the Irish government decided in 1999 to divide the country into two larger administrative regions in order to remain eligible for EU funding, see Committee of the Regions (2001: 145).

### 4.3.1 Empirical Considerations

The theoretical model presented in section 4.2 suggests that economic integration contributes to government decentralisation by lowering the relative costs associated with the decentralised provision of public goods. On the other hand, economic integration could also have the opposite effect, since it implies higher exposure to exogenous shocks which could counteract the benefits of decentralisation. Increased economic risk is expected to stimulate the demand for interpersonal income redistribution and risk-sharing across regions, thus enhancing central government activity.

The welfare-maximising approach employed above, however, abstracts from several important aspects in order to keep the model tractable and to derive empirically testable implications concerning the effect of preference heterogeneity, economies of scale, and integration on the degree of public sector decentralisation. These additional aspects are generally summarised by the inclusion of the shift parameters $\alpha$ and $\beta$. In the following, we discuss a couple of further considerations which could be taken into account in the empirical analysis.

By definition, the degree of public sector or fiscal decentralisation is determined both by the quantity and the number of different public goods provided by each level of government. The model presented here implicitly takes the preceding decision concerning the assignment of functions to different levels of government as given, and focuses instead on the quantity of public goods supplied by each level of government. However, interpreting $g^L$ and $g^C$ as bundles of different public goods instead, we can easily interpret a relative increase in the supply of $g^L$ as possibly being the result of devolved competencies.[22]

The model also abstracts from different local taxes. With increased factor mobility, local tax autonomy would imply welfare costs in terms of inefficiently low taxes due to enhanced fiscal competition between local governments.[23] Also, interjurisdictional spillovers of public goods or economies of scope are expected to favour centralisation or, at least, coordination of local policies. Since spillovers usually increase with factor mobility, increasing economic integration might therefore lead to higher centralisation.

Finally, due to the symmetric setting chosen, the model abstracts from inter-regional differences in income, population, and factor endowments, or even from aspects of intra-regional income and preference distribution. Cross-regional differences in preferences and income are likely to increase as a consequence of economic integration, regional specialisation and structural change. As pointed out by Bolton and Roland (1997), whereas well endowed regions benefit from extended fiscal autonomy and competition which permits them to escape from implicit inter-regional redistribution through national taxes, poor unproductive regions would call for higher central government transfers and

[22] See Appendix A for a generalised definition of the degree of fiscal decentralisation in case of $m$ public goods and $n$ local jurisdictions.

[23] See Bolton and Roland (1997).

income redistribution. Since economic integration strengthens the credibility of threats to secession, higher central government transfers to rich regions could even become necessary to prevent them from leaving. The case of Spain seems to best illustrate this argument. During intergovernmental negotiations on the system of financing, particularly Catalonia tends to regularly demand a higher share in yields from national taxes in exchange for political support of the central government.[24] These considerations therefore point to certain centralising effects of integration.

On the other hand, the New Economic Geography literature provides further support for the expected positive relationship between decentralisation and economic integration. In case of inter-regional differences in factor endowments, the market size effect of economic integration is expected to intensify regional specialisation in accordance with comparative advantages and to foster the inter-regional division of labour. This development is further supported by technical progress which reduces transaction and transport costs and increases factor mobility and interjurisdictional knowledge spillovers. Krugman (1991b), and Krugman and Venables (1996), among others, have shown that economic integration induces agglomeration effects in the industrial sector and leads to inter-regional specialisation of the production structure. Evidence for a causal relationship is found particularly for European Union regions.[25] Whereas per capita income of member countries increasingly converges, cross-regional disparities within countries tend to increase.

However, these considerations have not yet become established in the theories of fiscal federalism and secession. Since local public goods influence the location decisions of mobile factors, they are expected to play an important role in the process of agglomeration and specialisation at the regional level. As Baldwin and Krugman (2002) have recently shown, economic integration creates agglomeration rents for production factors located in the core which can be taxed away by local governments. Extending this approach to public spending, Brakman et al. (2002) point out that taxes stimulate the spread of production factors, whereas public goods foster agglomeration by enhancing the attractiveness of the location for mobile firms and workers. Yet, the resulting implications for the vertical government structure are not taken into account by these approaches. With increasing economic integration local governments would benefit from the decentralised provision of public goods and taxes, and, consequently, from extended fiscal autonomy which allows them to implement their own policies and compete internationally for mobile factors of production. In the end, fiscal decentralisation could trigger a process of repercussions intensifying industrial specialisation and agglomeration. Since investors benefit from fiscal competition and the implementation of market-conforming policies, economic interest groups are expected to support decen-

[24] See, also, Garrett and Rodden (2003) with respect to this.

[25] See, among others, Giannetti (2002), Stirböck (2002), and the survey of Krieger-Boden (2000).

tralisation of the public sector. Also, local autonomy allows investors to exert more influence on local decision-making.

Finally, as shown in chapter 3, apart from cost-benefit considerations, political decision-making processes in democracies and the underlying institutional rules are expected to influence the costs and benefits of decentralisation. For example, centralisation is expected to be more beneficial in federations which provide a guaranteed minimum representation of subnational jurisdictions in national decision-making. Since, in this case, the risk for minorities of being dominated by the national majority is reduced. In this case, demands for fiscal decentralisation in the course of economic integration might be prevented by collusive behaviour of local policy makers or the opposition of poor regions to fiscal competition. Integration would then enhance inter-regional redistribution instead.

Therefore, the implementation of demands for decentralisation depends on the degree of involvement of subnational entities in central decision-making and on the legal provisions regulating the transfer of powers. Decentralisation may be easier to achieve if the delegation of powers is laid down by simple law adopted by parliamentary majority instead of constitutional provisions which are difficult to change. Analogously, without the existence of rules for peaceful secession, the costs of separation are considerably higher, at worst taking the form of armed conflicts.[26]

### 4.3.2 Descriptive Statistics

The implications of the theoretical considerations are tested for the sample of 23 OECD countries presented in the previous chapters. By including both EU countries and other comparable industrial nations, the specific aspect of regional integration in Europe can be separated from the more general aspect of integration in the world economy.

Though indicating no uniform pattern, the expenditure and revenue figures presented in section 2.5 reveal a decentralisation trend for a majority of OECD countries, especially in terms of increased tax autonomy. When removing social security from the central government sector, the figures reveal a more significant rise of the average degree of expenditure decentralisation, particularly in European Union countries. However, whereas especially in Belgium and Spain the sub-central government share of public spending and revenue increased drastically, the development in the United Kingdom or Germany among others went in the opposite direction.

To contrast this development in the public sector to economic integration both in the global and the regional context, the analysis makes use of the degree of trade and financial openness, and of the share of trade with EU countries, as presented in Table 4.1.

[26] See, e.g., Bordignon and Brusco (2001), and Jehiel and Scotchmer (2001), with regard to credibility aspects of secession rules. In general, such mechanisms are usually not provided for in federal constitutions.

Table 4.1: Degree of economic openness, and trade with EU countries, 1970-2001

| Country | Trade openness (1) | | Quinn/Inclan index (2) | | EU trade (3) | |
|---|---|---|---|---|---|---|
| | 1970-1975 | 1996-2001 | 1970-1975 | 1996-2001 | 1970-1975 | 1995-2000 |
| AUS | 27.8 | 41.7 | 0.55 | 0.82 | 27.0 | 17.9 |
| AUT | 62.1 | 92.2 | 0.71 | 0.93 | 63.3 | 66.5 |
| BEL | 90.9 | 151.6 | 0.70 | 0.96 | 75.0 | 73.4 |
| CAN | 44.8 | 79.9 | 0.88 | 1.00 | 13.3 | 7.4 |
| DEN | 57.8 | 73.7 | 0.65 | 1.00 | 66.7 | 67.8 |
| FIN | 52.6 | 70.3 | 0.63 | 1.00 | 62.0 | 55.9 |
| FRA | 34.8 | 50.3 | 0.79 | 0.93 | 59.6 | 63.5 |
| GER | 45.4 | 59.1 | 0.99 | 1.00 | 58.7 | 55.9 |
| GRE | 35.6 | 50.4 | 0.32 | 0.96 | 56.0 | 63.1 |
| ICL | 81.0 | 75.4 | | | 55.4 | 60.2 |
| IRL | 84.8 | 161.3 | 0.60 | 1.00 | 76.5 | 61.9 |
| ITA | 34.9 | 50.7 | 0.75 | 1.00 | 53.6 | 58.1 |
| JAP | 22.2 | 19.6 | 0.55 | 0.79 | 11.1 | 15.3 |
| LUX | 171.2 | 241.0 | 0.70[a] | 0.96[a] | 75.0 | 77.8 |
| NED | 93.8 | 111.3 | 0.86 | 1.00 | 71.3 | 69.3 |
| NEZ | 48.8 | 63.2 | 0.44 | 0.96 | 22.4[b] | 17.3 |
| NOR | 75.7 | 74.4 | 0.54 | 0.96 | 71.0 | 73.2 |
| POR | 57.2 | 69.1 | 0.32 | 0.96 | 53.9 | 78.0 |
| SPA | 29.7 | 57.0 | 0.43 | 0.93 | 46.9 | 68.0 |
| SWE | 52.8 | 81.3 | 0.74 | 0.93 | 62.8 | 61.4 |
| SWI | 63.9 | 75.1 | 0.88 | 0.93 | 70.1 | 69.2 |
| UK | 48.3 | 56.5 | 0.59 | 1.00 | 41.8 | 55.0 |
| USA | 13.1 | 24.3 | 0.90 | 1.00 | 26.0 | 19.6 |
| Median: | | | | | | |
| *OECD* | *52.7* | *70.3* | *0.68* | *0.96* | *58.7* | *61.9* |
| *Non-EU15* | *46.8* | *68.8* | *0.55* | *0.96* | *26.5* | *18.7* |
| *EU15* | *52.8* | *70.3* | *0.70* | *0.96* | *62.0* | *63.5* |

Note: (1) sum of exports and imports in % of GDP; (2) index of financial openness, re-adjusted on a scale of 0-1, [a] BEL/LUX; (3) sum of exports and imports to/from EU15 countries in % of total foreign trade. Six-year-averages, [b] 1987. Source: (1) IMF; (2) Quinn and Inclan (1997), Armingeon et al. (2004); (3) OECD. Own calculations.

With few exceptions, both the share of exports and imports in GDP, and the Quinn/Inclan index which reflects the degree of financial openness according to currency, capital and current account restrictions have increased considerably in most OECD countries during the period of observation, clearly providing evidence for growing worldwide integration. Accordingly, the me-

Table 4.2: The budget of the European Union, 1960-2001

| | EU expenditure in % of total public exp. of EU countries | EU expenditure in % of EU-GDP |
|---|---|---|
| 1960-1965 | 0.20 | 0.07 |
| 1970-1975 | 1.38 | 0.54 |
| 1996-2001 | 2.33 | 1.10 |

Note: Six-year-averages. Source: Europäische Kommission (2000); own calculations.

dian degree of trade openness of OECD countries rose in 30 years from 52.7% during 1970/1975 to 70.3% during 1996/2001. As expected, due to the establishment of the Common Market, the degree of openness is on average higher for EU countries than for Non-EU countries. However, the process of global integration has been more pronounced for the latter. In line with this, EU trade flows indicate slightly increasing regional integration among EU countries, whereas other OECD countries traded even less with the EU. The extent of economic integration is therefore significantly higher among EU countries.

The process of political and economic integration took off in Europe with the set-up of the European Coal and Steel Community (ECSC) in 1951 and the European Economic Community (EEC) in 1958, which established common political institutions and a customs union. With the final accomplishment of the internal European market and the coming into force of the Maastricht Treaty on the European Union in 1993, and of the European Monetary Union in 1999, the process of integration reached a new quality which goes beyond economic considerations. In parallel with this, the number of member countries grew by more than four times from 6 to 25 from 1951 to 2004.

Table 4.2 portrays the process of political integration in Europe in terms of budgetary flows. The share of EU expenditure as % of total GDP or as % of total expenditure of the member countries has nearly doubled since the beginning of the 1970s. However, particularly in the case of the European Union, the actual level of political integration is strongly underestimated by the budgetary flows. Whereas the direct fiscal role of the EU is rather limited, EU legislative, regulatory and coordinating activities have grown considerably, entering nearly all domains of national legislation. Among other things, this development is particularly due to the unclarified allocation of competencies between the European Union and the member states. This enables the European Commission, for example, to extend its activity to all areas potentially affecting the Common Market. Using different indicators, Alesina et al. (2001b), e.g., confirm that the extent and intensity of policy-making by institutions of the European Union (European Council, Commission, Court of Justice) have increased sharply in most policy domains over the last 30 years.[27]

All things considered, the simultaneity of fiscal decentralisation and increasing economic integration in most OECD countries indicates a possible relationship between those two trends. At the same time, the "Sandwich" hypothesis seems to be partly endorsed. At least in terms of expenditure and revenue shares, the role of national governments in certain EU countries is considerably declining in the course of political integration.

### 4.3.3 Investigation Approach

In the following, an empirical investigation is carried out which includes, apart from integration, preference heterogeneity and economies of scale. By this, both differences in the costs and benefits of decentralisation, and possible interactions with integration are taken into account. The hypothesis of a decentralising effect of integration is tested for the panel of 23 OECD countries covering the period 1965/1970 to 2001.

The regression analysis relates the degree of fiscal decentralisation to economic and European integration, while controlling for further variables which explain the vertical division of government functions and the relative demand for certain public services provided by the central government. In this way, we take into account the fact that changes in the degree of fiscal decentralisation as measured by the share of sub-central government expenditure (revenue) in consolidated general government expenditure (revenue) are either due to changes in the assignment of functions and financial resources, or to changes in the budget share of certain expenditure and revenue categories.[28]

In order to focus on the impact of increasing integration, the model is estimated with country fixed effects, which depict all time-invariant country-specific factors, such as geographic area, institutions, traditions, or inter-regional diversities. In doing so, we concentrate on the factors which are assumed to determine the costs and benefits of decentralisation over time. Whereas the pooled OLS regressions in chapter 3 were primarily concerned with the determinants explaining cross-country variation at one point of time, the fixed effects approach focuses on the time variation in the data instead, by conditioning on the cross-sectional distribution of decentralisation. Moreover, it controls for characteristics which are unobserved or cannot be quantified,[29] thus solving simultaneity problems in the form of omitted-variable bias.

[27] See also Schmidt (1999) for an analysis of the degree of "Europeanisation" of government functions.

[28] See also the discussion in section 2.2.

[29] Just to give an example, the role of the public sector or of the central government in economy and society is usually deeply rooted in the country's history. In today's France, e.g., the strong role of the central government is the expression of the Jacobinism of the French revolution, which distrusted dispersed power because of the local support for the monarchy.

Since the fixed effects deal with long-lasting unobservable differences between countries, it will not surprise that these estimations might yield dramatically different results as compared to the specifications employed in the previous analysis, which did not include country fixed effects.

Formally, the basic estimation equation is

$$Decentr_{it} = \beta_{0i} + \beta_1 \cdot Cost_{it} + \beta_2 \cdot Heter_{it} + \beta_3 \cdot Diverse_{it} + \beta_4 \cdot Open_{it} \\ + \beta_5 \cdot EUInteg_{it} + \beta_6 \cdot (Fix_i \cdot Open_{it}) + u_{it}.$$

$Decentr_{it}$ denotes the share of sub-central government expenditure (revenue) in consolidated general government expenditure (revenue) in country $i$ in period $t$. Again, both conventional and corrected measures of fiscal decentralisation are used alternatively.

$Open_{it}$ denotes the degree of integration of each country in the world economy in period $t$. In order to capture the market size effect described in the theoretical framework, the degree of *trade openness* as measured by the share of exports and imports in GDP is used as an indicator of economic integration. Alternatively, we employ the Quinn/Inclan index of *financial openness* which reflects the degree of liberalisation of goods and capital markets according to legal provisions in order to account for other facets of economic integration.

To separate the effects, integration in the world economy and political integration are included in the regressions. As already noted, economic integration might have fostered both decentralisation in the member countries and the transfer of political and fiscal powers to the EU level. Both economic and political aspects of integration within the European Union ($EUInteg_{it}$) are taken into account on an annual basis by the inclusion of different indicators: First, in order to capture both the impact of the joining of the European Union and advancing political integration, a dummy variable for EU membership is interacted with the share of EU expenditure in consolidated public expenditure of the member countries ($EU \cdot EU\ exp.$). Alternatively, we use a country-specific index of *political integration* which assigns higher values to increasing degrees of integration of the respective country with the EU: from free-trade agreements, the establishment of the customs union, the European Economic Area, until the creation of the Economic and Monetary Union. By this, different degrees of participation in EU policy of both member countries, such as Denmark or the UK, and Non-EU countries, such as the EFTA, are taken into account. And, finally, the share of trade with EU countries in total foreign trade (*EU trade*) is used as an indicator of the regional concentration of each country's trade flows.[30]

The effect of integration is separated from other potential determinants of the degree of public sector decentralisation as described by the theoretical framework in section 4.2 and the positive theory of fiscal federalism through the inclusion of control variables. As in the econometric model presented in chapter 3, cost of decentralisation in terms of economies of scale and spillovers

[30] See Appendix C and D for more details on the variables.

of public goods ($Cost_{it}$), inter-regional heterogeneity ($Heter_{it}$), and further explanatory variables ($Diverse_{it}$) are taken into account. Since we cannot separately estimate the effects on policy of a country's institutions or of the degree of preference heterogeneity, which are mostly constant over time, and of other time-invariant country-specific characteristics represented by $\beta_{0i}$, we ask whether those factors have an indirect, non-linear effect on policy. For this reason, certain constant country-specific characteristics ($Fix_i$) are interacted with the degree of economic and, alternatively, European integration. By this, the institution or preference specific effect of integration can be captured.

Economies of scale and spillovers of public goods are again captured by the size of the country in terms of *population*, and the spatial allocation of the population, as measured by the degree of *urbanisation*. Since, in general, these factors change only gradually over time, the effects are expected to be rather moderate and have to be interpreted with caution. Further time-invariant factors, such as geographic area, or the number of constituent jurisdictions, which are assumed to affect economies of scale and spillovers, are captured by the country fixed effects.

As before, inter-regional heterogeneity of preferences is represented by the degree of linguistic fractionalisation (*Fractional*). Within this context, problems related to measurement of preference heterogeneity are less important, since omitted aspects are captured by the fixed effects. Given its time-invariance, fractionalisation is interacted with the degree of economic openness, and, alternatively, with indicators of European integration in the regression. In addition to this, the time-variant degree of *regional disparity* of per capita income is taken into account in order to control for changes in the degree of heterogeneity in the course of integration which are not captured by the fixed country effects. On the one hand, the degree of decentralisation is expected to increase with inter-regional heterogeneity. On the other hand, by controlling for regional economic disparity, we separate a possible centralising effect due to increased demand for inter-regional redistribution in the context of greater exposure to economic shocks from other possible effects of economic integration.

The next set of factors consists of standard control variables capturing the demand for certain public goods, such as *income* (GDP) *per capita*, or temporary expenditure and revenue effects of business and electoral cycles, such as the *growth rate* of real per capita income, the rate of *unemployment*, and a dummy variable for national *election* years.

Since the decentralisation trend seems to have accelerated in the 1990s, we also control for the role of international conflicts postulated by Spolaore and Alesina (2001). The authors show that the decline in international conflicts and the enforcement of international law raise the benefits of secession. Accordingly, disarmament and the end of the Cold War reduced the importance of extensive defence and security systems, which are original functions of the central government. Consequently, all other things being equal, the share of central government expenditure is expected to have declined during the last decade. Within this context, regional autonomy movements are also more likely to be tolerated since they are no longer perceived as a threat to national security and integrity. In order to verify this hypothesis, the share of military expenditure of the Warsaw Treaty states in GNP is set in relation to the respective share of NATO countries (*Coldwar*), and is used as a proxy of the potential military threat exerted by the communist block to western countries.

The role of institutions is finally taken into account by interacting integration with certain decision-making rules. First, a dummy variable for the existence of an upper chamber of parliament consisting only of representatives appointed by the regional governments or legislatures (*Regional parliam.*) takes into account the common-pool problem described by Brennan and Buchanan (1980). The analysis in chapter 3 has shown that particularly direct involvement of representatives subject to instructions of the regional authorities is expected to enhance logrolling and political cartelisation. In order to moderate competitive pressures, sub-central governments tend to establish tax cartels which are enforced by the central government. Therefore, direct participation in national decision-making enables especially poor regions to oppose the devolution of fiscal competencies, and, thus, pressures for interjurisdictional fiscal competition in the course of integration. Second, a dummy variable is included, which accounts for legal provisions concerning national *referendums* on constitutional and legislative matters. Direct democracy is expected to lead to more decentralisation, since referendums prevent elected representatives from exercising vote-trading and centralising government activities. However, the empirical analysis in chapter 3 detected an opposite relationship.

In light of the theoretical discussion in section 4.2, we expect a positive effect of integration on the degree of fiscal decentralisation, particularly in the context of the European Union. However, with increasing demand for interpersonal and inter-regional redistribution associated with higher exposure to economic shocks and growing regional disparities, the opposite effect may also prevail. Whether decentralisation ultimately occurs should also depend on the specific institutional framework.

## 4.4 Results

### 4.4.1 Basic Estimations

The results of the estimations for the degree of decentralisation of direct public expenditure (indicator ED1) are reported in Table 4.3.[31] The F tests indicate significant country effects in the data, Hausman specification tests mainly reject specifications using random effects. Checks for collinearity and influential observations have been carried out, detected large outliers being removed

[31] Due to the lack of fiscal and especially regional data for certain periods and countries, the sample is unbalanced.

from the sample. Changes in territorial structures which exerted considerable effects on the indicator of regional disparity are instead taken into account by the addition of dummy variables for the countries and periods in question.[32] Since Wooldridge's (2002) test indicates strong serial correlation in the panel data, the variance matrix estimates are corrected for both heteroscedasticity and autocorrelation according to Newey and West (1987).[33]

In contrast to theoretical expectations and the typical results of cross-sectional empirical studies, yet, in line with the pooled regression analysis in chapter 3, the estimates report a negative significant coefficient of urbanisation and, to a lesser extent, of population size on the degree of public sector decentralisation.[34] This possibly indicates that in case of focusing on the time dimension, growing demand for public goods provided by the central government dominates vis-à-vis economies of scale aspects at subnational levels of government which barely change in the course of time. As mentioned before, the centralising effect of increasing urbanisation might be due to the fact that urban agglomeration is typically associated with higher interjurisdictional spillovers[35] and increasing demand for social assistance, both enhancing central government activity. However, the secular relation between population changes and government expenditure or decentralisation is supposed to be complex and uncertain. The estimates also report a strong and highly significant negative effect of regional disparity of per capita income on the degree of decentralisation. The inclusion of this variable turns out to improve considerably the goodness of fit of the regression. Provided that economic integration increases cross-regional disparities, this might be indirect evidence of a stimulating effect of integration on the demand for inter-regional redistribution through central government expenditure.

With respect to economic development, the results are in line with previous studies reporting a decentralising effect of higher per capita income. Also, electoral and business cycles seem to play a certain role, the share of sub-central government expenditure being lower in years of national elections and higher unemployment. On the other hand, though having the expected signs, the coefficients of economic growth and military threat (Cold War) are not significant. Apparently, business cycles affect the activity of both central and

32 Apart from Germany after reunification, this is particularly the case for Canada, Netherlands, and Portugal. Regressions including dummy variables for further countries with minor territorial changes yielded similar results.

33 The alternative computation of robust White standard errors for within-groups estimators proposed by Arellano (1987), which accounts for the clustering of observations, yields less precise estimates in the present case. However, as already mentioned, the reliability of the White variance matrix estimator is questionable in case of small samples or cross-sections.

34 The results are the same when using the median regional population size instead of total population as a proxy for potential economies of scale at the subnational level.

35 This point is also made by Peacock and Wiseman (1961).

subnational governments in the same way, thus indicating similar expenditure and revenue elasticities of income of the different layers of government.

Surprisingly, note that the results of fixed effects estimates mostly correspond to those of the pooled regressions carried out in chapter 3. One important exception is the effect of inter-regional heterogeneity of per capita income. Whereas in the static context of pooled regressions, which focused on the cross-sectional variation, larger inter-regional disparities were associated with more decentralisation, the time dimension considered in the panel analysis provides a positive relationship between changes in regional disparities and centralisation.

Table 4.3: Fixed effects (within) estimates for fiscal decentralisation, direct expenditure (incl. social security), OECD countries, 1970-2001

| | Dep. var.: Degree of expenditure decentralisation (indic. ED1) | | | | | | |
|---|---|---|---|---|---|---|---|
| | (1) | (2) | (3) | (4) | (5) | (6) | (7) |
| *Population* | -.089 | -.131 | -.047 | -.090 | -.109 | .039 | .044 |
| | (.084) | (.085) | (.086) | (.086) | (.081) | (.080) | (.093) |
| *Urbanisation* | -.236** | -.239*** | -.207** | -.245*** | -.252*** | -.278** | -.183* |
| | (.096) | (.093) | (.093) | (.094) | (.092) | (.116) | (.101) |
| *Reg. disparity* | -.227*** | -.239*** | -.252*** | -.235*** | -.206*** | -.116** | -.180*** |
| | (.066) | (.066) | (.068) | (.068) | (.064) | (.050) | (.059) |
| *P.c. income* | .062** | .032 | .018 | .063** | .066** | .020 | .017 |
| | (.028) | (.033) | (.031) | (.029) | (.028) | (.024) | (.029) |
| *Growth rate* | -.056 | -.024 | -.059 | -.057 | -.037 | -.043 | -.093 |
| | (.075) | (.078) | (.069) | (.074) | (.073) | (.065) | (.063) |
| *Unemployment* | -.254 | -.297* | -.331** | -.267 | -.267 | -.377*** | -.369*** |
| | (.192) | (.177) | (.157) | (.186) | (.182) | (.143) | (.132) |
| *Election* | -.004* | -.003 | -.003* | .001* | -.003* | -.003 | -.004 |
| | (.002) | (.002) | (.002) | (.002) | (.002) | (.002) | (.002) |
| *Coldwar* | -.007 | -.004 | -.010* | -.006 | -.008 | -.008 | -.006 |
| | (.006) | (.006) | (.006) | (.006) | (.005) | (.005) | (.006) |
| *Trade openness* | .026 | | .091*** | .028 | -.056 | -.006 | .089*** |
| | (.031) | | (.035) | (.031) | (.062) | (.028) | (.032) |
| *Finan. openness* | | .088* | | | | | |
| | | (.048) | | | | | |
| *EU · EU exp.* | .012 | .009 | | | .017** | -.023* | |
| | (.008) | (.006) | | | (.007) | (.014) | |
| *EU trade* | | | .314*** | | | | -.032 |
| | | | (.111) | | | | (.127) |
| *EU polit. integr.* | | | | .008* | | | |
| | | | | (.005) | | | |

Table 4.3 (cont.): Fixed effects (within) estimates for fiscal decentralisation

| | Dep. var.: Degree of expenditure decentralisation (indic. ED1) | | | | | | |
|---|---|---|---|---|---|---|---|
| | (1) | (2) | (3) | (4) | (5) | (6) | (7) |
| *Fractional · Trade openness* | | | | | .235* (.134) | | |
| *Fractional · (EU · EU exp.)* | | | | | | .177*** (.039) | |
| *Fractional · EU trade* | | | | | | | 1.248*** (.367) |
| *Referendum · Trade openness* | | | | | -.042* (.025) | | |
| *Referendum · (EU · EU exp.)* | | | | | | .001 (.011) | |
| *Referendum · EU trade* | | | | | | | -.003 (.031) |
| *Regional parliam. · Trade openness* | | | | | -.219** (.093) | | |
| *Regional parliam. · (EU · EU exp.)* | | | | | | -.009 (.008) | |
| *Regional parliam. · EU trade* | | | | | | | -.219 (.154) |
| No. obs. (countries) | 484 (23) | 457 (22) | 482 (23) | 484 (23) | 484 (23) | 484 (23) | 482 (23) |
| Adj. $R^2$ | .959 | .962 | .962 | .960 | .962 | .969 | .967 |
| Within $R^2$ | .187 | .220 | .263 | .201 | .253 | .396 | .361 |

Note: All regressions include country fixed effects and dummies for the periods after territorial changes in Canada, Germany, Netherlands, and Portugal, whose coefficients are not reported. Newey-West heteroscedasticity and autocorrelation consistent standard errors (L=3) are in parentheses. ***, **, and * indicate significance at the 1%, 5% and 10% level, respectively.

Regarding integration, the estimates only partly support the hypothesis of a positive impact of integration on the degree of public sector decentralisation in OECD countries. A marginal rise in the degree of trade openness is associated with a smaller share of central government expenditure, the effect, however, being only significant when including additionally the share of trade with EU countries. Apparently, this is in line with the findings in section 4.3.2 which show no clear decentralisation trend in OECD countries when considering direct public expenditure inclusive of social security. A weakly significant decentralising effect of integration is found instead when using alternatively the Quinn/Inclan index of financial openness.

In the European context, particularly economic, and, to a lesser extent, political integration prove to have contributed to increased fiscal decentralisation. At first glance, the results therefore confirm the "Sandwich" hypothesis only in some respects. Central governments in EU member countries apparently have been pushed back both by the process of supranational political unification and by increasing regional and global economic integration. However, the simultaneous inclusion of EU trade and political integration variables shows that indeed the decentralising effect of regional trade integration ultimately dominates (not shown).[36]

The theoretical predictions concerning the decentralising impact of integration are more clearly supported when looking at the interaction terms. According to the estimates reported in the columns (5) to (7), the positive effect of European integration, and, to a lesser extent, of global economic integration, on the sub-central government share of public spending turns out to be particularly valid for linguistically heterogeneous countries.[37] Note that when the interaction terms are included, the corresponding direct effects of economic or European integration are reversed.

The results found also emphasise that institutional rules matter to some extent. Contrary to the expectations, but, again, consistent with the analysis in chapter 3[38], direct democracy tends to be associated with centralisation of public spending, particularly in the context of economic integration. This may not be surprising when considering that national referenda are mostly concerned with objects of general national interest, such as the ratification of international treaties or the validation of significant constitutional reforms, and to a lesser extent with the clear and precise assignment of responsibilities among levels of government or the central government budget.[39]

On the other hand, the centralising effect of subnational participation in central decision-making suggested by Brennan and Buchanan (1980) is clearly supported by the estimates. Countries having a chamber of parliament with indirectly elected regional representatives tend to centralise government activity in the course of integration in the world economy and, to a lesser extent, in the course of European integration.[40] According to this result, political

[36] Note that the correlation coefficient between trade within EU countries and the share of EU expenditures amounts only to 0.497. The share of trade with EU countries in GDP has been used alternatively as a measure of economic integration in the EU. However, the results coincide with those of trade openness, and both variables are highly correlated.

[37] The results are robust to the use of different fractionalisation indices, and we do not report them. In order to take the geographical distribution into account, we have also run alternative regressions interacting the index of linguistic fractionalisation with a dummy variable for the existence of regionally concentrated assertive minorities (*Regional*). The classification of these minorities is based, among other things, on the electoral results of regionalist parties as a possible indicator for regional distinctiveness. As expected, the results support the decentralising effect of heterogeneity to a greater extent (not shown).

[38] There, the use of a dummy variable for legal provisions concerning national referendums also yielded a negative, though insignificant result.

[39] See the institutional analysis in chapter 3. With the exception of Switzerland, most constitutions explicitly forbid budget referendums at the national level.

[40] Alternative regressions considering more general definitions of regional chambers of parliament in fact yielded opposite results. These results are not reported here.

bargaining at the national level enables especially poor regions to prevent competitive pressures related to fiscal decentralisation and economic integration, and to call for redistributive central government expenditures instead.

In order to address the problem of misrepresentation of decentralisation, and of differences between the expenditure and the revenue side of the public sector, the analysis proceeds using alternatively the measure of tax decentralisation constructed in section 2.3.2 (indicator *TD1*), which is based on data reported by the OECD Revenue Statistics.[41] Accounting for tax-raising autonomy of sub-central government, Table 4.4 reports a weakly significant de-

Table 4.4: Fixed effects (within) estimates for fiscal decentralisation, autonomous own tax revenue, OECD countries, 1965-2001

| | Dep. var.: Degree of tax decentralisation (indicator TD1) | | | | | | |
|---|---|---|---|---|---|---|---|
| | (1) | (2) | (3) | (4) | (5) | (6) | (7) |
| *Population* | -.051 | -.083 | -.012 | -.046 | -.061 | .016 | .016 |
| | (.079) | (.078) | (.078) | (.080) | (.078) | (.069) | (.086) |
| *Urbanisation* | -.275*** | -.266*** | -.275*** | -.276*** | -.284*** | -.291*** | -.279*** |
| | (.093) | (.087) | (.091) | (.091) | (.087) | (.105) | (.094) |
| *Reg. disparity* | -.193*** | -.205*** | -.186*** | -.194*** | -.190*** | -.152*** | -.171*** |
| | (.058) | (.060) | (.057) | (.057) | (.058) | (.051) | (.056) |
| *P.c. income* | .024 | .048 | .009 | .021 | .027 | -.002 | .009 |
| | (.030) | (.032) | (.031) | (.030) | (.031) | (.029) | (.032) |
| *Growth rate* | -.085 | -.082 | -.083 | -.089 | -.087 | -.072 | -.092 |
| | (.061) | (.064) | (.062) | (.062) | (.062) | (.058) | (.064) |
| *Unemployment* | .382*** | .368** | .381*** | .371*** | .370** | .330** | .382*** |
| | (.138) | (.156) | (.137) | (.138) | (.148) | (.141) | (.135) |
| *Election* | -.001 | -.001 | -.001 | -.001 | -.001 | -.001 | -.001 |
| | (.002) | (.002) | (.002) | (.002) | (.002) | (.002) | (.002) |
| *Coldwar* | -.011* | -.009 | -.010 | -.011* | -.011* | -.011* | -.008 |
| | (.006) | (.006) | (.006) | (.006) | (.006) | (.006) | (.006) |
| *Trade openness* | .051* | | .059* | .050* | .056 | .038 | .053 |
| | (.029) | | (.033) | (.028) | (.050) | (.026) | (.034) |
| *Finan. openness* | | -.000 | | | | | |
| | | (.041) | | | | | |
| *EU · EU exp.* | -.002 | -.001 | | | .000 | -.013 | |
| | (.005) | (.005) | | | (.005) | (.013) | |
| *EU trade* | | | .031 | | | | -.101 |
| | | | (.068) | | | | (.117) |
| *EU polit. integr.* | | | | -.000 | | | |
| | | | | (.003) | | | |

41 Alternative regressions for tax decentralisation not considering decision-making powers, are provided in Table B.31 in Appendix B. Apart from some differences in the level of significance, most results are quite similar.

Table 4.4 (cont.): Fixed effects (within) estimates for fiscal decentralisation

| | Dep. var.: Degree of tax decentralisation (indicator TD1) | | | | | | |
|---|---|---|---|---|---|---|---|
| | (1) | (2) | (3) | (4) | (5) | (6) | (7) |
| *Fractional · Trade openness* | | | | | .025 | | |
| | | | | | (.123) | | |
| *Fractional · (EU · EU exp.)* | | | | | | .086 ** | |
| | | | | | | (.034) | |
| *Fractional · EU trade* | | | | | | | .394 |
| | | | | | | | (.313) |
| *Referendum · Trade openness* | | | | | -.019 | | |
| | | | | | (.025) | | |
| *Referendum · (EU · EU exp.)* | | | | | | -.006 | |
| | | | | | | (.013) | |
| *Referendum · EU trade* | | | | | | | .024 |
| | | | | | | | (.025) |
| *Regional parliam. · Trade openness* | | | | | -.132 ** | | |
| | | | | | (.059) | | |
| *Regional parliam. · (EU · EU exp.)* | | | | | | -.004 | |
| | | | | | | (.007) | |
| *Regional parliam. · EU trade* | | | | | | | -.028 |
| | | | | | | | (.139) |
| No. obs. (countries) | 548 (23) | 522(22) | 535 (23) | 548 (23) | 548 (23) | 548 (23) | 535 (23) |
| Adj. $R^2$ | .968 | .970 | .969 | .970 | .968 | .969 | .969 |
| Within $R^2$ | .195 | .171 | .207 | .195 | .207 | .239 | .218 |

Note: See Table 4.3 for further details.

centralising effect of economic integration in terms of trade openness, whereas the corresponding positive effect of European integration is only significant for linguistically heterogeneous countries. A negative relationship between higher military threat during the Cold War and tax decentralisation is also confirmed. Note that, again, representation of subnational governments or legislatures in the upper chamber significantly reduces the degree of tax decentralisation, particularly when interacted with global economic integration. Finally, the positive coefficient of the rate of unemployment indicates a relatively stronger decline in central government tax revenues – mainly derived from broad-based income and corporate taxes – in times of rising unemployment, as compared to sub-central governments, which mostly rely on profit and property taxes.

### 4.4.2 Sensitivity Analysis and Robustness Checks

In order to check for the robustness of the results with regard to other measures of decentralisation and possible outliers, several sensitivity analyses have been carried out. As a first approach, additional concepts of expenditure and revenue decentralisation mentioned in chapter 2 are employed, allocating intergovernmental transfers to the grantor: *self-financed expenditure* inclusive of intergovernmental expenditure, but exclusive of intergovernmental revenue, and total *own revenue* exclusive of intergovernmental revenues. In doing so, we focus on the level of government actually financing public spending, irrespective of the degree of discretion.

According to the comparative overview in chapter 2, the increase in public sector decentralisation is more evident with respect to public revenue and in case of excluding social security from the central government. Indeed, the decentralising effect of increasing trade openness is more clearly supported for self-financed expenditure and own revenue, though without accounting for decision-making powers.[42] Integration is thus shown to increase subnational government reliance on – formally – own revenues. With respect to European integration, however, the results are less conclusive. Particularly the effect of political integration as depicted by the share of EU expenditure or by the composite index becomes less accurate, and is even reversed for public revenues. This corresponds to the previous findings for tax decentralisation. Regarding the indirect effects of integration and the other control variables, the previous results are mostly confirmed.

In order to separate the possible insurance effect of central government activity, additional regressions excluding social security expenditure and revenue are carried out.[43] The results found are with few exceptions consistent with the previous estimates. Again, increasing economic integration is associated with a higher sub-central government share of consolidated public expenditure and revenue, particularly when excluding grants received from central government. The effect of European integration is again reversed with respect to the revenue side. Interestingly, the relationship between the decline in large global conflicts associated with the end of the Cold War and the decentralisation of the public sector becomes more evident when excluding social security. More precisely, the reduction in the potential military threat of the Warsaw Treaty Organisation exerted a positive effect on the share of sub-central government expenditure and revenue in OECD countries.[44]

Generally speaking, the use of different measures of decentralisation mostly seems to corroborate the evidence of a positive effect of economic integration on the degree of fiscal decentralisation, particularly with respect to the revenue side. In contrast to this, the hypothesis of a decentralising impact of European integration is only clearly confirmed with respect to direct public spending in linguistically heterogeneous countries. Figures 2.7 and 2.8 in chapter 2, however, reveal two possible exceptional cases of considerable de-

---

[42] See Tables B.25 and B.26 in Appendix B. Due to gaps in the OECD Revenue Statistics, the regressions for own revenue draw on data derived from the GFS of the IMF, which provide longer time series.

[43] See Tables B.27 - B.29 in Appendix B.

[44] The results do not change when the military threat is considered only for NATO countries instead. Hence, the end of the Cold War seems to have affected public sector activity in neutral countries, too.

centralisation which deserve closer examination: Belgium and Spain.[45] From 1989 on, the share of sub-central government expenditure and tax revenue increased drastically in Belgium as a consequence of the transfer of competencies to the recently created regions and linguistic communities. At the same time, Belgium represents a small open economy whose degree of openness rose considerably in the last decades (see Table 4.1). With regard to Spain, the transfer of fiscal powers to the autonomous regions, and, simultaneously, economic opening and integration in the EU made considerable progress after the end of the Franco regime. Apart from this, both countries are characterised by significant linguistic diversity.

Table 4.5: Quantile (median) estimates for fiscal decentralisation, direct expenditure (incl. social security), OECD countries, 1970-2001

| | Dep. var.: Degree of expenditure decentralisation (indic. ED1) | | | | | | |
|---|---|---|---|---|---|---|---|
| | (1) | (2) | (3) | (4) | (5) | (6) | (7) |
| *Population* | -.039 | -.052 | -.045 | -.048 | -.078 | .127 | -.008 |
| | (.050) | (.067) | (.070) | (.076) | (.074) | (.094) | (.093) |
| *Urbanisation* | -.168*** | -.141* | -.183*** | -.148*** | -.216*** | -.341*** | -.150* |
| | (.051) | (.072) | (.054) | (.057) | (.067) | (.079) | (.090) |
| *Reg. disparity* | -.132*** | -.123*** | -.148*** | -.142** | -.119*** | -.124*** | -.114 |
| | (.045) | (.038) | (.040) | (.061) | (.037) | (.039) | (.071) |
| *P.c income* | .057*** | .023 | .056*** | .058*** | .075*** | -.001 | .039* |
| | (.021) | (.025) | (.019) | (.016) | (.028) | (.015) | (.022) |
| *Growth rate* | -.071 | -.039 | -.066 | -.086* | -.080 | -.043 | -.055 |
| | (.058) | (.050) | (.049) | (.052) | (.067) | (.048) | (.047) |
| *Unemployment* | -.301*** | -.332*** | -.292** | -.305*** | -.357*** | -.435*** | -.356*** |
| | (.078) | (.095) | (.115) | (.092) | (.079) | (.092) | (.114) |
| *Election* | -.000 | .000 | -.001 | .000 | -.001 | -.001 | -.001 |
| | (.002) | (.001) | (.002) | (.002) | (.002) | (.002) | (.001) |
| *Coldwar* | -.002 | .000 | -.003 | -.002 | -.004 | -.004 | -.001 |
| | (.004) | (.004) | (.004) | (.003) | (.003) | (.003) | (.004) |
| *Trade openness* | -.011 | | .014 | -.011 | -.030 | -.014 | .021 |
| | (.020) | | (.034) | (.019) | (.043) | (.019) | (.041) |
| *Finan. openness* | | .068* | | | | | |
| | | (.035) | | | | | |
| *EU · EU exp.* | .006 | .004 | | | .009* | -.018 | |
| | (.006) | (.004) | | | (.005) | (.016) | |
| *EU trade* | | | .097* | | | | .070 |
| | | | (.052) | | | | (.148) |
| *EU polit. integr.* | | | | .003 | | | |
| | | | | (.003) | | | |

45 France constitutes another example of significant decentralisation, however, only with respect to tax autonomy.

Table 4.5 (cont.): Quantile (median) estimates for fiscal decentralisation

| | Dep. var.: Degree of expenditure decentralisation (indic. ED1) | | | | | | |
|---|---|---|---|---|---|---|---|
| | (1) | (2) | (3) | (4) | (5) | (6) | (7) |
| *Fractional* · *Trade openness* | | | | | .126 (.104) | | |
| *Fractional* · (*EU* · *EU exp.*) | | | | | | .156*** (.043) | |
| *Fractional* · *EU trade* | | | | | | | .383 (.546) |
| *Referendum* · *Trade openness* | | | | | -.043 (.031) | | |
| *Referendum* · (*EU* · *EU exp.*) | | | | | | -.000 (.013) | |
| *Referendum* · *EU trade* | | | | | | | -.008 (.030) |
| *Regional parliam.* · *Trade openness* | | | | | -.142** (.060) | | |
| *Regional parliam.* · (*EU* · *EU exp.*) | | | | | | -.005 (.012) | |
| *Regional parliam.* · *EU trade* | | | | | | | -.227*** (.086) |
| No. obs. (countries) | 484 (23) | 457 (22) | 482 (23) | 484 (23) | 484 (23) | 484 (23) | 482 (23) |
| Pseudo $R^2$ | .850 | .857 | .850 | .850 | .856 | .861 | .852 |

Note: All regressions include country dummies, as well as period dummies for territorial changes in Canada, Germany, Netherlands, and Portugal, whose coefficients are not reported. Bootstrap standard errors are reported in parentheses. ***, **, and * indicate significance at the 1%, 5% and 10% level, respectively.

In fact, after carrying out a sensitivity analysis, it turns out that particularly the coefficients of economic and EU integration vary with the use of different samples (see Table B.30 in Appendix B). Note, first, that due to the limited size of the cross-section[46] and to the fixed effects approach, it is not surprising that even though we have checked for outliers, individual cases have a considerable influence on the results. Obviously, least squares estimations are severely distorted by outlying observations concerning the distribution of the dependent variable, especially when the sample size is moderate. When dropping Belgium from the sample, the effect of economic openness becomes less precisely estimated, and the sign is even partly reversed. The same occurs for European integration, in case of excluding Spain. Yet, the sign of the interaction term remains unchanged.

[46] Belgium and Spain make up about 6% and, respectively, 4% of the observations in the sample.

Table 4.6: Quantile (median) estimates for fiscal decentralisation, autonomous own tax revenue, OECD countries, 1965-2001

| | Dep. var.: Degree of tax decentralisation (indic. TD1) | | | | | |
|---|---|---|---|---|---|---|
| | (1) | (2) | (3) | (4) | (5) | (6) |
| *Population* | .097* | .062 | .121*** | .103*** | .073** | .013*** |
| | (.054) | (.052) | (.041) | (.027) | (.037) | (.035) |
| *Urbanisation* | -.197*** | -.180*** | -.173*** | -.196*** | -.191*** | -.182*** |
| | (.043) | (.046) | (.059) | (.037) | (.061) | (.064) |
| *Reg. disparity* | -.072 | -.072** | -.056 | -.064* | -.071 | -.053 |
| | (.049) | (.033) | (.056) | (.038) | (.045) | (.041) |
| *P.c. income* | -.005* | -.007 | -.016 | -.008 | .005 | -.018 |
| | (.014) | (.016) | (.016) | (.014) | (.017) | (.019) |
| *Growth rate* | -.017 | .008 | -.004 | -.008 | -.041 | -.011 |
| | (.034) | (.035) | (.042) | (.037) | (.032) | (.032) |
| *Unemployment* | .213** | .206*** | .193** | .213*** | .226*** | .201*** |
| | (.085) | (.064) | (.075) | (.064) | (.074) | (.060) |
| *Election* | .001 | .001 | .001 | .001 | .001 | .001 |
| | (.002) | (.001) | (.002) | (.002) | (.001) | (.001) |
| *Coldwar* | -.005 | .004 | -.004 | -.004 | -.005** | -.003 |
| | (.003) | (.003) | (.003) | (.003) | (.002) | (.003) |
| *Trade openness* | -.002 | | -.001 | -.004 | .052* | .003 |
| | (.015) | | (.018) | (.013) | (.031) | (.015) |
| *Finan. openness* | | .007 | | | | |
| | | (.020) | | | | |
| *EU · EU exp.* | -.002 | -.002 | | | -.004** | |
| | (.004) | (.003) | | | (.002) | |
| *EU trade* | | | .012 | | | -.031 |
| | | | (.030) | | | (.075) |
| *EU polit. integr.* | | | | -.001 | | |
| | | | | (.001) | | |
| *Fractional · Trade openness* | | | | | -.099 | |
| | | | | | (.091) | |
| *Fractional · EU trade* | | | | | | .178 |
| | | | | | | (.194) |
| *Referendum · Trade openness* | | | | | -.010 | |
| | | | | | (.012) | |
| *Referendum · EU trade* | | | | | | .002 |
| | | | | | | (.015) |
| *Regional parliam. · Trade openness* | | | | | -.057* | |
| | | | | | (.032) | |
| *Regional parliam. · EU trade* | | | | | | -.014 |
| | | | | | | (.083) |
| No. obs. (countries) | 548 (23) | 522 (22) | 535 (23) | 548 (23) | 548 (23) | 535 (23) |
| Pseudo $R^2$ | .867 | .869 | .870 | .867 | .868 | .870 |

Note: See Table 4.5 for further details.

As a test for robustness, "robust" estimators, like the least absolute deviations (LAD) estimator, are proposed by Koenker and Bassett (1978).[47] A special case of generalised quantile regressions estimates the median of the dependent variable, conditional on the values of the independent variables. It generally turns out that this estimator is very robust with respect to outliers in both the dependent and the independent variables. Table 4.5 shows the corresponding results of median regressions for direct public expenditure using country-specific dummy variables. Since the usual standard errors tend to be understated in the presence of heteroscedasticity, bootstrap standard errors are reported according to Efron and Tibshirani (1993). The robust estimations confirm that, indeed, integration in the world economy as described by the degree of trade openness has no clear direct effect on the degree of expenditure decentralisation. Note, however, that the index of financial openness used alternatively maintains a positive significant coefficient.[48] Similarly, the results with respect to European integration and the interaction terms remain unchanged, though less accurately estimated.

Corresponding quantile (median) estimates for tax decentralisation (Table 4.6) yield even less conclusive results with respect to the direct effects of economic and European integration.[49] Only the centralising effect of representation of subnational governments or legislatures in the upper chamber is weakly supported. In general, quantile estimates give less accurate results in our case.

## 4.5 Discussion and Conclusions

The aim of this chapter was to investigate empirically the relationship between economic integration in general, and political integration in the European Union in particular, and the recent process of public sector decentralisation.

The theoretical framework presented here shows that by increasing the market size and enhancing economies of scale in the private sector, integration increases the benefits from the decentralised provision of public goods. Within this context, political unification in Europe is supposed to support decentralisation, since market integration is intensified and government functions formerly allocated to the central level are taken over by a supranational authority. On the other hand, with increasing exposure to economic shocks the demand for central government redistribution and macroeconomic stabilisation may prevail, too.

---

47 See, e.g., Judge et al. (1988) for an overview of quantile regressions.

48 This is probably due to the fact that, unlike the degree of trade openness, this indicator is not correlated with the size of the economy and exhibits no distinct pattern for Belgium.

49 The specification considering the interaction between $EU \cdot EU\ exp.$ and the other constant variables yielded no reasonable results and is therefore excluded here.

Using a panel data approach, we tested the hypothesis of a positive impact of global economic and European integration on the degree of decentralisation of the public sector for OECD countries. The estimates mostly indicate a significant positive relationship between economic integration as measured by the share of foreign trade in GDP and the degree of fiscal decentralisation, especially with respect to public revenues and in case of excluding social security. The results are valid even in case of considering tax-raising powers of sub-central governments. Some limited evidence is also provided for the "Sandwich" hypothesis postulating a diminishing role of national governments in the course of European integration. European integration as measured either by the share of trade with EU countries or the volume of EU expenditure exerts a positive effect on the sub-central government share of direct expenditure, the relationship being particularly valid for linguistically heterogeneous countries.

In line with the common-pool argument, direct involvement of subnational governments in central decision-making through a regional chamber of parliament is found to be associated with stronger centralisation, both in terms of public expenditure and tax revenue. Contrary to the expectations, integration also seems to lead to higher centralisation in countries providing for direct democracy at the national level. The estimates also indicate that growing inter-regional income disparity significantly decreases the sub-central government share of expenditure and revenue, thus supporting the hypothesis of growing demand for inter-regional redistribution by the central government with increasing exposure to economic shocks. Finally, a negative relationship is reported between the extent of military threat and the relative size of sub-central government activity.

However, the results prove to be sensitive to the measurement of decentralisation and to the inclusion of individual countries. It turns out that the decentralising impact of economic, as well as European integration is particularly induced by the exceptional cases of Belgium and Spain. At least, economic and political integration seem to have played a significant role in the remarkable process of fiscal decentralisation observed in these two countries. Indeed, robust estimates confirm that, strictly speaking, European integration contributed to the relative increase of sub-central government expenditure and revenue in linguistically heterogeneous countries, whereas participation of subnational governments in national decision-making induced centralising trends in the course of global integration.

Despite some inconclusive results and general problems related to the measurement of fiscal decentralisation, the empirical analysis provides us with some new results. The approach taken in this chapter focused on the particular interaction between integration on the one hand, and public sector decentralisation on the other hand, revealing a significant relationship between those two broad trends among OECD countries, especially in the context of preference heterogeneity. This result therefore supports both the "Decentralisation Theorem" and the theoretical literature on secessions.

Despite circumstantial evidence for this tendency, nation-states formed during long historical processes are not expected to disappear in the near future with advancing European integration, as these national governments continue to exert considerable power through the European Council. In line with this, up to now the European Union has been vested particularly with regulatory and legislative competencies, and to a lesser extent with direct expenditure and revenue powers. The analysis also indicates that institutional rules play an important role in determining the impact of integration on the vertical government structure and that the end of the Cold War has partly contributed to the enforcement of demands for local autonomy.

# 5

# Long-Term Trends in the Public Sector: An Inquiry into German History

## 5.1 Introduction

The studies carried out for OECD countries in the previous chapters have shown that, in spite of some exceptions, vertical government structures and institutional rules barely have changed over time. Therefore, the conclusions derived from those analyses might only be valid in the specific historical and economic context of the period of time considered there, and the role of other determining forces remains obscure. This suggests to take a long-term view on the development of the public sector in order to determine those factors actually underlying changes in the degree of fiscal decentralisation over time.

An often expressed view postulates that public sector structures evolve in conformity with some natural laws. De Tocqueville (1840), for example, predicted a natural tendency towards increasing centralisation among democratic nations which results from the striving for equality and uniformity. Also, according to Wagner (1876) and Popitz (1927), the long-term trend seems to suggest an almost ever-expanding role of the public sector in general, and of the central government in particular, in the process of social and economic development. Among other factors which contribute to increased government centralisation, Popitz explicitly mentions economic integration.[1] Whereas this reasoning corresponds indeed with the "supranationalising" effect of economic integration and globalisation described above, it fails to account for the concomitant decentralisation trends reported by the empirical analysis for OECD countries.

The case of Germany seems particularly interesting to address these questions. First and foremost, despite considerable political differences, there are striking economic and fiscal parallels between the current process of European integration and the formation of Germany as a unified country in the

[1] "Die Entwicklung des Deutschen Reiches [...] zeigt, [...] dass eine einheitliche Wirtschaft auf dem Gebiete des Rechts und der Gewerbeförderung zum mindesten gemeinsame Gesetzgebung voraussetzt [...]", Popitz (1927: 347).

19th century. The process of integration of the previously strongly fragmented German states took off with the creation of the customs union (*Zollverein*) in 1834, and culminated in the political unification of 1871 and the introduction of the Mark as a single currency in 1876. During this time, the transfer of competencies from the sovereign German states to the newly created central authority was mostly undergone at the expense of the state level. However, like in the EU, tax authority at that time remained largely with the states, whereas tariff revenues and state contributions constituted the primary resource of the central level. Also, similarly to today's EU, state governments exerted a dominant influence on central policy-making in Germany through the upper chamber of the national parliament. Though less comparable, reunification of West and East Germany in 1990 provides another interesting example for economic and political integration.

Apart from this, the German experience is expected to shed some light on the institutional determinants of changing fiscal structures. In particular, significant institutional changes and the alternating dominance of state and central level in national policy-making during its history are expected to have affected the formation of tax and expenditure cartels between subnational governments in line with the collusion hypothesis of Brennan and Buchanan (1980). Therefore, we can gain some general insight into the workings of decision-making institutions by looking at different historical periods.

For this purpose, this chapter investigates the long-term development of the public sector in Germany from 1871 to the present day. The following questions circumscribe the core of this examination. First, to what extent is it possible to detect, as Wagner (1876) and Popitz (1927) suggested, a long-term trend of public sector growth and centralisation in Germany's federal system? And, second, which are the factors determining this development? Within this context we address the question whether the decentralising effect of economic and European integration partly revealed in the panel analysis is also specifically supported for Germany, by focusing on a longer time period. Generally speaking, the determinants of variations in the vertical government structure may considerably differ across countries and over time.

Long-term trends in public expenditure and centralisation have largely been investigated, both for Germany and for other industrial nations.[2] These studies generally find no clear evidence in support of a continuous centralising trend in the public sector following a law of nature. Rather, there are several, frequently disconnected, developments. As illustrated by Peacock and Wiseman (1961) for the United Kingdom, most significant phases of fiscal centralisation are only attributed to the "displacement effect" of wars. Nonetheless,

---

[2] See, e.g., Recktenwald (1962) and Hansmeyer (1967) for Germany, and Hansmeyer and Zimmermann (1984), Recktenwald (1984), Kraus (1983), Pryor (1968) and Peltzman (1980) for Germany and other countries. Blankart (2001) also provides an investigation of Popitz' "law" for Prussia.

Blankart (1999, 2000) detects a "hidden" centralisation process in Germany after World War II.

In the present work, the long-term development in Germany is assessed both in terms of government size and allocation of decision-making powers and government functions and revenues among the fiscal tiers. In order to investigate the validity of the collusion hypothesis, particular emphasis is put on the analysis of the institutional framework providing for subnational participation in central decision-making. The effect of economic development and of economic and European integration on the degree of fiscal decentralisation are finally tested empirically for the period 1950 to 2001, controlling for other time-variant determinants of the vertical government structure.

The investigation proceeds according to the following plan. First, section 5.2 presents a historical description of Germany's vertical government structure since the foundation of the German Reich until today. Then, in the next section, the long-term development is quantified in terms of size and allocation of public expenditure and revenues. The regression analysis is carried out in section 5.4, and conclusions are finally drawn in section 5.5.

## 5.2 A Brief History of German Federalism

This section aims at providing an inquiry into Germany's fiscal federal structure in historical terms from the creation of a unified state to the present day.[3]

### 5.2.1 The German *Kaiserreich* (1871-1918)

There had been no unified German state until the foundation of the German *Kaiserreich* in 1871. Although a single German economic area was already brought into being with the creation of the customs union (*Zollverein*) in 1834, the first attempt to unite all independent German states failed in 1848-49. The *Norddeutsche Bund*, a confederation of still sovereign states founded in 1867 and dominated by Prussia, represented the first political union, which was based on a customs union, common law, institutions and armed forces, and which was endowed with some own financial resources derived from individual state contributions.

After the final unification of all German states in 1871, Germany's federal system until World War I was characterised by a strong asymmetry between a dominant Prussia, which had more than two thirds of total population and economic power, and provided both the German Kaiser and the Reichskanzler, and a multitude of smaller states and principalities. Though formally

[3] For the period before World War II, the description draws particularly on Burg (1992), Witt (1992), Neumark (1976), Gerloff (1913), Terhalle (1952), Schremmer (1994), and Döhler (2002), who also provide some historical figures.

having equal powers, the democratically elected lower chamber of parliament, the *Reichstag*, remained rather weak as compared to the upper chamber, the *Bundesrat*, which consisted of representatives delegated by the state governments. The representative body of the sovereign states was the dominant legislative authority, being vested with certain prerogatives, such as an absolute veto power with respect to the federal budget and all federal legislation, and the right to dissolve the lower chamber and to take part in other important decisions of the central government, such as the declaration of war. Taking furthermore into account that small states had disproportionately strong representation in the *Bundesrat*, formally in the position to outvote Prussia, the German *Kaiserreich* can be described as a highly federalised state with the state level constituting the most important level prior to World War I.

In general, during the *Kaiserreich* government functions were clearly distributed between the central and the state level. The federal government was exclusively responsible for defence, foreign affairs, trade policy and certain economic services, particularly postal operations, and had to maintain the legal and economic unity. Within this context, federal laws were generally executed by state governments on their own behalf. The state as well as the local levels were predominantly responsible for almost all other expenditures. As a general rule, the state level was mainly concerned with higher authority functions, including administration, justice and police. Expenditure on culture and education were shared between the state and the local levels, the former being primarily responsible for universities, and science and research, the latter for schools. On the other hand, tasks related to welfare state and population, such as social assistance, health, housing, and environmental services were mainly performed at the local level.

Similarly to the USA and Switzerland, the Constitution of 1871 established a strict division of revenue sources and taxing powers, without providing any systematic mechanisms of policy coordination between the different fiscal tiers. Though not explicitly laid down in the constitution, indirect taxes and tariffs exclusively belonged to the central, direct taxes to the state and local levels. The states were completely autonomous to set up their own tax and financial system, and were exclusively responsible for tax administration.[4] State taxes included first and foremost income, wealth, inheritance and profit taxes. Local governments generally shared in these revenues or were allowed to autonomously determine the rates for business and property taxes subject to certain limits and to raise additional charges to the state income taxes. Yet, the degree of local discretion varied significantly between the states. Finally, surpluses from state-owned enterprises constituted a further important revenue source, particularly for state and local levels.

Apart from this, according to Art. 70(2) of the Constitution, the Reich's current budget deficit had to be balanced by fiscal transfers of the states

---

[4] Note that no inter-state fiscal equalisation existed at that time, neither by vertical, nor by horizontal intergovernmental transfers.

according to their population size, the *Matrikularbeiträge*. Though in principle the central level was allowed to introduce own taxes in parallel with the states,[5] the expansion of central taxing powers was strongly opposed by the states. Therefore, the state contributions constituted initially the third most important financial resource of the central government. In contrast to this, exceptional expenditures, mostly for military purposes, were predominantly financed by public debts. In theory, the central level could indefinitely incur debts which, indeed, led to a strong rise of the Reich's public debt from zero in 1871 to approximately 9.1% relative to GNP in 1914.[6] At least with regard to its military expenditures, therefore, the central level was independent of the individual states.

Although the state level was able to defend its dominant position until the end of the *Kaiserreich*, nonetheless, the central level and, particularly, the *Reichstag* continuously gained ground at the expense of the states and the *Bundesrat*. This was particularly due to the introduction of social insurance in the 1880s, and to the fact that new tasks, such as the building of a modern navy and the acquisition of colonies were taken on by the central government. Particularly the central level's unlimited power to incur public debts was perhaps a major driving force of centralisation during the German *Kaiserreich*. In the course of time, the central level was also increasingly involved in certain areas of traditional state competency, like science and academic research.

This process of growing importance of the central level was also reflected in increasing financial independence from state governments. With the introduction of the Reich's inheritance tax in 1906 – a central tax shared with the states – and even more so with the war contribution (*Wehrbeitrag*) created in 1913, the central level established its first own direct taxes. On the other hand, as revenues from tariffs increased in consequence of the protectionist trade policy,[7] the states prevented the central government's independence by enacting the *Frankensteinsche Klausel* in 1879. According to this settlement, which was in force until 1904, the central level had to transfer all tariff and tobacco tax revenues exceeding 130 million Mark to the states, despite running a budget deficit. This led in the end to net payments to the states and rising debts of the central government. Due to the induced budget deficit, the individual states could continue to transfer its *Matrikularbeiträge*, therefore keeping the central level financially dependent on the states (Bismarck: "*Kostgänger der Einzelstaaten*"). However, the share of transfers received from the states in total tax and tariff revenues of the central government declined from 15-20% before 1880 to 3% in 1913.[8]

---

[5] This provision was, however, abolished in 1904.

[6] See Neumark (1976: 99f.) and also Gerloff (1913).

[7] According to Schremmer (1994), the share of revenue from tariffs in total revenue of the central government rose from 25% in the 1870s to 40-50% at the end of the 1890s.

[8] See Neumark (1976).

### 5.2.2 The Inter-War Period (1919-1938)

Besides abolishing the monarchy, the Weimar Constitution of 1919 crucially altered the German federal system. The central level, represented by a directly elected president who had extraordinary competencies, and the *Reichstag* as the lower chamber, now became the dominant level of government. The upper chamber of the German parliament representing the Länder governments, the *Reichsrat*, though formally having equal rights in terms of legislation, retained only a suspensive veto power which could be overruled by a qualified two thirds majority in the lower chamber.

The inevitable concentration of government functions at the central level, which usually occurs during long military conflicts, was consolidated after the war. The new Weimar Constitution transferred certain government functions from the state to the central level and also introduced new expenditures on social assistance and education which were previously assigned to the local level. Apart from this, war damage compensation formed a considerable part of the central budget.

The process of centralisation during the Weimar Republic becomes even more evident with respect to the financial constitution. With the financial reform of Erzberger[9] in 1919 the different tax laws of the states were replaced by a standardised tax system, the central government also receiving the exclusive right to raise and legislate most taxes (*Kompetenzkompetenz*). Besides having exclusive competency for tariffs and consumption taxes, the central government had the ultimate decision-making power in terms of concurrent legislation over most direct and indirect taxes and framework legislation over state taxes and charges (Art. 8 of the Weimar Constitution), the *Reichsrat* having only a suspensive veto power. State governments were not allowed to levy surcharges on central taxes, and tax administration and collection was centralised. Consequently, the states lost their fiscal autonomy and became on their part financially dependent on the central level. Only few taxes, like business, property, building and other minor indirect taxes remained in the competency of state governments, though limited by central rules.[10] To compensate them for the loss in financial autonomy, state and local levels shared in the yields of income, corporate and value-added taxes. Apart from this, fiscal equalisation through vertical transfers was introduced for the first time, both at the state and the local levels.

With the beginning of the Nazi period in 1933, Germany ceased to be a federal system. The states were consolidated and entirely lost both their fiscal and political autonomy and the *Reichsrat* was dissolved. Consequently, and particularly with begin of remilitarisation in 1935, most public expenditures and financial resources were allocated to the central level. Tax sharing was replaced by vertical central grants and the few remaining state taxes were

[9] Note that this tax legislation was mainly in force until 1977.

[10] In 1920 business and property taxes were transferred from the local to the state government.

finally allocated to the central or to the local level. By regaining in 1936 their right to determine the rates of the business and property taxes under certain limits imposed by the Reich, local governments retained a certain degree of fiscal autonomy. Terhalle (1952) suggests that the share of total tax revenues which was determined by central legislation increased from 50% in 1913-14 to 98% in 1938.[11]

### 5.2.3 The Postwar Period (since 1949)

After World War II, the government structure of the Federal Republic of Germany emerged as a compromise between two tendencies. On the one hand, a federalist current, represented by the Constitutional Convent and the Allies, supported strong autonomy of state governments and strict separation of expenditure and taxing powers. On the other hand a unitarist current, represented by the Parliamentary Council, was in favour of a centralised federal state in the tradition of the Weimar Republic.[12] Due to the pressures exerted by the Allies against the emergence of a strong central government, the newly created Länder finally obtained a stronger position as compared to the Weimar period.

In the tradition of the Weimar Constitution, Art. 72(1) and 105(2) of the new German Basic Law of 1949 provide for a wide range of concurrent legislation giving the central government the power to exhaust all aspects of a specific matter, the subnational entities retaining the power to legislate only as long as that matter has not been exhausted by the central government (*Kompetenzkompetenz*). Apart from this, the majority of general framework legislation is allocated at the central level, too. However, in contrast to the Weimar Republic, the upper chamber of the national parliament, the *Bundesrat*, which represents the state governments,[13] is now involved with equal powers in decision-making concerning constitutional revision, the distribution of competencies and revenues, and national legislation carried out by state administrations. Particularly this last aspect led to an increase in the proportion of ordinary bills which had to be approved by the regional chamber from initially 10% to nearly two thirds nowadays.[14]

Apart from concurrent and framework legislation, a new striking feature of today's federal system consists in increased policy coordination between the different levels of government. In line with this, joint public activities (*Gemeinschaftsaufgaben*), formally defined in Art. 91 of the Basic Law, are particularly carried out in areas related to transport and communication and other economic services. In addition, the primary responsibility of the state

[11] See Terhalle (1952: 317).

[12] See, also, Döhler (2002) with respect to this controversy.

[13] Carrying on the tradition since 1871, the present upper chamber of parliament is composed of representatives delegated by the Länder governments and subject to their instructions, each Land having a uniform vote.

[14] See http://www2.bundesrat.de

level in matters of culture and education is counterbalanced by considerable policy coordination after 1949, both between the different Länder and between the state and the federal level.

To comply with the demands of the Allies, a strict division of financial resources was initially implemented, however, mostly with respect to tax yields and tax administration, and less in terms of tax legislation. Despite allocating income and corporate tax yields exclusively to the Länder governments, Art. 106(3) of the Basic Law in its initial version of 1949 generally allowed the central government to participate in these revenues, provided approval of the *Bundesrat*. Following the financial reforms of 1955 and 1969, income and corporate taxes were ultimately transformed into shared taxes, along with the value-added tax.[15] Shared taxes constitute since then on average 85% of total tax revenues of consolidated sub-central government. In addition to this, a complex system of fiscal equalisation was set up in 1955 which, besides vertical grants, provided for the first time for financial transfers from rich to poor Länder, intended for the adequate equalisation of divergent tax efforts.

On the other hand, concurrent legislative powers over most taxes, including state and local taxes, are assigned to the federal level in line with Art. 105(2).[16] Only local governments regained in 1956 their pre-war autonomy, being allowed to determine the rates of the business and property taxes within certain limits set by federal legislation. According to the indicator presented in chapter ??, from 1973 to 2001 a relatively constant average share of 93% of total tax revenue of consolidated general government resulted from federal or concurrent legislation. Even though the yields of most important taxes were initially allocated to the state level, concurrent tax legislation on these taxes was de facto already assigned to the federal level from the beginning. Therefore, except for the transfer of certain minor taxes from the state to the central level, no significant increase in tax centralisation can be noticed since then. There is, however, circumstantial evidence for a continuing tendency to cede or abolish certain state and local taxes, such as the wealth tax, the wage sum tax, or the tax on business capital, and, more recently, the motor tax, in exchange for increased participation in the common tax pool.

Consequently, although being able to exercise a crucial veto power on most legislative issues in the upper chamber of parliament, in return the state level today enjoys only a limited extent of complete autonomy, particularly with respect to tax-raising powers. This applies even more so for rather poor Länder which are dependent on central grants. Therefore, whereas the *Kaiserreich* and the Weimar Republic were characterised by the predominance of the state and, alternately, the central level, the Federal Republic of Germany is

[15] Note that since 1969 and 1998, local governments also receive a fixed share in revenues from income and, respectively, value-added taxes.

[16] See also Blankart (2000) on these issues. Note, also, that in line with Art. 123(1) the previous uniform tax system of the Weimar Republic remained in force, thus not allowing different tax laws of the states.

characterised by complex connections between governments at all levels, which is frequently referred to as *Politikverflechtung*.[17] This framework has probably grown out of the desire for uniform living conditions after the war, and of the historically rooted fear of state fragmentation (*Kleinstaaterei*). Although there are policy areas in which one level's competency clearly supercedes other levels' competency, it can be said that no fiscal tier really enjoys complete autonomy in today's Germany.

Given this type of cooperative federalism, Hesse (1962) argued that the close interrelationship between governments at the federal, state, and local levels establishes a "unitary federation". However, it should be noted that this specific kind of horizontal and vertical cooperation is not equivalent to centralisation of policies resulting in a higher share of federal public goods and taxes. One should rather expect state governments to use their funds in their own interest, even if the general legal framework for their policies is laid down centrally and uniformly. The evidence indicates that despite very low tax autonomy, there is significant variation in expenditure patterns across the Länder.[18]

Despite significant centralisation after World War I, the review of German history from the foundation of the German Reich in 1871 until today therefore could not detect any continuous rise of central government's power, but rather some distinct developments. Whereas the Weimar Republic clearly emerged as a highly centralised federal state, Länder governments regained importance after World War II, though only in terms of extended participation in cooperative decision-making at the central level.

The historical overview, however, supports the collusion hypothesis of Brennan and Buchanan (1980). Today's institutional framework certainly facilitates the creation of revenue cartels between the state and the central levels aimed at mitigating fiscal competition. The analysis in section 3.3.1 has shown that both equal participation of the state level in decision-making concerning the distribution of revenues, and the allocation of concurrent powers to the central government seem to have made this possible. These mechanisms furthermore tend to impede any alteration of the status quo. It is not surprising then, that the recently failed efforts to reform Germany's federal structures excluded from the outset the transfer of autonomous taxing powers to the state governments.[19]

In contrast to this, despite participation in central decision-making, no cartelisation was possible among state governments during the previous periods. Whereas the Weimar Republic was characterised by a predominant central government and weak state governments, during the *Kaiserreich* the

---

[17] See Scharpf et al. (1976).

[18] See, e.g., Buettner et al. (2004).

[19] The only attempts are aimed at exchanging the yields of some minor taxes between the central and the state levels, without, however, providing for separate taxing powers.

central government lacked the power to ensure such revenue cartels among the highly autonomous state governments. In the next section, these findings with respect to centralisation of decision-making structures are verified more thoroughly by means of quantitative figures.

## 5.3 Quantification of Long-Term Trends in the Public Sector

In order to examine public sector growth and centralisation in terms of the "laws" formulated by Wagner (1876) and Popitz (1927), this section quantifies the development of the public sector in Germany since the middle of the 19th century until today, both in general, as well as differentiated with regard to fiscal tiers.

### 5.3.1 Growth of the Public Sector

To begin with, according to Wagner (1876), state activity and particularly public expenditure are supposed to rise at a faster rate than output in the process of cultural and economic development, that is with increasing industrialisation and agglomeration.[20] This "historically inevitable" expansion of the public sector originates in the pressure of social and economic progress, and, particularly, in the rising complexities involved, which require increased enforcement of law and order, and direct state participation in production and provision of economic and social services. Generally speaking, goods produced by the public sector are assumed to have a high income elasticity of demand, and so rising income per capita implies an increase in the public sector's share in economy.

However, this claim is rather based on statistical observation than on clear empirical evidence.[21] Based on an empirical study of public expenditures in Germany, Brecht (1932) provided some evidence that local expenditure per capita is supposed to increase disproportionately with population size and urbanisation. However, the German literature has criticised this result because of lacking theoretical foundation and because the empirical evidence is doubtful.[22]

Taking into account that there are neither gross national product (GNP) figures for the nineteenth century, nor reliable public expenditure data for the period before World War I available, the public sector's role in Germany

---

20 See Wagner (1876: 892–908). See, also, Peacock and Wiseman (1961), and Recktenwald (1962) for a critical assessment.

21 Ram (1987), e.g., provides some mixed results from a cross-country analysis. While there is some support for Wagner's hypothesis in time series, there is no clear evidence in cross-section estimates.

22 See Kuhn (1993) for a survey of this literature.

will be analysed according to the ratio of total public expenditures according to national income statistics as percentage of net national product (NNP). For the pre-1950 period, the analysis draws on the work of Hoffmann (1965) which, despite statistical deficiencies, comprises the most consistent and detailed compendium of historical data on Germany.[23]

However, note that any quantitative analysis of the public sector's role in the economy faces fundamental difficulties. First and foremost, the entire range of state activities tends to be understated by fiscal measures which represent only budgetary flows. Apart from this, for reasons of frequent changes in both the geographical as well as the statistical boundaries which delineate the public sector, it is quite complicated to measure exactly the scope of the public domain over a long period of time. One should bear in mind that especially in the 19th century statistics were incomplete and methodologically controversial and many economic terms, such as investments and national income, not clearly defined. Also because of significant changes in German territory and population, a comparison of the development after World War II with earlier periods is, even in relative figures, controversial.

Given this qualification, Figure 5.1 plots the ratio of total public expenditures as percentage of net national product at market prices (NNP). Concerning the period prior to 1913, the growth of the public sector (including social security) is characterised by a relatively steady, but not rapid, expansion.[24] From a minimum at 7.1% in 1856, the share of total public expenditures as a percentage of NNP more than doubled to 14.8% in 1913. According to Neumark (1976) this can particularly be explained by the increase of military and social spending, and increasing demands for public goods with economic development and population growth.

The period after World War I takes off with significantly higher public spending, which demonstrates the "displacement effect" of social and political upheavals, such as wars, noted by Peacock and Wiseman (1961).[25] As any modern war economy transforms itself typically into a public sector-controlled state economy, the public sector's importance will almost naturally be much greater immediately after any war as in comparison to the pre-war level. According to the authors, large social and economic crises induce people to accept dramatic changes in tax burdens and institutions, and will impose new functions upon the government. This increase in the share of the public sector in economy is less likely to return to the old level before the crisis. However, besides the effect of the war, by far the biggest and most rapid growth of the

[23] See Appendix C for a description of data sources and definitions. Note that no reliable data are available for the periods around World War I and II.

[24] The two exceptional peaks in 1866 and 1871 are both due to temporarily extended military spending in relation to the Prussian-Austrian and Franco-German War, respectively.

[25] See Pryor (1968) for a critical discussion and an empirical test of the "displacement effect".

Fig. 5.1: Growth of the public sector in Germany, 1850-2003

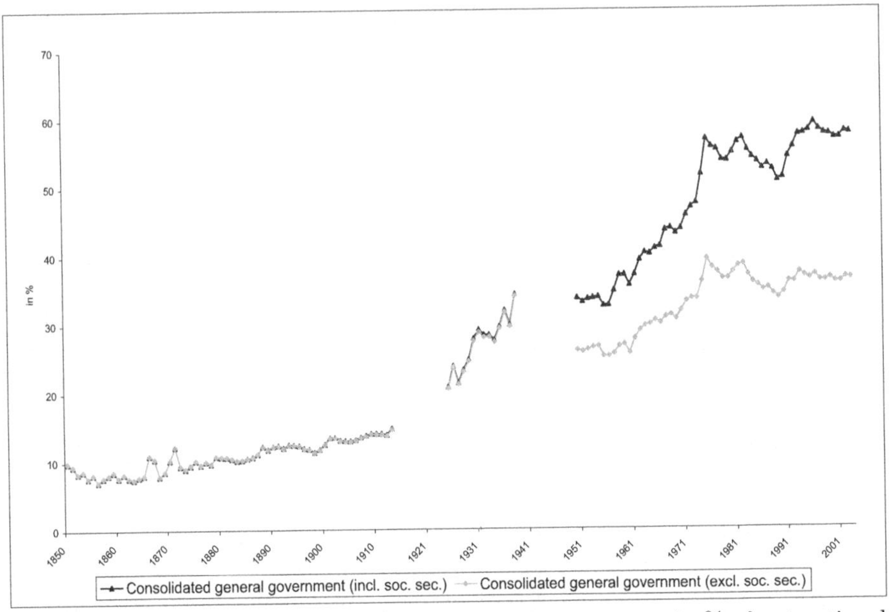


Note: Public expenditures of consolidated general government in % of net national product at market prices, according to national income accounts. Social security figures reported by Hoffmann (1965) are understated for the period 1850-1938. See Appendix C for data sources and definitions.

public sector occurred from 1925 to 1938, the share of public expenditure in NNP increasing from 20.8% to 34.4%.[26]

In order to explain this extraordinary expansion of the public sector, three factors seem to play a crucial role.[27] First, there is a significant rise in public expenditures regarding education, housing, and social affairs (even without social insurance) due to the extension of the welfare system during the Weimar Republic. Second, war damage compensation in accordance with the treaty of Versailles amounted to more than 10% of total public expenditures.[28] Later on, Nazi Germany started its remilitarisation and military expenditures increased considerably. Third, finally, whereas, in consequence of the Great Depression from 1929 to 1932, the national product actually declined, public expenditures remained mostly at their high levels, or even increased as, for example, in the case of welfare expenditures.

26 Including all social insurance expenditure, Andic and Veverka (1963) even report an increase of the public sector's share from 23.4% to 37.9% during this time. However, these figures are not strictly comparable.

27 See, in general, Gerloff (1913), Recktenwald (1962, 1975), and Neumark (1976).

28 See Statistisches Bundesamt (1972).

For World War II there is no such "displacement effect" observable. Starting with a level of 33.8% in 1950, the ratio of public expenditures to NNP grew significantly during the sixties and seventies, and particularly during the period 1973 to 1975. After reaching a peak of 57.1% in 1982, there is a small decline in the public sector's share to 51.3% in 1990. However, after German reunification, additional public spending concerning the reconstruction of East Germany led again to an increase of the public sector size to another peak of 59.3% in 1996 and a modest decline thereafter. As for the inter-war period, the rapid growth of the public sector after World War II is mainly due to the extension of the welfare state. Excluding social security, the size of the public sector only increases from 26.1% in 1950, which is slightly lower than the pre-Nazi era level (1933: 28.1%) to 36.5% in 2003.

In conclusion, the general trend from the middle of the nineteenth century to the present day indicates an increase of the public sector share by more than six times over the past 150 years: from an average of 9% for 1850-1855 to nearly 58% in 1998-2003. An empirical verification strongly supports this positive trend for the entire period, as well as for the individual periods, even in case of accounting for the "displacement effects" of the two world wars (see Table 5.1 below). However, if extra expenditures due to German reunification are regarded as short-time exceptional, the development since 1982 seems to point to a considerable slowdown in public sector growth.

### 5.3.2 The Process of Public Sector Centralisation

#### Positive Theories of Government Centralisation

Certain authors postulated that there is an inevitable tendency towards centralisation of the public sector in the course of social and economic development. With respect to Germany, Popitz (1927) observed that the central government got increasingly involved in the affairs of state and local governments during the transition from the *Kaiserreich* to the Weimar Republic.[29] Assuming that apart from a few original tasks of central and local governments, there are no clear criteria for the distribution of most functions among different levels of government, he predicts that particularly competencies of state governments tend to be attracted by the central government over time. Apart from this, as a consequence, the delimitations of areas of central and state government activity are expected to become increasingly blurred.

Different reasons are given in support of the increasing dominance of the central government. First, Popitz argues that an integrated economic area and the uniform supply of welfare services and living conditions require central legislation. The resulting costs for the state governments may subsequently be taken over by the central government, too. Second, lacking financial resources

[29] A similar centralising tendency in the public sector is also predicted by Bryce's law for the USA, see Blankart (2001).

and considerable interjurisdictional differences in size and tax efforts impede state and local governments to execute central government legislation and to overcome emergency situations. Since the central level naturally benefits from a larger elasticity of revenues, it can provide financial assistance to the state governments, and also possesses more opportunities to extend its scope of public expenditures. For example, it can be observed that new and innovative public policy areas, such as transport in the 1920s, tended to be allocated first and foremost at the central level. And finally, it is because of the political preponderance of the lower chamber of parliament, the *Reichstag*, that popular demands, particularly related to the welfare state, tend to be increasingly addressed to the central state.

Generally speaking, the automatic "force of attraction of the central state" (Popitz, 1927: 349) is expected to entail an upward shift of both functions and financial resources from the state to the central level of government. However, Popitz mixes normative and positive perspectives on the development of the public sector, and his conclusions are highly controversial.[30] For example, he postulates that efficiency and economical budget appropriation is only achieved through centralised administration. Whereas the increasing political dominance of the democratically elected lower chamber of parliament and the demand for uniform living conditions certainly acted in favour of a stronger central government, it is not necessarily clear that an integrated economic area requires policy centralisation and that smaller state governments naturally lack financial resources to fulfil their tasks. Also, inter-state disparities may be addressed by fiscal equalisation payments without the intervention of the central state.

The predictions of Popitz' "law" have to be assessed against the specific historical and political background of the Weimar Republic, particularly the consequences of the war and the collapse of the monarchy which generated a centralist democratic current and led to the deprivation of powers of the state governments after the financial reform of Erzberger in 1919. Therefore, it rests an open issue whether Popitz' conclusions represent a law of nature and can be simply extrapolated to other periods of time.

Peacock and Wiseman (1961) also suggest that the process of economic growth generates pressures for the movement of responsibility for public functions to higher levels of government, however, without stating whether this applies at the central or at intermediate levels.[31] They mention particularly technical progress and improvements in transport and communication, which are assumed to generate pressures for improved and more uniform standards of public services and to increase the efficient size of economic and administra-

---

30 See Albers (1964), Recktenwald (1984), Hansmeyer and Zimmermann (1984), Hansmeyer (1967), Kraus (1983) and Blankart (2001) for a critical discussion of Popitz' law. According to Meyer (1998), Popitz' approach provides no adequate explanation of the process of centralisation at the European level either.

31 Note, however, that the authors also mention the possibility of opposite effects, consisting in concomitant pressures to preserve local autonomy.

tive units. Increasing externalities of public goods, especially associated with the advancing of urbanisation in the course of economic development, tend to further support centralisation. However, strictly speaking, spillovers could be dealt with alternatively by policy coordination or fiscal transfers between the jurisdictions involved.

The "displacement effect" of wars is also mentioned by Peacock and Wiseman (1961) as another reason for increasing centralisation. They suggest that public sector growth and centralisation may occur concomitantly as the result of the same social crises. Accordingly, people are supposed to accept more easily centralisation of government functions and revenues and abrogations of local autonomy during periods of war, increased social cohesion further supporting demands for uniform standards and policies. After the war, along with war-related commitments, such as public debt and war damage compensation which are generally incurred by the central level, higher central government expenditure does not return to the pre-war levels.

## Allocation of Expenditure and Revenue by Fiscal Tiers

In the following, these hypotheses are verified for Germany by means of descriptive statistics. A quantitative examination of long-term trends in the vertical structure of public expenditure and revenue faces serious difficulties, in particular regarding the period until 1913.[32] We focus, first, on the allocation of public expenditure by fiscal tiers, excluding social security.

According to Figure 5.2, starting from 29.3% in 1881, the central government's share of total public expenditures seems to have remained rather stable until 1913. At the same time, there is a concomitant increase of spending at the local level. In line with Brecht's "law", Tilly (1997) notes that municipal government expenditures, especially driven by investment activity, grew clearly faster than the national product during this period. Particularly the process of urbanisation is assumed to have forced municipalities to expand their traditional activities and to take on new functions, such as the provision of local

[32] Although the Reichsschatzamt (1908) provides data for some single years, it is important to note that these figures are only of limited use and reliability, since the local level is not adequately taken into account. Hoffmann (1965) also provides some long times series, yet, only for the allocation of administrative public spending across levels of government since 1850. We use the estimates of Andic and Veverka (1963) for the period until 1913 which rely on expenditures made directly by the different levels of government (*Unmittelbare Ausgaben*) and reported by financial statistics (*Finanzstatistik*), which exclude transfers to other levels of government. Only five observations are available for this early period. After 1925, data reported by Kraus (1983) and the Statistisches Bundesamt are employed, which, however, draw on self-financed expenditure (*Nettoausgaben*), that is total expenditure excluding transfers received from other levels of government. These concepts correspond to the indicators *ED1* and, respectively, *ED2*, derived in section 2.2.2. See Appendix C for more details on data sources and definitions.

infrastructure.[33] This development seems to have taken place at the expense of the state level, as there is a strong decline of the state level's share of total public expenditures from 44.4% in 1881 to 35.5% in 1913. Consequently, in quantitative terms, with a share of 36.7% in 1913 local government emerged as the most important fiscal tier in the run-up to World War I, replacing the state level which, however, continued to play an important role.

Fig. 5.2: Allocation of total public expenditures (excluding social security) by fiscal tiers, Germany, 1881-2001

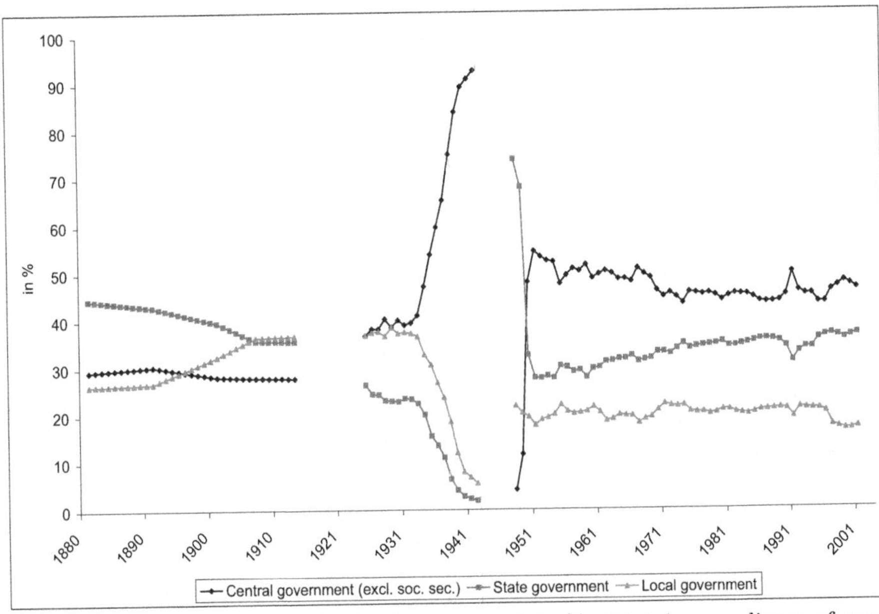


Note: Public expenditure by level of government in % of total expenditure of consolidated government, excluding social security and payments to the EU. Due to different expenditure definitions, the time series 1881-1913 and 1925-2001 are not strictly comparable. See Table B.33 in Appendix B for detailed figures.

As regards the period after World War I, the evidence supports the "displacement effect" of wars with respect to the vertical government structure. During the Weimar Republic from 1925 to 1932, the quantitative picture reflects the constitutional re-assignment of powers noted above, showing that particularly the central level increased in importance, whereas the state level's role continued to decline. Accordingly, the central level started with a much higher share of total public expenditures of 36.8% in 1925, particularly due

[33] For example, Legler et al. (1988) find a similar increase of local spending towards the end of the 19th century in the U.S., arguing that this gain in local spending reflects the process of urbanisation.

to spending on social assistance and war damage compensation, and further expanded, while the state government's share declined at 26.4% in 1925 and even 23.4% in 1932, being clearly surpassed by the local government which mostly rested at its pre-war level of approximately 37%.[34] This development is in line with Popitz' observation that state government competencies are increasingly taken over by the central government.

During the Nazi era, the central government's share of total public expenditures made up as much as 75% in 1938 before the outbreak of World War II. With gradual transformation into a war economy, the local and, above all, the state level become insignificant, with a share of 18.6% and 6.4%, respectively.

The figures also reflect the significant system change which occurred after World War II. The most important consequence of the war was the re-emergence of the state level, which in effect exchanged its position with the local level. The Federal Republic of Germany starts in 1950 with a substantially higher share of central government expenditures as compared to the pre-Nazi period. However, particularly due to decreasing defence and war compensation spending, the central level's share of total public expenditures significantly declined from 54.5% in 1951 to 46.3% in 2001.[35] The state level's share increased during the same period of time from 27.8% to 36.7%, which comes closer to its level at the end of the *Kaiserreich*. On the other hand, starting at its pre-World War II level, the local level's share increased only slightly from 17.8% in 1950 to 20.9% in 1990, only to decline again after the German reunification to 17.1% in 2001. Therefore, despite the higher initial level of centralisation, the decrease in the share of central government expenditure thereafter and the simultaneous gain in importance of the state level clearly contradict Popitz' predictions for the period after World War II.

This long-term development on the expenditure side is mostly confirmed when taking a look at the revenue side. Note that due to the lack of sufficiently disaggregated historical data, the figures are not adjusted for tax-raising powers. As depicted by Figure 5.3, the share of tax revenue accrued to the central level increased considerably, particularly during the inter-war period, from 40.3% in 1913 to 49% in 1932 and to 67.3% in 1937. However, it decreased again after the war from a peak of 62.3% in 1955 to its former level at the end of the Weimar Republic until 2001. At the same time, the state level's share of tax revenue decreased continuously from 35.1% in 1881 to only 10.7% in 1937, whereas after the war the development went in the opposite direction, from 26.3% in 1955 to 38.7% in 2001, which is even higher as compared to the level during the *Kaiserreich*. Note, however, that the state level's tax revenue share does not take account of the extremely low degree of tax-raising auton-

[34] Note that due to different expenditure definitions, the time series before and after World War I are not strictly comparable. Generally, the degree of decentralisation is slightly lower in case of self-financed expenditure reported after 1925.

[35] The great leap in Figure 5.2 after 1948 results from the fact that a central government was not installed until creation of the Federal Republic in 1949.

omy of the states after World War II. Unadjusted tax revenue figures therefore overestimate the role of the state level more seriously than expenditure figures.

This development, again, took place at the expense of the local government. The share of total tax revenues accrued to local governments first increased from 25.9% in 1881 to 37.2% in 1913, surpassing the state government's share since the 1890s. This development is particularly due to the expansion of tax revenues of Prussian local communities, which accounted for the largest part of local government expenditure and revenue in Germany and enjoyed considerable tax autonomy. Apart from the local business and property taxes, particularly their right to levy a local surcharge on the state income tax significantly contributed to this development.[36] After the war, however, the local governments' share of tax revenues continuously decreased from a share of 30.3% in 1925 to 11.9% in 1950, and remained relatively constant until the present day.

Fig. 5.3: Allocation of total tax revenue (excluding social security) by fiscal tiers, Germany, 1881-2001

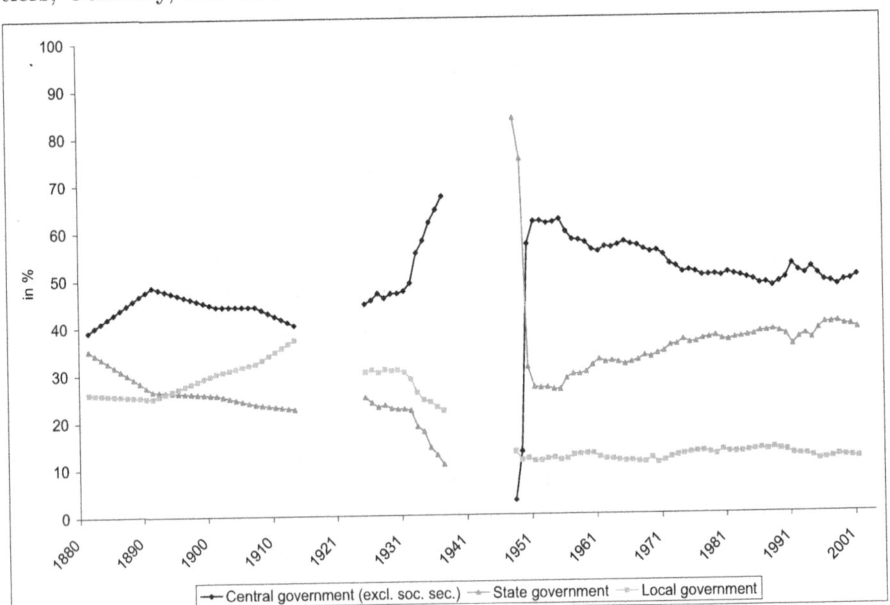


Note: Tax revenue by level of government in % of consolidated tax revenue, excluding social security and payments from the EU. See Table B.34 in Appendix B for detailed figures.

36 See also Neumark (1976) and Blankart (2001) with respect to this.

This picture changes, however, when taking social security as a part of the central level into account.[37] Beginning with the introduction of the social insurance in 1885, the share of central government in total public expenditure including social security nearly doubled, increasing from 34% in 1891 to 67.2% in 2001. Whereas in the pre-1914 and post-1950 periods there is only a moderate increase, the figures for the inter-war period reflect the drastic expansion of the welfare state, particularly induced by the economic crises.

Indeed, a quantitative verification indicates significant centralisation trends in public expenditure for all periods only in case of including social security (see Table 5.1). When excluding social security (columns 4 and 6), a centralisation trend is statistically confirmed only for the inter-war period, whereas during the period before World War I and from 1950 to 1990, the central government's share of public expenditure and tax revenue tended to decrease. The decentralisation trend since 1950 is also confirmed when focusing on government functions which might be provided at sub-central levels according to the theory of fiscal federalism, thus also excluding defence spending (column 5).[38]

## Allocation of Government Functions by Fiscal Tiers

In general, changes in the degree of fiscal decentralisation over time are either due to shifts in the assignment of functions and revenues between fiscal tiers, including also the introduction of new tasks, or to divergent rates of growth of expenditure and revenue across levels of government related to different demand patterns. Therefore, next, we take a closer look at changing patterns in the allocation of government functions by level of government in order to assess Popitz' predictions concerning the appropriation of state functions by the central government.

A general problem consists in changing classifications of expenditure according to government functions in the course of time. Based on financial statistics and the classifications used by Andic and Veverka (1963) and the Statistisches Bundesamt, Figures B.2 to B.4 in Appendix B illustrate significant changes in the functional composition of the expenditure of the different levels of government from 1913 until today. In general, the common trend in the central government budget indicates a decrease in the proportion of expenditure related to administration, defence, and law & order, and a concomitant rise of activities related to social assistance, economic services, and education. These changes are also reflected by the degree of centralisation of selected government functions, as presented in Figure 5.4.

In terms of the vertical assignment of government functions, the figures indicate a clear centralisation trend particularly with respect to economic

[37] See Figure B.1 in Appendix B.

[38] A test of the "displacement effect" might furthermore imply the exclusion of other expenditure resulting from wars, which are, however, difficult to identify. See, e.g., Kraus (1983).

Table 5.1: Trends in public sector growth and decentralisation, Germany

| Period | Publ. exp. (1) | Publ. exp. (2) | Decen. exp. (3) | Decen. exp. (4) | Decen. exp. (5) | Decen. taxes (6) |
|---|---|---|---|---|---|---|
| *1850-2003* | .005*** | .003*** | -.004*** | -.002*** | -.005*** | -.001*** |
| | (.000) | (.000) | (.000) | (.000) | (.000) | (.000) |
| No. obs. | 132 | 132 | 84 | 99 | 99 | 98 |
| $R^2$ | .911 | .908 | .775 | .447 | .705 | .176 |
| Adj. $R^2$ | .910 | .908 | .772 | .442 | .702 | .168 |
| *1850-2003* [a] | .002*** | .002*** | -.001*** | .001* | .000 | .002*** |
| | (.000) | (.000) | (.000) | (.001) | (.000) | (.000) |
| *Dum25-38* | .078*** | .103*** | -.195*** | -.182*** | -.301*** | -.125*** |
| | (.015) | (.008) | (.017) | (.022) | (.013) | (.016) |
| *Dum50-90* | .196*** | .109*** | -.219*** | -.235*** | -.343*** | -.199*** |
| | (.018) | (.010) | (.027) | (.032) | (.019) | (.023) |
| *Dum91-03* | .257*** | .113*** | -.220*** | -.248*** | -.374*** | -.206*** |
| | (.025) | (.014) | (.038) | (.048) | (.028) | (.034) |
| No. obs. | 132 | 132 | 84 | 99 | 99 | 98 |
| $R^2$ | .957 | .962 | .923 | .714 | .961 | .612 |
| Adj. $R^2$ | .955 | .961 | .919 | .702 | .959 | .595 |
| *1850-1913* | .001*** | .001*** | -.002*** | .001*** | -.001*** | .000 |
| | (.000) | (.000) | (.000) | (.000) | (.000) | (.000) |
| No. obs. | 64 | 64 | 33 | 33 | 33 | 33 |
| $R^2$ | .848 | .844 | .785 | .765 | .805 | .010 |
| *1925-1938* | .009*** | .009*** | -.023*** | -.027*** | -.014*** | -.019*** |
| | (.001) | (.001) | (.003) | (.005) | (.004) | (.002) |
| No. obs. | 14 | 14 | 14 | 14 | 14 | 13 |
| $R^2$ | .860 | .864 | .823 | .685 | .555 | .848 |
| *1950-1990* | .007*** | .003*** | -.000** | .002*** | .001*** | .003*** |
| | (.000) | (.000) | (.000) | (.000) | (.000) | (.000) |
| No. obs. | 41 | 41 | 26 | 41 | 41 | 41 |
| $R^2$ | .857 | .767 | .169 | .757 | .420 | .906 |
| *1991-2003* | .001 | -.000 | -.003* | -.000 | -.001 | .003*** |
| | (.001) | (.000) | (.001) | (.002) | (.002) | (.001) |
| No. obs. | 13 | 13 | 11 | 11 | 11 | 11 |
| $R^2$ | .197 | .038 | .314 | .001 | .037 | .547 |

Note: Coefficients and standard errors (in parentheses) of OLS regressions on a linear trend. ***, **, and * indicate significance at the 1%, 5% and 10% level, respectively. Total public expenditure according to national income statistics, either including (1) or excluding social security (2), as per cent of net national product at market prices. Degree of expen. decentralis. (indic. ED1, ED2 in section 2.2.2): sub-central government expenditure according to financial statistics, including social security (3), excluding social security (4), or excluding social security and defence (5). Degree of tax decentralis. (indic. TD3 in section 2.3.2): sub-central government tax revenue according to financial statistics (6). [a] including dummy variables for the periods 1925-38, 1950-90, 1991-2003. See Appendix C for data sources and definitions.

Fig. 5.4: Degree of centralisation by government function, Germany, 1913-2001

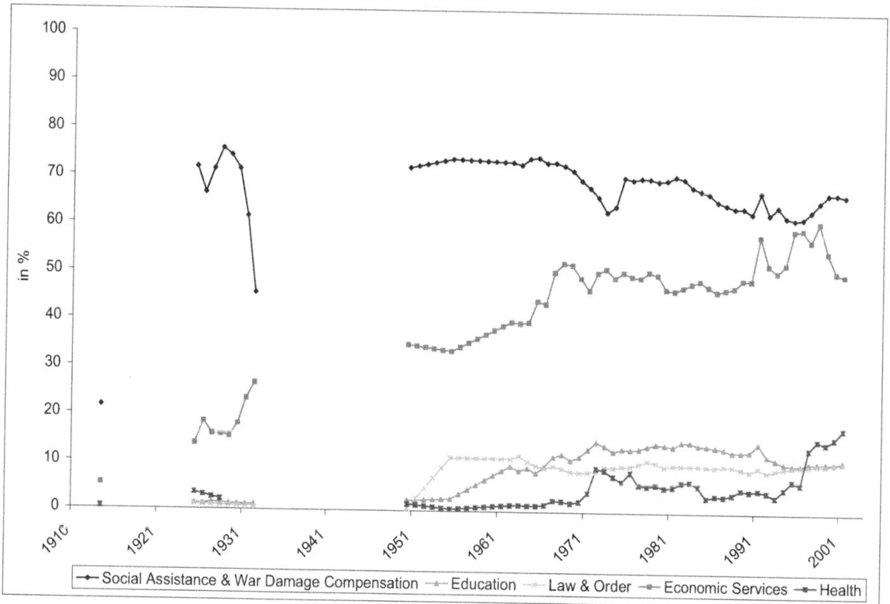


Note: Central government expenditure in % of total public expenditure by government function, as reported in national financial statistics. See Table B.32 in Appendix B for detailed figures, and Appendix C for a breakdown by government functions.

services which include transport, communication and economic development, among others, and to a lesser extent, with respect to law & order, education and health after 1950. Accordingly, the central government's share of total transport and communication expenditures rose from 6.2% in 1913 to a peak of 50.8% in 1976, subsequently decreasing to 42.6% in 2001.[39] A similar development pattern can be observed for other expenditure on economic services, too. Alternatively, with a share of 64.0%, the local level was by far the most important fiscal tier regarding transport spending in 1913. According to Tilly (1997), local authorities played a significant role during the process of industrialisation, especially from 1897 to 1912, by providing public infrastructure. This role was then quickly taken over by the state and, in particular, the central level. After rising to its absolute peak of 69.7% in 1929, the local level's share thus dropped to 21.3% in 1975, until reaching 31.1% in 2001. Nonetheless, the distribution of expenditure shares between the central and the sub-central levels indicate significant joint activities in this area after 1950. This development seems to correspond to an increasing tendency to provide

[39] Table B.32 in Appendix B provides some period-averaged figures on the allocation of public expenditure by government functions.

uniform public services as suggested by Popitz (1927) and Peacock and Wiseman (1961).

In accordance with the constitutional assignment, apart from law & order, the state level clearly emerged as the most important fiscal tier in charge of education and science. Particularly during the Weimar Republic, school expenditures were increasingly allocated from the local to the state level. The share of total school expenditure made at the local level thus decreased to 28.7% in 2001, representing less than half of its share in 1913. However, after World War II, the central government became increasingly involved in activities related to law & order and universities and science, areas of original state competency. Accordingly, the central government's share in total science & research expenditure increased from 40.7% in 1950 to 80.2% in 1982, and decreased at 69.8% thereafter.[40]

Moreover, whereas expenditures on health and communal services persisted mainly in local responsibility, further tasks, like social assistance during the Weimar Republic, and housing and cultural affairs after World War II, have been transferred from the local to the central, and respectively, to the state level. As shown by previous studies, too, the disaggregated long-term trend indicates an upward shift of government functions to state and central government at the expense of the local level.[41]

Altogether, the budgetary figures clearly support the institutional analysis in the previous section, partly indicating a secular centralisation trend in Germany from 1871 to the present day. However, rather than showing a monotonous pattern, the development is characterised by stepwise increases corresponding to exogenous shocks and changes in the political system. When excluding the upward shifts caused by the wars, only the inter-war period is characterised by increasing fiscal centralisation. Though remaining the most important fiscal tier, the central government's share in total public expenditure and tax revenue decreased significantly after 1950, while at the same time the state government's share increased, at least in budgetary terms. Interestingly, the German reunification in 1990 which exerted an important economic and political effect, produced no significant change in the vertical government structure.

Therefore, Popitz' "law" of increasing centralisation is only confirmed from 1871 until World War II. After 1950 a significant structural break occurred, the state level regaining importance at the expense of the local level. Only from the point of view of the local level, the development after World War II indicates a shift of competencies to upper levels of government, albeit local governments still have a higher degree of tax autonomy than state govern-

40 For earlier periods, Pfetsch (1974) reports a rise of the central level's percentage of expenditure on science and technology in relation to the state level by 2.6 times from 9.7% in 1871 to 24.9% in 1914.

41 For example, Hansmeyer and Zimmermann (1984) report a significant shift of expenditure competencies from state to central government only for the areas of health and general public finances.

ments. This development, however, runs counter to Popitz' additional prediction that centralisation occurs at the expense of the states. These results are consistent with previous studies for Germany. On the other hand, Popitz' second hypothesis concerning increasing overlap of state and central government functions seems to be confirmed for the period after 1950. However, instead of the predicted rise in policy centralisation, as during the Weimar Republic, the increasing overlap resulted in a new type of "hidden" centralisation consisting of joint central/state decision-making and financing.[42] The descriptive analysis for Germany therefore provides no clear support for a general continuous and unavoidable process of government centralisation.

## 5.4 Determinants of Fiscal Decentralisation in Germany

In the following, a time series analysis is carried out to explore the factors determining the development of the degree of fiscal decentralisation in Germany after 1950. The particular focus lies on the role of economic and social development and on the dynamic impact of economic and European integration.

### 5.4.1 Quantitative Approach

In order to determine whether integration or other socioeconomic factors exert a causal influence on decentralisation over time, the most common method suggests regressing the degree of fiscal decentralisation on lagged values of itself and of other determinants. The quantitative analysis covers only the period 1950-2001, since no continuous time series for the degree of fiscal decentralisation is available before World War I and the inter-war period is not only short, but also plagued with strong fluctuations. Since no significant institutional changes occurred since 1950, the focus of the analysis lies on the effect of time-variant factors, all other things being equal.

Formally, the basic estimation relates the degree of fiscal decentralisation to economic development and integration, and controls for other possible determinants investigated in chapters 3 and 4:

$$Decentr_t = \beta_0 + \beta_1 \cdot Decentr_{t-1} + \beta_2 \cdot Econ_{t-1} + \beta_3 \cdot Integ_{t-1}$$
$$+ \beta_4 \cdot Diverse_{t-1} + \beta_5 \cdot Trend + u_t.$$

$Decentr_t$ denotes the degree of fiscal decentralisation in period $t$, $Econ_{t-1}$, $Integ_{t-1}$ and $Diverse_{t-1}$ the past values of variables capturing economic development, economic and European integration, and other determinants of decentralisation, respectively.[43] Fiscal decentralisation is again measured as the share of sub-central government expenditure or revenue in total public

[42] See, also, Blankart (1999), and Hansmeyer (1967) with respect to this.
[43] See Appendix C for data sources and definitions of the variables.

expenditure or revenue. In order to solve the problems of spurious regressions mentioned in the literature and to account for the effect of history, the lagged value of decentralisation, $Decentr_{t-1}$, is included on the right-hand side of the equation, too. The dynamic behaviour of series is further accounted for by the direct inclusion of a linear function of time (*Trend*) in the regression model.[44]

In order to test the hypothesis of a centralising effect of economic development set up by Peacock and Wiseman (1961), the natural log of real *per capita income* is included in the regression. In addition to this, we control for the effect of *population* size and *density*, or alternatively, the degree of *urbanisation*, and for other possible determinants like the *dependency ratio* or the *rate* of *unemployment*. In order to account for changes in the degree of fiscal decentralisation related to the business cycle, the contemporaneous value of the *rate* of *growth* of real per capita income is included, too. As in chapter 4, economic integration is captured again by the degree of *trade openness*, whereas European integration is represented in terms of the share of *EU expenditure* in total public expenditure of EU member countries and, respectively, the share of *EU trade* in total German foreign trade.

Since our interest is in the investigation of the determinants of fiscal decentralisation, we consider only the single aspect of Granger causality in one direction and refrain from running vector autoregressive regressions.[45] As already noted by Pryor (1968), the results of time series and of cross-section analyses of the determinants of fiscal decentralisation vary considerably. First, due to specific institutional factors, the degree of variation in decentralisation across countries at one or even different points in time is generally higher than for single nations over time. Second, the determinants of the composition of public expenditures, such as technology, population or income structures are expected to be different for both dimensions. Whereas, for example, cross-country variation in population size is rather expected to reflect potential economies of scale in the provision of public goods, variation over time might represent changing demand patterns. Also, time series analyses for single countries have the advantage that statistical and fiscal definitions

[44] Granger and Newbold (1974) point to the problem of trending behaviour and high autocorrelation in the residuals in the analysis of macroeconomic data. In case of co-integrated series, that is series that drift together at roughly the same rate, standard significance tests are misleading, regressions typically yielding apparently significant results, even if the series are completely independent. Admittedly, the inclusion of a trend alone might not solve entirely the problem of non-stationarity if the series are co-integrated. However, differencing the series would provide no reasonable alternative either, since it would obscure information on the long-run relationship between dependent and independent variables. Also, the economic relationship is expected to be different between levels and between increments. See also Greene (2000: 778f, 789f) with respect to this.

[45] See Granger (1969). In this regard, the equation is a reduced form which neglects the contemporaneous relationship between the variables.

are mostly consistent. Apart from this, one has to take into account that issues of multicollinearity and serial correlation are more severe in time series than in panel analysis. Though partly accounting for the time dimension, the results of the panel analysis for OECD countries might therefore differ from the estimates for Germany.

### 5.4.2 Results

Table 5.2 shows the results from OLS regressions of the degree of expenditure decentralisation (excluding social security) using different specifications.[46] Checking for influential observations, the year 1991 has been excluded from the sample due to the distortionary statistical effect of reunification. In addition to this, dummy variables are included to control for distinct developments in the *post-war* period (1950-55) due to reconstruction and for the territorial and structural changes caused by *re-unification* in 1990. Due to severe problems of multicollinearity encountered in time series analysis, additional variables are included only insofar as they contribute to the goodness of fit of the regression. The estimation takes account of just one lag, since the inclusion of higher order lags was rejected on grounds of the Akaike criterion (AIC). Note that the Breusch-Godfrey (BG) tests allowing for 1 or 2 lags mostly do not indicate the presence of residual autocorrelation. The inclusion of quadratic or cubic trends did not alter the results of the estimations and did not improve the goodness of fit of the regression.

The estimates are clearly consistent with the previous descriptive overview, running counter the prediction of Peacock and Wiseman (1961) concerning increasing centralisation in the course of economic development. At least for the period after 1950, per capita income is shown to have a positive impact on the degree of expenditure decentralisation in Germany, even controlling for a trend and the possible effects of post-war reconstruction and later reunification. In terms of elasticity, an increase in real per capita income by 1% raises the degree of decentralisation by 0.4%.[47] This result is robust to the exclusion of the trend variable or of other variables, such as population density. Moreover, F-tests for joint significance of 1 and 2 lags strongly support this causal relationship at the 0.3% level.

On the other hand, again in line with the results of the cross-sectional time-series analysis for OECD countries carried out above, increasing population density or urbanisation are associated with higher centralisation. This result may be explained by the fact that, whereas rapidly increasing urbanisation and technological progress actually boosted municipal governments' investments in local infrastructure at the end of the 19th century, once the

[46] Social security is excluded, since no consistent data are available for the period before 1974.

[47] The standard error is 0.114. The elasticity has been calculated by running a log-linear regression, the results are available upon request.

Table 5.2: OLS estimates of fiscal decentralisation, self-financed expenditure (excl. social security), Germany, 1950-2001

| | Dep. var.: Degree of expen. decentralis. (indic. ED2) | | | | | |
|---|---|---|---|---|---|---|
| | (1) | (2) | (3) | (4) | (5) | (6) |
| *Decentr*$_{t-1}$ | .440*** | .484*** | .488*** | .378*** | .453*** | .422*** |
| | (.101) | (.152) | (.104) | (.103) | (.118) | (.098) |
| *Per capita income*$_{t-1}$ | .267*** | .268*** | .279*** | .260*** | .268*** | .312*** |
| | (.047) | (.084) | (.047) | (.046) | (.048) | (.051) |
| *Population*$_{t-1}$ | | -.069 | | | | |
| | | (.113) | | | | |
| *Density*$_{t-1}$ | -.371*** | | -.321** | -.392*** | -.356** | -.774*** |
| | (.119) | | (.120) | (.116) | (.138) | (.233) |
| *Urbanisation*$_{t-1}$ | | -1.904*** | | | | |
| | | (.637) | | | | |
| *Growth rate*$_t$ | .279*** | .224** | .295*** | .257*** | .281*** | .274*** |
| | (.073) | (.096) | (.072) | (.072) | (.075) | (.071) |
| *Dependency ratio*$_{t-1}$ | | | | | | .594* |
| | | | | | | (.298) |
| *Trade openness*$_{t-1}$ | | | .074 | | | |
| | | | (.045) | | | |
| *EU exp.*$_{t-1}$ | | | | .013* | | |
| | | | | (.007) | | |
| *EU trade*$_{t-1}$ | | | | | -.021 | |
| | | | | | (.095) | |
| *Re-unification* | -.003 | .046 | .017 | -.004 | -.000 | -.044* |
| | (.011) | (.037) | (.016) | (.011) | (.017) | (.023) |
| *Postwar* | .041*** | | .046*** | .033*** | .042*** | .037*** |
| | (.010) | | (.010) | (.010) | (.012) | (.010) |
| *Trend* | -.005*** | | -.006*** | -.006*** | -.005*** | -.005*** |
| | (.001) | | (.001) | (.001) | (.001) | (.001) |
| No. obs. | 49 | 39 | 49 | 49 | 49 | 49 |
| $R^2$ | .899 | .838 | .906 | .908 | .900 | .909 |
| adj. $R^2$ | .882 | .808 | .887 | .889 | .880 | .890 |
| BG(1) | 2.199 | 2.184 | 1.410 | 1.433 | 2.295 | 1.420 |
| BG(2) | 2.283 | 2.227 | 1.417 | 1.439 | 2.427 | 1.425 |

Note: Standard errors are in parentheses. ***, **, and * indicate significance at the 1%, 5% and 10% level, respectively.

large-scale construction of the basic infrastructure had been accomplished, the advance of urbanisation after 1950 generated other pressures instead, particularly demands for social assistance.[48] The effects of both population density and urbanisation are, however, quite sensitive to the inclusion of per capita income, being plagued by problems of multicollinearity.

Apart from the lagged degree of decentralisation, which points to a significant role of history, the estimates also indicate a significant and robust influence of business cycles. Accordingly, higher economic growth rates seem to increase sub-central government expenditures to a larger extent than central government expenditures. An increase in the share of population aged below 15 or above 64, the dependency rate, is also found to have a weak positive effect on the degree of decentralisation. Note, also, that both the trend variable and the dummy variable for the post-war period yield significant signs, whereas no distinct pattern can be made out for the period after reunification. Other variables employed in the previous panel analyses, such as the rate of unemployment, the share of persons employed in agriculture, national elections or the share of leftist parties in government had no significant coefficients (not shown).

With respect to the effect of integration, only political integration in the EU as depicted by the level of EU expenditure exerts a weakly significant decentralising effect.[49] F-tests, however, cannot reject the hypothesis of no effect of both economic and European integration. When excluding the trend variable or per capita income, the time pathes of which are highly correlated with those of the integration variables, the results of the regression remain unchanged. The time series analysis for Germany therefore tends to support the results of the panel analysis for OECD countries in chapter 4, according to which economic and European integration foster fiscal decentralisation particularly in case of strong preference heterogeneity and missing direct implication of subnational governments in central policy-making, both conditions which are not met in the German case. Despite this evidence, a mutual causal relationship between economic development and integration on the one hand, and changes in the vertical assignment of public expenditures on the other hand cannot be completely ruled out in the present analysis.

To test for the robustness of the results, alternative regressions have been run for the degree of decentralisation of public expenditure excluding defence (not shown), for different government functions (Tables B.35 and B.36 in Appendix B) or for total tax revenues (Table B.37 in Appendix B). The results are quite similar, particularly concerning the effect of economic development. Since the descriptive figures presented above indicated a significant

[48] Note that time series for the degree of urbanisation are only available since 1960. Also, due to very high collinearity, urbanisation is included in the regression without the trend variable.

[49] The Quinn/Inclan index of financial openness employed alternatively had no significant effect either.

centralisation trend in the area of economic services, we focused on government functions which are supposed to play an important role in locational competition in the course of integration in the world economy. The regression analysis, however, detects instead a highly significant decentralising effect of economic integration for public expenditures related to economic development and state-owned enterprises (other economic services).

In interpreting these results, one has to take again into account the limitations related to the measurement of fiscal decentralisation by means of unadjusted budgetary data. Apart from non-quantifiable legislative or regulatory activities, the extent of subnational discretion in decisions regarding public expenditures and taxation are not taken into account in the present time series analysis. However, since no significant changes in matters of legislative taxing powers occurred during the period of investigation, the distortionary effect of incorrect measurement is expected to be rather limited in size.

## 5.5 Discussion and Conclusions

The purpose of the present chapter was to investigate the long-term trend and the underlying determinants of public sector centralisation in Germany from the creation of a unified state in 1871 to the present day. Both the institutional and the quantitative review of the German history in fact document a significant expansion of the public sector in line with Wagner's "law", together with a stepwise increase in the role of the central government.

However, similarly to earlier studies for other countries, there is no clear support for a continuous and unavoidable process of centralisation in the public sector as suggested by Popitz (1927), but rather for some distinct developments caused by the distortionary effects of wars and regime changes. The rise of the central government since 1871 seems to have come to an end in the aftermath of World War II, being replaced by a new type of "hidden" centralisation (Blankart, 1999), which is characterised by complex interconnections between the central and the state levels. A significant difference consists in the fact that whereas prior to 1950 competencies were transferred particularly from the state to the central level, after 1950 the upward shift occurred from local to state and central government. It rests unclear which tendency would have dominated in the public sector without the event of significant exogenous shocks like the two world wars or drastic changes in the political system. Therefore, Popitz' claims have to be assessed against the historical and political background specific to the inter-war period.

The historical analysis, however, sheds some light on the role of institutional rules of decision-making, supporting the collusion hypothesis of Brennan and Buchanan (1980). Accordingly, only the specific institutional set-up after World War II, which provided for equal participation of the state level in decision-making concerning the distribution of revenues, as well as for the allocation of concurrent powers to the central government, enabled the creation of revenue cartels between the state and the central levels aimed at mitigating fiscal competition.

The results of the time series regression analysis of the determinants of fiscal decentralisation during the period 1950 to 2001 contrast with common predictions in the literature, indicating a significant decentralising effect of per capita income growth during this time. On the other hand, however, except for public expenditure on certain economic services, there is no clear evidence for a causal relationship between economic and European integration and fiscal decentralisation in the case of Germany.

In the end, these findings suggest that public sector growth and centralisation are not inevitable features of government following certain laws of nature. Therefore, this analysis allows no clear forecast with respect to the future allocation of functions and revenues across levels of government. In addition, as shown by the case of Germany, the long-term development of vertical government structures crucially depends on the country-specific institutions and preferences.

# 6

# Summary and Conclusions

Motivated by increasing interest in public finance and government practice on the comparison of vertical government structures, and by recent decentralising tendencies in the public sector, the aim of this work was to investigate empirically the determinants of vertical government structures across countries and over time. The particular focus was on the relationship between those two broad trends in today's world, increasing economic integration at the world and regional scale on the one hand, and concomitant supranationalisation and decentralisation of government structures, on the other hand.

Chapter 2 dealt with the problems encountered in defining and measuring the degree of fiscal decentralisation. We investigated how decentralized the public sector is in OECD countries and whether there is a real decentralisation trend observable among them. Drawing on a recent analytical framework of the OECD, different measures of fiscal autonomy and revenue decentralisation were presented which consider tax-raising powers of sub-central governments. Taking account of changes in the assignment of decision-making competencies during the course of time, new time series of annual data on the degree of fiscal decentralisation were provided for 23 OECD countries in the time period between 1965 and 2001. It is shown that common measures usually employed tend to considerably overestimate the extent of fiscal decentralisation. Evidence is also provided for increasing fiscal decentralisation in a majority of OECD countries during the last three decades.

Subsequently, based upon the decentralisation measures developed in chapter 2, chapter 3 addressed empirically the question about the general determinants of differences in vertical government structures of OECD countries, focusing on the role of preferences and decision-making institutions. Based upon a detailed investigation of decision making rules, an empirical analysis was conducted for a panel of OECD countries. The results indicate that apart from preference heterogeneity, economies of scale, and other demand side factors, institutions are significant in explaining cross-national differences in the degree of fiscal decentralisation. When using a new indicator of decentralisation which accounts for tax-raising powers of sub-central government (*TD1*), the evidence strongly supports the collusion hypothesis according to which delegation of decision-making concerning the assignment of powers and national legislation to subnational representatives leads to increased tax centralisation, whereas direct participation of the citizens of the subnational entities has the opposite effect. On the other hand, direct democracy at the national level is mostly found to be associated with increased centralisation.

Drawing on recent work on the creation and breakup of countries, chapter 4 investigated the impact of economic and political integration on the vertical government structure. The question was whether there exists a causal relationship between increasing economic and political integration on the one hand, and increasing fiscal decentralisation on the other hand, particularly among EU member countries? We argued that by increasing the market size and the benefits from the decentralised provision of public goods, integration might have triggered the recent process of fiscal decentralisation in OECD countries. A theoretical framework was therefore set up, which related the degree of fiscal decentralisation to economic integration, preference heterogeneity, and economies of scale. The results of the empirical panel analysis mostly support a decentralising effect of global economic and European integration. This is particularly true in countries with strong preference heterogeneity, whereas participation of subnational governments in central decision-making is associated with increasing centralisation.

Finally, chapter 5 focused on the German experience from the second half of the 19th century until the present in order to address the question whether there is an unavoidable long-term centralisation trend in the public sector, as suggested by Popitz (1927). Apart from this, we investigated empirically whether those factors identified above in the quantitative studies for OECD countries were also underlying the development in the public sector in Germany over a longer period of time. The historical analysis of decision-making institutions and of the allocation of public expenditure and revenue by fiscal tiers provides no conclusive evidence for a natural continuous process of government centralisation as suggested by Popitz' "law", but rather for some distinct developments caused by the distortionary effects of wars and regime changes. Whereas the role of central government increased continuously at the expense of the state governments until World War II, after 1950 the state level regained importance and a new type of "hidden" centralisation characterised by joint central/state decision-making and financing finally emerged. The effects of economic development and of economic and European integration on fiscal decentralisation in Germany were also tested empirically for the period 1950 to 2001, controlling for other time-variant determinants of the vertical government structure. The results of the time series analysis indicate a significant positive decentralizing effect of per capita income growth during this time. On the other hand, there is no clear evidence for a causal relationship between economic and European integration and fiscal decentralisation in the case of Germany.

In summary, the most important contributions of this work can be briefly outlined as follows. First, a new attempt was made to improve the measurement of fiscal decentralisation, helping to compare countries and to detect common trends over time, and providing a new data set for future empirical work. The different results yielded in the empirical analyses show how important it is to use an indicator of decentralisation which accounts for subnational decision-making autonomy instead of received expenditure and revenue shares. Second, the work contributes to the positive theory of fiscal federalism by providing empirical evidence from panel analyses on the determinants of the degree of fiscal decentralisation, particularly highlighting the role of costs, preferences and institutions. Third, the implications of the recent literature on secessions for the vertical government structure were investigated on theoretical and empirical grounds, providing some evidence for a causal relationship between the two current trends, integration and decentralisation, particularly with respect to EU countries. And, finally, the historical experience of Germany was used to explore the "laws" and determinants governing the long-term development of the public sector.

Before drawing some conclusions from the present work, it has to be admitted that the results derived from these studies are concerned with developed industrial countries mostly with long-standing democratic traditions. In the case of the developing countries or the East European transition countries, other factors are assumed to have determined the process of government decentralisation. Particularly transition from totalitarianism to democracy – as illustrated by Spain, Portugal, and Greece –, the advance of economic and social development, and external political pressures might have played an important role in these cases. On the other hand, the pre-accession strategy of the European Union certainly triggered the regionalisation process in the post-communist East European countries, too. These are some interesting issues to be addressed in future studies. Another subject which need to be dealt with are the efficiency and growth enhancing prospects of decentralisation.

The investigation also suggests that integrating the New Economic Geography with fiscal federalism theory, and with the literature on secessions would provide an interesting starting-point for more comprehensive future theoretical and empirical research. Future research should also deal with the problem of aggregation of different government functions in analysing the degree of public sector decentralisation. Since government functions represent different public goods, a disaggregated approach would automatically take account of different spillover and economies of scale effects and provide a better understanding of the factors determining vertical government structures. Finally, the analysis could be extended to the correct measurement of expenditure decentralisation, too.

Which final conclusions can be drawn from the present work? From a normative point of view, the assessment of the empirically verified pressures exerted by economic integration and globalisation to decentralise government activity depends first and foremost on the perception of the state. Even without considering the extreme case of Leviathan governments, if one accepts the view, that political and fiscal decentralisation is beneficial since it fosters competition among governments, thereby enhancing accountability of policy makers, correspondence between local preferences and costs/benefits of local public goods, and policy innovation and efficiency in the public sector, then, integration has to be welcomed. The famous alternative to political decision-making, "voting with the feet" (Tiebout, 1956) is expected to work best with advancing mobility and technical progress, thus further enhancing efficiency in the public sector. However, this does not imply that policy coordination or centralisation were useless. These instruments are useful particularly in the case of technical or fiscal externalities, which are also expected to grow with integration, or in the case of public goods the preferences for which are rather homogeneously distributed.

With respect to the European Union, which increasingly turns into a conglomerate of culturally, ethnically and linguistically distinct communities, this suggests to allocate only those functions to the supranational authority for which there exists a high degree of preference identity. Particularly in the face of globalisation, the status and competitiveness of local and regional governments should be enhanced by providing them with adequate fiscal autonomy. Despite circumstantial evidence for a diminishing role of national governments in the global economy and in the European Union, nation-states formed during long historical processes are not expected to disappear in the near future with advancing economic and political integration. By clarifying the division of government functions between the European and the national levels, the European Constitution takes a significant step towards modernisation of the EU. In the end, however, the future development depends on the desired finality of the process of European integration.

Given the evidence provided in this work, which are the long-term prospects for the development of vertical government structures? First of all, vertical government structures are shown to exhibit significant inertia over time, important structural changes being mostly caused by strong exogenous shocks, such as wars or political system changes like the transition to democracy. In international comparison there are indeed a number of indicators for a substantial "retreat of the state" in a global economy (Strange, 1996). However, whether the observed shift of government functions to the private sector, for example in terms of privatisations of state enterprises or the emergence of public-private partnerships, and the rise of the "regulatory state" (Majone, 1997) actually lead to increased centralisation or decentralisation of the public sector, rests an open question. Areas of public sector activity continuously change over time, both quantitatively and qualitatively. Nonetheless, the present work and recent developments indicate a decline in traditional areas of central government activity, such as welfare state, defence, and security, together with a loss of importance of national factors of location with advancing globalisation and the transfer of powers to supranational authorities. The concomitant rise in local and regional economies as well as cultural identities and increasing demands for citizen participation in local decision-making, leads one to suppose that the decentralisation of the public sector has not yet come to an end.

# A

# Theoretical Model

## Different Regional Population Sizes

A possible extension of the theoretical model presented in section 4.2 consists in the consideration of different regional population sizes $N_i$. In this case, the amount of the local public good supplied to each region $g_i^L$, and consequently, the total amount of public goods $g_i = g^C + g_i^L$ as well as the degree of decentralisation of the public sector $\theta_i$ in each region, are assumed to differ across regions. The utility function (4.3) now becomes

$$U_i = ln(g_i^L)^{\alpha} + ln(g^C)^{\beta(1-\delta)} + lnA_i(g_i^L)^{\omega} - \left(\frac{g^C}{N} + \frac{g_i^L}{N_i}\right), \qquad (A.1)$$

and after inserting for $g_i^L = \theta_i g_i$ and $g^C = (1-\theta_i)g_i$ finally

$$\widetilde{U_i} = \alpha ln\theta_i g_i + \beta(1-\delta)ln(1-\theta_i)g_i + lnA_i + \omega ln\theta_i g_i - \frac{g_i\left(\theta N + (1-\theta_i)N_i\right)}{NN_i}. \qquad (A.2)$$

Accordingly, the optimal degree of decentralisation from the viewpoint of a region $i$ now depends on the population size of the federation $N$, as well as on the region's population size $N_i$:

$$\theta_i^* = \frac{N_i(\alpha+\omega)}{N_i(\alpha+\omega) + N\beta(1-\delta)}, \quad g_i^* = N\beta(1-\delta) + N_i(\alpha+\omega). \qquad (A.3)$$

All other things being equal, the optimal degree of decentralisation decreases with the size of the federation, $\theta_{iN}^* < 0$, but increases with the region's population size, $\theta_{iN_i}^* > 0$. In the latter case, economies of scale are exploited at the subnational level of government. However, since in reality changes in both regional and total population size are likely to be concomitant, both effects on centralisation might balance out on aggregate.

### General Definition of the Degree of Fiscal Decentralisation

Considering the provision of a bundle of public goods, the degree of decentralisation is defined as the share of total public services provided by sub-central government. Accordingly, the aggregate measure of public sector or fiscal decentralisation corresponds to the weighted sum of the degree of decentralisation of each public service, using as weights the shares of the different public services in aggregate public output.[1]

In order to obtain an operational measure, each public service is attributed to the central or the local government or both of them, and has to be weighted according to its relative importance in public sector activity. Applying the model presented in section 4.2 to a federation consisting of two levels of government and $i = 1...n$ local jurisdictions, with $j = 1...m$ public goods provided either locally ($g_{ji}^L$) or centrally ($g_j^C$), we obtain the *degree of decentralisation*

$$D = \sum_{j=1}^{m} \left( \frac{\sum_{i=1}^{n} g_{ji}^L}{g_j} \right) \left( \frac{g_j}{g} \right) = \frac{\sum_{j=1}^{m} \sum_{i=1}^{n} g_{ji}^L}{g},$$

with

$$g = \sum_{j=1}^{m} \sum_{i=1}^{n} g_{ji}^L + \sum_{j=1}^{m} g_j^C .$$

[1] See Oates (1972).

# B

# Tables and Figures

Table B.1: Levels of government in OECD countries

| Country | Regional level of governm. | Local level of governm. | Special territories |
|---|---|---|---|
| Australia (AUS) | states, territories | municipalities | |
| Austria (AUT) | Länder | municipalities | |
| Belgium (BEL) | regions, communities | provinces, municip. | |
| Canada (CAN) | provinces, territories | municipalities | |
| Denmark (DEN) | | counties, municip. | Faroe, Greenl. |
| Finland (FIN) | | municipalities | Aland |
| France (FRA) | regions, départements | municipalities | TOM, Corsica |
| Germany (GER) | Länder | districts, municip. | |
| Greece (GRE) | | prefect., municip. | |
| Iceland (ICL) | | municipalities | |
| Ireland (IRL) | | counties, boroughs districts | |
| Italy (ITA) | regions, provinces | municipalities | special regions |
| Japan (JAP) | | prefect., municip. | |
| Luxembourg (LUX) | | municipalities | |
| Netherlands (NED) | provinces | polder b., municip. | |
| New Zealand (NEZ) | regional councils | territ. authorities | |
| Norway (NOR) | | counties, municip. | |
| Portugal (POR) | | municip., parishes | Azores/Madeira |
| Spain (SPA) | auton. communities | provinces, municip. | histor. regions |
| Sweden (SWE) | county councils | municip., parishes | |
| Switzerland (SWI) | cantons | municip., parishes | |
| United Kingdom (UK) | | counties, districts unitary authorities | Scotland, Wales, N.Ireland |
| United States (USA) | states | counties, districts municipalities | |

Note: Only units of government endowed with own or assigned tax revenues are taken into account. Own compilation.

Table B.2: Fiscal decentralisation in OECD countries (competencies, polit. autonomy)

| | |
|---|---|
| AUS | 1970s increasing overlap of central/state gov. competencies |
| AUT | 1974, 1983/84, 1988 role of federal chamber and competencies of Länder strengthened |
| | 1992 agreement const. reform (n. implemented): devolution, abolition of dir. state admin. |
| BEL | 1970 creation of commun./regions, devolution of competen. to commun., co-decision rules |
| | 1980, 1988 devolution of legislative competencies to elected regional and community gov. |
| | 1994 constitutional reform: federal state |
| CAN | 1982 constitutional reform: strengthening of the provinces |
| | 1987 const. reform (failed): strengthening of the provinces and of the autonomy of Québec |
| | in the course of time federal gov. competencies delegated to provinces |
| DEN | 1970 competencies of local gov. extended to all local affairs, reduced state supervision |
| | 1976 responsibility for social security transferred to local gov. |
| | 1980s, 1990 further devolution of competencies |
| FIN | 1976 strengthening of local self-government |
| | 1994-97 creation of self-governed regional councils responsible for regional development |
| FRA | 1982-83 devolution competencies, election region. govern., reduced state supervision |
| | 2002 devolution of competencies to subnat. gov. |
| | 2003-04 constitutional reform: devolution of competencies to subnat. gov. |
| GER | in the course of time increased Länder participation in federal legislation |
| | 1992 extended participation of Länder gov. in EU policy-making |
| GRE | 1975 democracy: creation of 1st level of local self-government |
| | 1986-87 administrat. decentralisation, creation of development regions |
| | 1994 2nd level local self-govern. (prefectures), extended competencies local/reg. gov. |
| | 1997 development regions with own budgets |
| | 1997-2001 devolution of competencies to local gov. |
| | 2001 const. reform: strengthened local self-govern., reduced state superv. |
| IRL | 1977, 1983, 1987 certain minor functions devolved to local gov. |
| | 1986, 1994 creation of regions as decentralised units of central gov. |
| | 1999 constitutional reform: recognition of elected local government bodies |

Table B.2 (cont.): Fiscal decentralisation in OECD countries (compet., pol. auton.)

| | |
|---|---|
| ITA | 1970 creation of regions with ordinary statute |
| | 1972, 1977 devolution of admin. competencies to ordinary regions, local gov. |
| | 1990-92 extended local/reg. competencies, local self-govern., reduced state supervision |
| | 1993 direct election of mayors and province presidents |
| | 1997-98 "admin. federalism": devolution competencies to reg./local gov. |
| | 1999 direct election of regional presidents |
| | 2001-03 const. reform: federalisation, devolution legisl. competencies to regions, strenthening of autonomy, end of state supervision |
| JAP | 1995 law to promote decentralisation |
| LUX | 1979 constitutional reform: local self-government |
| | 1988 extension of local self-government, reduction of state supervision |
| NED | 1983, 1994 strengthening of provincial and local gov. vs. central gov. |
| NEZ | 1974 creation of self-governed regional councils |
| NOR | 1977 admin. independence of counties, strengthening of municipalities |
| POR | 1976 democracy: local self-govern., devolution of competencies, autonomy Madeira/Azores |
| | 1979 creation of development regions |
| | 1999 devolution of competencies to local gov. and Madeira/Azores |
| SPA | 1978 democracy: regional and local autonomy |
| | 1981-83 creation auton. regions, abolition state supervision, devolution regional competencies |
| | 1992-93 extension of regional competencies |
| SWE | 1970 reduction of provincial gov. competencies |
| | 1997, 1999 creation of self-governed pilot regions for reg. development |
| SWI | reform of distribution of government functions currently planned |
| UK | 1972 N. Ireland: abolition self-govern., dissolution of regional parliam. |
| | 1973 extension of competencies of local gov. |
| | 1980-85 reduction of competencies of local gov. |
| | 1994 creation of administrative government offices for the regions (GOR) |
| | 1998 N. Ireland: restoration of self-government, election regional parliam. |
| | 1999 Scotl., Wales: elected parliaments, legisl./admin. competencies, reduced state supervision; |
| | England: regional development agencies (RDA), elected bodies planned |
| | 2000 London: direct election of council and mayor |
| USA | extension federal legislation in areas of state/local gov. (social affairs) |

Source: Constitutions and legal provisions, see also Table 2.3. Own compilation.

Table B.3: Fiscal decentralisation in OECD countries (finan. autonomy)

| | |
|---|---|
| AUS | 1971 cession of payroll tax to the states |
| | 2000 cession of general sales tax receipts to the states |
| BEL | 1980 own revenues with limited legisl. power assigned to commun./regions |
| | 1989, 1994, 2001-02 extension of own sources and tax-rising powers of communities/regions, co-decision on financing system |
| DEN | 1996 complete cession of county land tax yield to the counties |
| FRA | 1980 tax-raising autonomy for direct local taxes |
| | 1983 cession of national taxes and legisl. competencies to départ./regions |
| | 1999-2001 abolition of certain local/regional tax bases |
| | 2003 constitutional reform: financial autonomy of subnat. gov. |
| GER | 1969 const. reform: concurrent competencies extended, cession of Länder taxes to central gov., sharing of personal, corporate income tax, VAT |
| | 1996 abolition of the Länder wealth tax |
| | 1997 communal business capital tax replaced with a share in VAT |
| GRE | 1990 local gov. shares in national taxes |
| | 2001 constitutional reform: financial autonomy of subnat. gov. |
| IRL | 1997 local gov. share of motor tax yield |
| ITA | 1973-74 abolition of local taxes, centralisation of tax administration |
| | 1989-93 substitution of grants with local/regional taxes, legisl. powers |
| | 1998 introduction of further reg./loc. taxes, surcharges on nat. taxes |
| | 2000 substitution of grants with regional share in national taxes |
| | 2001 constitutional reform: financial autonomy of local/regional gov. |
| LUX | 1979 financial autonomy of local gov. |
| NED | in the course of time abolition of certain local taxes |
| NOR | 1979 tax-raising power of counties, county income tax |
| POR | 1979 own local taxes; special taxing powers for Madeira and Azores |
| | 1989-90 new local taxes, legislative competencies of local gov. |
| | 1997 constitutional reform: local tax-raising powers |
| | 1999 local gov. share in national taxes |
| SPA | 1981-82 national/own taxes ceded to regions, reg. share in nat. taxes |
| | 1987 regional co-decision on financing system, extended regional shares in national taxes |
| | 1988-90 new local and provincial taxes |
| | 1993 regional share in national income tax, extended legisl. competencies for regional shared taxes |
| | 1997 extended regional share in national income tax and additional, surcharge, extended legisl. competencies for regional shared taxes |
| | 2002 extended reg. share in national income tax and surcharge, cession of further taxes to the regions |
| SWE | 1986 reduction of the local income tax base |
| | 1991-2000 temporary limits on local tax rates set by central gov. |
| SWI | 1993 harmonisation of cantonal tax legislations |
| UK | 1980-84 reduction of legislative competencies for local taxes |
| | 1990 transfer of certain local taxes to central gov. |
| | 1999 tax legislative competencies for Scottish Parliament |

Source: Constitutions and legal provisions, see also Table 2.3. Own compilation.

Table B.4: Degree of expenditure decentralisation, 1970-2001

| Country | Direct expenditure (ED1) | | | | Self-financed expend. (ED2) | | | |
|---|---|---|---|---|---|---|---|---|
| | 1970-1975 | | 1996-2001 | | 1970-1975 | | 1996-2001 | |
| | (1) | (2) | (1) | (2) | (1) | (2) | (1) | (2) |
| AUS | 49.3 | 49.3 | 48.3 | 48.3 | 27.4 | 27.4 | 31.6 | 31.6 |
| AUT | 33.1 | 45.8 | 32.0 | 47.5 | 25.2 | 34.9 | 22.8 | 33.8 |
| BEL | 14.6 | 21.0 | 27.8 | 39.5 | 7.7 | 10.0 | 25.2 | 33.8 |
| CAN | 57.7 | 58.5 | 60.0 | 63.7 | 48.3 | 49.6 | 53.2 | 56.5 |
| DEN | 59.2 | 61.8 | 55.6 | 59.9 | 29.4 | 30.7 | 33.5 | 36.1 |
| FIN | 36.8 | 42.6 | 38.3 | 45.2 | 26.3 | 30.3 | 29.4 | 34.7 |
| FRA | 17.5 | 29.0 | 18.2 | 32.2 | 10.8 | 18.0 | 12.1 | 21.5 |
| GER | 44.1 | 65.9 | 36.1 | 64.6 | 39.7 | 59.3 | 33.4 | 60.2 |
| GRE | 3.9 | 5.0 | | | 3.7 | 4.8 | | |
| ICL | 17.7 | 21.8 | 28.2 | 33.7 | 17.8 | 21.9 | 25.1 | 30.1 |
| IRL | 28.3 | 34.5 | 24.9 | 28.4 | 16.5 | 18.1 | 6.6 | 7.4 |
| ITA | 17.8 | 26.2 | 24.9 | 36.3 | 7.9 | 11.7 | 11.7 | 17.2 |
| JAP | 48.4 | 65.5 | 35.8 | 62.8 | 22.9 | 28.4 | 18.4 | 27.6 |
| LUX | 16.4 | 26.7 | 15.5 | 27.6 | 8.8 | 14.3 | 10.0 | 17.5 |
| NED | 33.4 | 53.2 | 28.3 | 45.9 | 7.4 | 11.6 | 8.5 | 13.7 |
| NEZ | 12.5[a] | 12.5[a] | 11.1 | 11.1 | 10.4[a] | 10.4[a] | 10.0 | 10.0 |
| NOR | 36.9 | 48.1 | 34.1 | 46.1[b] | 32.7 | 42.2 | 21.8 | 32.7[b] |
| POR | 6.8 | 9.3 | 10.1 | 13.7 | 3.4 | 4.7 | 6.6 | 9.0 |
| SPA | 9.8 | 15.6 | 35.8 | 63.4 | 5.4 | 8.7 | 17.4 | 30.8 |
| SWE | 43.5 | 48.0 | 36.3 | 42.0 | 32.5 | 35.8 | 30.1 | 34.8 |
| SWI | 57.8 | 74.4 | 49.6 | 78.2 | 49.9 | 63.3 | 44.0 | 62.2 |
| UK | 32.1 | 36.9 | 21.9 | 31.6[b] | 19.6 | 22.4 | 7.2 | 19.3[b] |
| USA | 44.4 | 53.1 | 47.6 | 60.2 | 35.7 | 42.8 | 39.5 | 49.0 |
| Median[c]: | | | | | | | | |
| *OECD* | *33.2* | *44.2* | *33.1* | *45.6* | *21.3* | *24.9* | *22.3* | *31.2* |
| *EU15* | *30.2* | *35.7* | *28.1* | *40.8* | *13.7* | *18.1* | *14.8* | *26.2* |

Note: Total expenditure and lending minus repayments of sub-central government in % of consolidated general government expenditure, without EU payments, including (1) or excluding (2) social security; for JAP only current expenditure. Six-year-averages, [a] 1978-80, [b] 1988-90, [c] without GRE. Indicator ED1: total expenditure excluding transfers to other levels of government. Indicator ED2: total expenditure excluding grants received from other levels of government. Source: IMF, Government Finance Statistics Yearbook (except for: BEL – Banque Nationale de Belgique, JAP – OECD, National Accounts). Own calculations.

Table B.5: Own revenue of sub-central government, 1970-2001

| Country | Lev. gov. | 1970-1975 | 1996-2001 |
|---|---|---|---|
| AUS | Regional | 46.0 | 61.0 |
| | Local | 80.6 | 84.3 |
| AUT | Regional | 56.3 | 51.2 |
| | Local | 85.7 | 82.6 |
| BEL | Regional | | 91.4 |
| | Local | 49.7 | 54.4 |
| CAN | Regional | 76.1 | 85.1 |
| | Local | 51.2 | 61.8 |
| DEN | Local | 50.7 | 59.5 |
| FIN | Local | 70.0 | 76.1 |
| FRA | Local | 54.5 | 66.1 |
| GER | Regional | 81.5 | 81.9 |
| | Local | 69.5 | 66.7 |
| GRE | Local | 85.6 | |
| ICL | Local | 90.6[a] | 89.3 |
| IRL | Local | 42.9 | 22.3 |
| ITA | Local | 26.9 | 43.2 |
| JAP | Local | 49.4 | 51.6 |
| LUX | Local | 53.0 | 63.5 |
| NED | Local | 12.0 | 33.5 |
| NEZ | Local | 81.7[b] | 91.1 |
| NOR | Local | 82.8 | 61.4 |
| POR | Local | 50.0 | 63.0 |
| SPA | Regional | 19.3[c] | 26.5 |
| | Local | 51.9 | 65.9 |
| SWE | Local | 70.6 | 82.6 |
| SWI | Regional | 71.1 | 69.1 |
| | Local | 82.2 | 84.1 |
| UK | Local | 51.9 | 28.6 |
| USA | Regional | 74.2 | 77.9 |
| | Local | 60.4 | 62.1 |

Note: Revenue (irrespective of the degree of autonomy) exclusive of intergovernmental grants received from other levels of government, in % of total revenue and grants by level of government. Six-year-averages; [a] 1983-84, [b] 1978-80, [c] 1980. Source: IMF, Government Finance Statistics Yearbook (except for: BEL – Banque Nationale de Belgique, JAP – OECD, National Accounts). Own calculations.

Table B.6: Degree of revenue autonomy of sub-central government, 1975-2001

| Country | Lev. gov. | Auton. own taxes (RA1) | | Auton. own & shared taxes (RA2) | |
|---|---|---|---|---|---|
| | | 1975-1980[a] | 1996-2001 | 1975-1980[a] | 1996-2001 |
| AUS | Regional | 46.5 | 61.2 | 46.5 | 61.2 |
| | Local | 76.9 | 84.4 | 76.9 | 84.4 |
| AUT | Regional | 14.8 | 16.0 | 57.9 | 53.1 |
| | Local | 38.9 | 39.7 | 83.4 | 82.8 |
| BEL | Reg./Loc.[b] | 35.3 | 45.4 | 35.3 | 80.4 |
| CAN | Regional | 76.8 | 84.6 | 76.8 | 84.6 |
| | Local | 50.3 | 59.8 | 50.3 | 59.8 |
| DEN | Local | 47.7 | 56.8 | 47.7 | 56.8 |
| FIN | Reg./Loc.[b] | 64.8 | 67.4 | 64.8 | 67.4 |
| FRA | Reg./Loc.[b] | 34.0 | 65.9 | 34.0 | 65.9 |
| GER | Regional | 11.6 | 14.5 | 81.1 | 80.6 |
| | Local | 54.5 | 54.7 | 54.5 | 54.7 |
| GRE | Local | | | | |
| ICL | Local | 88.2 | 88.1 | 88.2 | 88.1 |
| IRL | Local | 32.0 | 24.7 | 32.0 | 24.7 |
| ITA | Reg./Loc.[b] | 12.4[b] | 26.8 | 12.4[b] | 26.8 |
| JAP | Local | | | | |
| LUX | Local | 51.1 | 63.6 | 51.1 | 63.6 |
| NED | Reg./Loc.[b] | 16.7 | 31.1 | 16.7 | 31.1 |
| NEZ | Reg./Loc.[b] | 80.6 | 90.5 | 80.6 | 90.5 |
| NOR | Local | 64.6 | 61.3 | 64.6 | 61.3 |
| POR | Reg./Loc.[b] | 21.1[c] | 37.9 | 21.1[c] | 37.9 |
| SPA | Reg./Loc.[b] | 64.5 | 33.6 | 64.5 | 39.3 |
| SWE | Reg./Loc.[b] | 74.3 | 82.4 | 74.3 | 82.4 |
| SWI | Regional | 68.1 | 64.0 | 73.5 | 69.7 |
| | Local | 84.0 | 82.8 | 84.0 | 82.8 |
| UK | Local | 50.1 | 27.9 | 50.1 | 27.9 |
| USA | Regional | 74.6 | 77.7 | 74.6 | 77.7 |
| | Local | 55.9 | 62.1 | 55.9 | 62.1 |

Note: Revenue by degree of autonomy, as % of total own revenue of sub-central government. In case of various regional or local tiers of government, these are consolidated at each corresponding level of government. Six-year-averages, [a] earliest available years; [b] due to problems of identification, local and regional level of government are consolidated. No subnational non tax revenue data available for Greece and Japan. Source: see Table 2.3. Own calculations.

Table B.7: Decentralisation trends, fixed effects estimates, 23 OECD countries, 1965-2001

| | Dep. var.: Degree of fiscal decentralisation | | | | | |
|---|---|---|---|---|---|---|
| | ED1 | ED2 | TD1 | TD3 | RD1 | RD3 |
| OECD | .185*** | .163*** | .087*** | .133*** | .110*** | .156*** |
| | (.026) | (.019) | (.012) | (.016) | (.019) | (.030) |
| No. obs. | 594 | 603 | 760 | 760 | 466 | 466 |
| Within $R^2$ | .084 | .114 | .065 | .085 | .068 | .057 |
| EU15 | .238*** | .200*** | .108*** | .178*** | .104*** | .176*** |
| | (.038) | (.027) | (.017) | (.024) | (.027) | (.045) |
| No. obs. | 379 | 387 | 491 | 491 | 303 | 303 |
| Within $R^2$ | .097 | .132 | .076 | .106 | .048 | .050 |

Note: Fixed effects (within) regressions on a linear trend. Standard errors are reported in parentheses. ***, **, and * indicate significance at 1%, 5% and 10% levels, respectively. Public expenditure is excluding social security.

Table B.8: Degree of tax decentralisation (indic. TD1), annual figures, 1965-2001

| | 1965 | 1966 | 1967 | 1968 | 1969 | 1970 | 1971 | 1972 | 1973 | 1974 | 1975 | 1976 | 1977 | 1978 | 1979 | 1980 | 1981 | 1982 | 1983 |
|---|---|---|---|---|---|---|---|---|---|---|---|---|---|---|---|---|---|---|---|
| AUS | | | | | | | | | 19.68 | 19.28 | 19.94 | 19.77 | 19.72 | 19.58 | 18.85 | 18.19 | 18.30 | 19.24 | 19.49 |
| AUT | | | | | | | | | 2.90 | 3.09 | 3.62 | 3.61 | 3.47 | 3.36 | 3.35 | 3.39 | 3.50 | 3.53 | 3.67 |
| BEL | 6.59 | 6.73 | 3.64 | 7.30 | 6.18 | 6.69 | 6.40 | 7.07 | 6.33 | 6.72 | 6.30 | 6.09 | 5.98 | 6.11 | 6.19 | 5.31 | 5.65 | 6.48 | 6.33 |
| CAN | 52.14 | 52.58 | 51.86 | 51.21 | 49.15 | 49.79 | 49.56 | 49.27 | 47.26 | 46.31 | 47.08 | 49.37 | 52.91 | 54.28 | 52.77 | 51.64 | 49.43 | 51.24 | 53.03 |
| DEN | | | | | | | | | 27.35 | 25.96 | 29.02 | 29.17 | 28.65 | 27.89 | 28.62 | 28.68 | 28.92 | 29.63 | 30.22 |
| FIN | 23.14 | 23.47 | 23.54 | 22.67 | 24.37 | 24.19 | 24.82 | 23.88 | 23.85 | 24.62 | 26.90 | 25.90 | 27.13 | 26.41 | 27.30 | 25.65 | 26.21 | 26.60 | 26.50 |
| FRA | | | | | | 1.13 | | | 1.93 | 1.63 | 2.18 | 2.06 | 2.25 | 2.28 | 2.39 | 11.85 | 11.96 | 11.97 | 12.83 |
| GER | | | | | | | | | 7.49 | 7.58 | 7.76 | 8.01 | 7.91 | 7.62 | 7.34 | 7.65 | 7.15 | 7.09 | 7.38 |
| GRE | | | | | | | | | | | 0.31 | 0.25 | 0.57 | 0.54 | 0.37 | 0.40 | 0.47 | 0.43 | 0.28 |
| ICL | | | | | | | | | | | 19.19 | | | | | 17.54 | 17.06 | 16.94 | 17.81 |
| IRL | 13.78 | 12.98 | 11.68 | 11.75 | 11.14 | 10.99 | 11.63 | 11.71 | 9.68 | 9.64 | 8.66 | 8.33 | 7.33 | 4.90 | 4.66 | 4.08 | 3.27 | 2.54 | 2.46 |
| ITA | 6.43 | 6.38 | 3.05 | 5.96 | 5.78 | 5.20 | 5.34 | 5.76 | 4.87 | 1.99 | 1.07 | 0.84 | 0.29 | 0.23 | 0.15 | 0.47 | 0.53 | 0.50 | 0.40 |
| JAP | 28.33 | 28.71 | 28.83 | 28.44 | 27.98 | 28.50 | 29.42 | 28.78 | 28.46 | 30.95 | 32.17 | 32.40 | 33.01 | 30.68 | 32.13 | 32.39 | 32.71 | 33.30 | 33.33 |
| LUX | 10.03 | 9.28 | 10.69 | 10.80 | 11.27 | 12.81 | 10.82 | 10.30 | 10.49 | 10.61 | 9.53 | 10.03 | 9.88 | 10.49 | 10.09 | 9.43 | 8.45 | 8.51 | 9.50 |
| NED | | | | | | | | | 2.19 | 2.29 | 1.92 | 2.35 | 2.83 | 3.56 | 3.36 | 3.21 | 3.73 | 4.13 | 4.13 |
| NEZ | 9.07 | 8.91 | 3.42 | 8.86 | 8.64 | 7.78 | 7.07 | 7.39 | 6.29 | 6.51 | 7.18 | 7.00 | 6.67 | 7.19 | 6.79 | 6.93 | 6.80 | 6.99 | 7.18 |
| NOR | | | | | | | | | 30.45 | 31.18 | 31.51 | 31.48 | 31.40 | 31.06 | 29.18 | 24.75 | 23.96 | 24.62 | 24.51 |
| POR | 0.00 | 0.00 | 0.00 | 0.00 | 0.00 | 0.00 | 0.00 | 0.00 | 0.00 | 0.00 | 0.00 | 0.00 | 0.35 | 0.39 | 0.33 | 0.32 | 0.31 | 0.27 | 0.30 |
| SPA | | | | | | | | | 4.84 | 5.07 | 5.33 | 6.08 | 7.74 | 7.85 | 9.20 | 5.94 | 5.68 | 10.11 | 10.04 |
| SWE | 30.77 | 32.45 | 32.81 | 33.04 | 33.49 | 34.59 | 34.59 | 35.93 | 36.40 | 37.64 | 36.31 | 36.95 | 38.32 | 41.47 | 42.85 | 44.80 | 45.61 | 44.62 | 43.31 |
| SWI | 54.33 | 52.41 | 55.16 | 54.10 | 55.57 | 54.97 | 56.22 | 55.21 | 59.01 | 59.01 | 61.50 | 58.17 | 59.87 | 58.60 | 59.99 | 58.66 | 58.68 | 57.68 | 58.41 |
| UK | 13.77 | 13.80 | 13.08 | 12.47 | 11.56 | 11.41 | 12.41 | 13.75 | 14.25 | 13.02 | 13.56 | 13.18 | 13.03 | 12.94 | 13.28 | 13.04 | 13.90 | 14.07 | 13.45 |
| USA | 34.38 | 34.62 | 34.41 | 34.56 | 33.42 | 34.80 | 36.55 | 37.31 | 38.12 | 37.31 | 38.30 | 38.40 | 38.00 | 37.48 | 36.29 | 35.64 | 33.91 | 34.72 | 36.26 |

| | 1984 | 1985 | 1986 | 1987 | 1988 | 1989 | 1990 | 1991 | 1992 | 1993 | 1994 | 1995 | 1996 | 1997 | 1998 | 1999 | 2000 | 2001 |
|---|---|---|---|---|---|---|---|---|---|---|---|---|---|---|---|---|---|---|
| AUS | 18.64 | 18.55 | 18.50 | 19.10 | 19.78 | 19.83 | 20.50 | 22.45 | 23.40 | 24.23 | 22.88 | 22.47 | 22.45 | 22.31 | 21.33 | 21.05 | | 17.16 |
| AUT | 3.45 | 3.31 | 3.34 | 3.45 | 3.50 | 3.66 | 3.58 | 3.40 | 3.41 | 3.53 | 3.59 | 3.76 | 3.45 | 3.39 | 4.03 | 3.50 | 2.96 | |
| BEL | 7.06 | 6.88 | 3.98 | 6.95 | 6.69 | 17.54 | 18.51 | 19.86 | 20.71 | 21.36 | 22.02 | 23.61 | 23.78 | 24.27 | 24.34 | 24.55 | | |
| CAN | 51.98 | 52.44 | 51.26 | 50.65 | 51.78 | 51.62 | 52.70 | 52.90 | 53.53 | 55.36 | 54.64 | 54.66 | 53.86 | 52.25 | 52.86 | 52.20 | 51.57 | 51.65 |
| DEN | 28.73 | 27.63 | 26.46 | 28.03 | 29.42 | 29.65 | 30.61 | 30.91 | 31.16 | 30.84 | 30.96 | 31.48 | 31.19 | 31.46 | 31.97 | 31.82 | 32.57 | |
| FIN | 26.07 | 26.15 | 26.08 | 25.89 | 24.88 | 24.30 | 26.74 | 26.23 | 26.69 | 31.15 | 32.18 | 29.50 | 28.21 | 25.85 | 25.10 | 24.64 | 22.48 | 25.49 |
| FRA | 15.21 | 15.59 | 15.63 | 15.53 | 16.16 | 16.28 | 16.55 | 16.89 | 19.05 | 19.81 | 20.05 | 19.96 | 19.93 | 19.65 | 19.53 | 18.74 | 18.01 | |
| GER | 7.74 | 7.89 | 7.91 | 7.59 | 7.90 | 7.62 | 7.81 | 7.00 | 6.81 | 6.96 | 6.79 | 6.49 | 7.20 | 7.65 | 7.61 | 7.47 | 7.29 | 6.87 |
| GRE | 0.23 | 0.25 | 0.05 | 0.10 | 0.28 | 0.31 | 0.26 | 0.24 | 0.21 | 0.19 | 0.17 | 0.19 | 0.17 | 0.17 | 0.24 | 0.27 | 0.25 | |
| ICL | 19.34 | 19.65 | 18.73 | 19.20 | 20.01 | 20.41 | 20.52 | 21.69 | 22.29 | 22.54 | 21.62 | 22.17 | 21.60 | 25.69 | 24.95 | 24.80 | 24.86 | 26.39 |
| IRL | 2.56 | 2.72 | 2.71 | 2.78 | 2.61 | 3.07 | 3.00 | 2.99 | 2.94 | 2.87 | 2.76 | 2.81 | 2.66 | 2.46 | 2.33 | 2.14 | 2.11 | 2.26 |
| ITA | 0.43 | 0.42 | | 0.18 | 0.48 | 1.18 | 1.25 | 1.25 | 1.31 | 5.32 | 5.01 | 5.23 | 5.67 | 5.90 | 6.19 | 5.86 | 13.74 | 14.12 |
| JAP | 33.53 | 34.07 | 33.18 | 33.18 | 33.44 | 32.74 | 31.79 | 32.68 | 34.34 | 33.69 | 33.72 | 34.13 | 35.00 | 35.17 | 37.54 | 37.68 | 37.00 | 37.91 |
| LUX | 5.75 | 9.27 | 3.15 | 8.69 | 8.58 | 9.25 | 8.74 | 9.18 | 7.95 | 8.42 | 7.98 | 9.07 | 8.91 | 8.42 | 8.60 | 7.79 | 7.84 | 8.14 |
| NED | 4.19 | 4.41 | 3.98 | 4.23 | 4.08 | 4.17 | 3.88 | 3.75 | 3.95 | 3.40 | 4.45 | 4.73 | 5.02 | 5.19 | 5.20 | 5.12 | 5.05 | |
| NEZ | 6.69 | 6.37 | 3.02 | 5.72 | 5.52 | 5.19 | 5.97 | 6.04 | 5.33 | 5.45 | 5.31 | 5.17 | 5.51 | 5.29 | 5.77 | 6.19 | 6.05 | 5.53 |
| NOR | 23.48 | 23.11 | 24.73 | 27.12 | 28.58 | 28.53 | 27.56 | 27.15 | 27.78 | 27.53 | 27.47 | 25.53 | 24.74 | 23.53 | 23.44 | 23.45 | 20.53 | 20.15 |
| POR | 0.42 | 0.41 | 0.57 | 0.64 | 0.73 | 1.76 | 2.73 | 2.76 | 2.61 | 2.85 | 2.68 | 2.85 | 2.92 | 2.89 | 3.14 | 3.36 | 3.18 | |
| SPA | 12.66 | 11.82 | 3.16 | 7.56 | 7.62 | 7.25 | 8.00 | 7.98 | 11.32 | 12.09 | 12.50 | 12.69 | 12.86 | 21.98 | 23.07 | 22.55 | 22.26 | 22.12 |
| SWE | 42.96 | 40.46 | 38.03 | 35.74 | 37.16 | 38.29 | 40.18 | 43.56 | 47.41 | 47.56 | 46.41 | 47.02 | 46.26 | 44.28 | 43.45 | 41.12 | 42.57 | 44.65 |
| SWI | 57.31 | 57.06 | 55.49 | 56.61 | 55.03 | 56.29 | 55.24 | 55.78 | 55.69 | 58.67 | 57.12 | 56.99 | 55.67 | 55.14 | 52.52 | 54.54 | 51.55 | |
| UK | 13.17 | 12.89 | 13.57 | 14.04 | 13.86 | 13.75 | 7.29 | 4.74 | 5.28 | 5.20 | 5.04 | 4.88 | 4.77 | 4.81 | 4.76 | 4.98 | 4.82 | 5.07 |
| USA | 37.54 | 37.52 | 38.03 | 37.64 | 38.33 | 37.98 | 38.15 | 38.55 | 39.08 | 39.03 | 38.81 | 38.58 | 37.84 | 37.00 | 36.18 | 35.92 | 34.99 | 35.88 |

Table B.9: Degree of tax decentralisation, 1965-2001

| Country | Auton. own taxes (TD1) | | Auton. own & sh. taxes (TD2) | | Total tax reven. (TD3) | |
|---|---|---|---|---|---|---|
| | 1965-1970 | 1996-2001 | 1965-1970 | 1996-2001 | 1965-1970 | 1996-2001 |
| AUS | 19.6[a] | 20.9 | 19.6[a] | 20.9 | 19.6[a] | 20.9 |
| AUT | 3.2[a] | 3.5 | 29.5[a] | 28.7 | 29.5[a] | 28.7 |
| BEL | 6.7 | 24.2 | 6.7 | 44.2 | 7.1 | 44.5 |
| CAN | 51.1 | 52.4 | 51.1 | 52.4 | 51.1 | 52.4 |
| DEN | 27.4[a] | 31.8 | 27.4[a] | 31.8 | 28.4[a] | 33.6 |
| FIN | 23.6 | 25.3 | 23.6 | 25.3 | 26.3 | 30.4 |
| FRA | 1.1[b] | 19.2 | 1.1[b] | 19.2 | 9.4[b] | 19.4 |
| GER | 7.6[a] | 7.3 | 48.3[a] | 49.6 | 48.3[a] | 49.6 |
| GRE | 0.3[a] | 0.2 | 0.3[a] | 0.2 | 4.9[a] | 2.0 |
| ICL | 19.2[a] | 24.7 | 19.2[a] | 24.7 | 19.2[a] | 24.7 |
| IRL | 12.1 | 2.3 | 12.1 | 2.3 | 12.1 | 3.9 |
| ITA | 6.0 | 8.6 | 6.0 | 8.6 | 6.2 | 13.1 |
| JAP | 28.5 | 36.7 | 28.5 | 36.7 | 32.5 | 40.5 |
| LUX | 10.8 | 8.3 | 10.8 | 8.3 | 10.8 | 8.3 |
| NED | 2.1[a] | 5.1 | 2.1[a] | 5.1 | 2.1[a] | 5.1 |
| NEZ | 8.6 | 5.7 | 8.6 | 5.7 | 8.6 | 5.8 |
| NOR | 31.0[a] | 22.6 | 31.0[a] | 22.6 | 31.0[a] | 23.0 |
| POR | 0.0 | 3.1 | 0.0 | 3.1 | 0.3 | 8.4 |
| SPA | 5.1[a] | 20.8 | 5.1[a] | 23.2 | 7.8[a] | 25.2 |
| SWE | 32.9 | 43.7 | 32.9 | 43.7 | 32.9 | 43.7 |
| SWI | 54.4 | 53.9 | 56.7 | 57.8 | 56.7 | 57.8 |
| UK | 12.7 | 4.9 | 12.7 | 4.9 | 12.7 | 4.9 |
| USA | 34.4 | 36.3 | 34.4 | 36.3 | 34.4 | 36.3 |
| Median: | | | | | | |
| *OECD* | *12.1* | *20.8* | *19.2* | *23.2* | *19.2* | *24.7* |
| *EU15* | *6.7* | *8.3* | *10.8* | *19.2* | *10.8* | *19.4* |
| Mean: | | | | | | |
| *OECD* | *17.3* | *20.1* | *20.3* | *24.1* | *21.4* | *25.3* |
| *EU15* | *10.1* | *13.9* | *14.6* | *19.9* | *15.9* | *21.4* |
| Std.dev.: | | | | | | |
| *OECD* | *15.39* | *15.97* | *16.46* | *17.26* | *15.89* | *16.87* |
| *EU15* | *9.87* | *12.46* | *14.01* | *16.31* | *13.34* | *15.84* |

Note: Tax revenue of sub-central governments by degree of autonomy in % of consolidated general government tax revenue, without social security and EU payments. Six-year-average. [a] 1973-75, [b] 1970. Source: see Table 2.3.

Table B.10: Degree of revenue decentralisation (indic. RD1), annual figures, 1975-2001

| | 1975 | 1976 | 1977 | 1978 | 1979 | 1980 | 1981 | 1982 | 1983 | 1984 | 1985 | 1986 | 1987 | 1988 |
|---|---|---|---|---|---|---|---|---|---|---|---|---|---|---|
| AUS | 23.86 | 23.36 | 24.11 | 24.20 | 23.51 | 22.96 | 23.10 | 24.18 | 25.18 | 24.29 | 24.95 | 25.48 | 25.53 | 26.74 |
| AUT | 13.42 | 13.28 | 13.23 | 13.10 | 12.99 | 13.78 | 13.85 | 14.29 | 14.71 | 14.04 | 13.87 | 13.58 | 14.00 | 14.55 |
| BEL | | | | 7.23 | 7.34 | 6.69 | 6.55 | 7.19 | 7.24 | 7.97 | 7.88 | 8.07 | 8.16 | 8.03 |
| CAN | | | | | 54.66 | 53.46 | 51.47 | 53.55 | 54.62 | 53.61 | 54.43 | 53.24 | 52.82 | 54.55 |
| DEN | 31.90 | 31.48 | 32.14 | 31.07 | 31.27 | 30.40 | 30.84 | 31.39 | 31.69 | 30.04 | 29.09 | 27.92 | 29.30 | 30.49 |
| FIN | 33.51 | 32.41 | 33.43 | 33.28 | 32.02 | 31.38 | 31.10 | 31.48 | 31.62 | 31.44 | 32.02 | 30.78 | 30.65 | 30.42 |
| FRA | | | | 6.15 | 6.13 | 14.67 | 14.66 | 14.82 | 15.64 | 17.76 | 18.26 | 19.21 | 19.31 | 19.86 |
| GER | 21.70 | 21.96 | 21.53 | 21.44 | 21.06 | 21.67 | 21.85 | 21.91 | 22.41 | 22.12 | 21.92 | 21.98 | 21.91 | 22.44 |
| GRE | | | | | | | | | | | | | | |
| ICL | 18.95 | | | | | 22.97 | 22.70 | 22.70 | 19.16 | 20.22 | 20.31 | 19.85 | 20.60 | 21.18 |
| IRL | 14.79 | 14.04 | 14.00 | 11.91 | 11.90 | 10.67 | 10.01 | 9.02 | 9.10 | 9.43 | 10.13 | 10.17 | 10.41 | 9.53 |
| ITA | | | | | | | | | | | 6.25 | 6.15 | 5.24 | 5.31 |
| JAP | | | | | | | | | | | | | | |
| LUX | 10.33 | 10.37 | 10.79 | 11.12 | 10.93 | 10.07 | 9.13 | 9.82 | 10.52 | 9.77 | 10.03 | 10.22 | 9.41 | 9.28 |
| NED | 7.05 | 7.66 | 8.16 | 8.98 | 9.00 | 8.71 | 9.29 | 9.93 | 10.44 | 10.62 | 10.64 | 10.00 | 10.51 | 9.89 |
| NEZ | | | | 11.99 | 11.18 | 11.25 | 11.17 | | | | | | | |
| NOR | | | | | | 27.15 | 26.58 | 26.70 | 25.34 | 24.99 | 24.61 | 25.59 | 27.61 | 28.71 |
| POR | | | | | | | | | | | | | 4.13 | 4.46 |
| SPA | | | 11.77 | 11.79 | 11.55 | 10.36 | 9.96 | 13.50 | 14.00 | 15.23 | 16.90 | 13.01 | 11.69 | 11.92 |
| SWE | | | | 42.86 | 43.90 | 45.86 | 46.63 | 45.21 | 43.83 | 43.71 | 41.65 | 38.70 | 36.05 | 37.50 |
| SWI | 64.69 | 62.52 | 64.18 | 63.51 | 64.68 | 63.81 | 63.97 | 63.30 | 64.04 | 63.31 | | | | |
| UK | 20.04 | 17.90 | 18.53 | 18.45 | 18.77 | 18.45 | 19.33 | 19.81 | 18.52 | 17.99 | 17.53 | 18.31 | 18.79 | 19.33 |
| USA | | | | | | 41.08 | 39.63 | 40.73 | 42.31 | 43.75 | 44.00 | 45.34 | 45.33 | 45.85 |

| | 1989 | 1990 | 1991 | 1992 | 1993 | 1994 | 1995 | 1996 | 1997 | 1998 | 1999 | 2000 | 2001 |
|---|---|---|---|---|---|---|---|---|---|---|---|---|---|
| AUS | 27.77 | 28.56 | 31.25 | 32.27 | 32.94 | 31.93 | 31.70 | 31.82 | 32.03 | 31.79 | 30.80 | | |
| AUT | 14.94 | 14.66 | 15.08 | 15.08 | 15.64 | 15.89 | 17.66 | 16.16 | 13.00 | 13.95 | 13.21 | | |
| BEL | 18.04 | 18.88 | 20.42 | 20.99 | 21.34 | 22.12 | 23.95 | 24.13 | 25.03 | 24.96 | | | |
| CAN | 54.56 | 55.58 | 55.54 | 56.30 | 58.18 | 57.95 | 57.87 | 57.17 | 56.20 | | 56.57 | 56.99 | 56.39 |
| DEN | 30.61 | 31.39 | 31.08 | 31.16 | 30.43 | 30.94 | 31.94 | 31.66 | 32.04 | 32.41 | 32.52 | 32.83 | |
| FIN | 30.01 | 31.96 | 33.41 | 34.70 | 32.33 | 33.07 | 33.74 | 32.63 | 31.37 | 29.95 | | | |
| FRA | 20.03 | 20.40 | 20.42 | 22.47 | 23.24 | 23.68 | 23.58 | 23.34 | 22.79 | | | | |
| GER | 21.57 | 22.13 | 20.89 | 20.35 | 20.42 | 19.86 | 20.72 | 20.85 | | | | | |
| GRE | | | | | | | | | | | | | |
| ICL | 21.49 | 21.55 | 22.84 | 23.21 | 23.75 | 23.01 | 23.55 | 23.47 | 26.66 | 26.19 | | | |
| IRL | 10.15 | 10.87 | 9.49 | 9.39 | 9.51 | 9.80 | 9.68 | 9.82 | 9.08 | | | | |
| ITA | 5.93 | | | | | | 8.50 | 9.68 | 9.84 | 9.91 | 10.01 | | |
| JAP | | | | | | | | | | | | | |
| LUX | | 13.58 | 13.97 | 12.93 | 13.32 | 12.91 | 13.81 | 13.68 | 12.87 | | | | |
| NED | 10.41 | 9.64 | 13.25 | 13.01 | 11.87 | 14.70 | 13.88 | 15.66 | 13.70 | | | | |
| NEZ | | | | 7.25 | 7.56 | 7.57 | 7.54 | 8.27 | 8.66 | 8.78 | 11.74 | 9.68 | 8.13 |
| NOR | 28.01 | 26.57 | 26.93 | 27.83 | 27.52 | 27.56 | 25.86 | 25.10 | 24.10 | 25.41 | 25.11 | | |
| POR | 4.99 | 5.00 | 6.33 | 4.94 | 5.35 | 4.99 | 5.19 | 5.46 | 6.04 | 7.38 | | | |
| SPA | 12.11 | 12.62 | 12.55 | 14.69 | 15.27 | 16.65 | 16.14 | 16.75 | 24.67 | | | | |
| SWE | 38.29 | 39.69 | 41.69 | 44.62 | 39.89 | 38.94 | 42.87 | 42.01 | 39.67 | 39.65 | 38.53 | | |
| SWI | | 64.03 | 61.38 | 61.95 | 64.44 | 63.26 | 62.97 | 61.91 | 61.70 | 59.76 | 61.41 | 58.79 | |
| UK | 19.73 | 13.98 | 10.73 | 10.92 | 11.02 | 10.45 | 9.80 | 9.45 | 9.17 | 9.11 | | | |
| USA | 45.46 | 46.02 | 46.21 | 47.25 | 46.86 | 46.76 | 46.25 | 46.97 | 46.50 | 46.38 | 46.07 | 45.60 | |

Table B.11: Degree of revenue decentralisation, 1975-2001

| Country | Auton. own taxes (RD1) | | Auton. own & sh. taxes (RD2) | | Total tax revenue (RD3) | |
|---|---|---|---|---|---|---|
| | 1975-1980[a] | 1996-2001 | 1975-1980[a] | 1996-2001 | 1975-1980[a] | 1996-2001 |
| AUS | 23.7 | 31.6 | 23.7 | 31.6 | 23.7 | 31.6 |
| AUT | 13.3 | 14.1 | 34.9 | 34.7 | 34.9 | 34.7 |
| BEL | 7.1 | 24.7 | 7.1 | 43.8 | 7.2 | 44.0 |
| CAN | 54.1 | 56.7 | 54.1 | 56.7 | 54.1 | 56.7 |
| DEN | 31.4 | 32.3 | 31.4 | 32.3 | 32.4 | 33.8 |
| FIN | 32.7 | 31.3 | 32.7 | 31.3 | 34.8 | 35.1 |
| FRA | 9.0 | 23.1 | 9.0 | 23.1 | 15.3 | 23.2 |
| GER | 21.6 | 20.8 | 54.8 | 50.1 | 54.8 | 50.1 |
| GRE | | | | | 4.2[b] | |
| ICL | 21.0 | 25.4 | 21.0 | 25.4 | 21.0 | 25.4 |
| IRL | 12.9 | 9.4 | 12.9 | 9.4 | 12.9 | 10.3 |
| ITA | 6.2 | 9.9 | 6.2 | 9.9 | 8.9 | 15.0 |
| JAP | | | | | 36.2[b] | 38.3[b] |
| LUX | 10.6 | 13.3 | 10.6 | 13.3 | 10.6 | 13.3 |
| NED | 8.3 | 14.7 | 8.3 | 14.7 | 8.3 | 14.7 |
| NEZ | 11.5 | 9.2 | 11.5 | 9.2 | 11.7 | 9.3 |
| NOR | 27.2 | 24.9 | 27.2 | 24.9 | 27.2 | 25.2 |
| POR | 4.1 | 6.3 | 4.1 | 6.3 | 10.3 | 10.5 |
| SPA | 11.4 | 20.7 | 11.4 | 24.2 | 13.8 | 25.8 |
| SWE | 44.2 | 40.0 | 44.2 | 40.0 | 44.2 | 40.0 |
| SWI | 63.9 | 60.7 | 66.5 | 63.6 | 66.5 | 63.6 |
| UK | 18.7 | 9.2 | 18.7 | 9.2 | 18.7 | 9.2 |
| USA | 41.1 | 46.3 | 41.1 | 46.3 | 41.1 | 46.3 |
| Median[c]: | | | | | | |
| *OECD* | *18.7* | *23.1* | *21.0* | *25.4* | *21.0* | *25.8* |
| *EU15* | *12.1* | *17.7* | *12.1* | *23.6* | *14.6* | *24.5* |
| Mean[c]: | | | | | | |
| *OECD* | *22.6* | *25.0* | *25.3* | *28.6* | *26.3* | *29.4* |
| *EU15* | *16.5* | *19.3* | *20.4* | *24.4* | *21.9* | *25.7* |
| Std.dev.[c]: | | | | | | |
| *OECD* | *16.24* | *15.14* | *17.88* | *16.45* | *17.16* | *15.94* |
| *EU15* | *11.45* | *9.74* | *15.56* | *13.91* | *14.78* | *13.37* |

Note: Own revenue of sub-central government by degree of autonomy, excluding grants received from other levels of government, in % of consolidated general government revenue, without social security and EU payments. Six-year-averages. [a] earliest years available; [b] GRE (Source: IMF, GFSY), JAP (Source: OECD, National Accounts, current revenue); [c] without GRE and JAP. Source: see Table 2.3.

Table B.12: Overview of empirical studies on the determinants of fiscal decentralisation

| Authors | Sample | Econ. scale/ Spillovers | Hetero- geneity | Demand/ Prefer. | Instit. | Other |
|---|---|---|---|---|---|---|
| Schaltegger/ Feld (2001) | CSTS (Switz.) | Popul.:<br>exp. (-),tax +<br>Urbanis.:<br>exp. +, tax - | | P.c. income -<br>Language +<br>Inequality (-)<br>Left gov. + | Referen. + | Grants to subnat. gov.:<br>exp. - / tax +<br>Coalition +/-<br>History + |
| Panizza (1999) | CS, 3-y. (Intern.) | Popul. (-)<br>Area +<br>Density + | Eth.-ling. fraction. + | P.c. income + | Democracy + | |
| Oates (1972) | CS (Intern.) | Popul. +<br>Area +/(+)<br>Density + | Dummy (+)/+ | P.c. income + | Federal + (Dummy) | Soc. sec. - |
| Wasylenko (1987) | CS (Intern./ separate) | Popul. (-)/(+)<br>Area (+)/(-)<br>Urbanis. + | | P.c. income +<br>Language + | Federal + (Dummy) | |
| Kee (1977) | CS (Intern./ Devel.) | Urbanis. + | | P.c. income:<br>inter.+/devel.(-)<br>Language:<br>develop. - | Federal + (Dummy) | Grants to subnat. gov. + |
| Patsouratis (1990) | TS (EU) | Popul. +/-<br>Density (+)/(-) | | P.c. inc. +/(-) | | |
| Pryor (1968) | CS/TS (Intern./ USA) | Popul.<br>CS (+)/+, TS -<br>Density (+)/(-) | | P.c. inc. +/- | | |
| Pommerehne (1977) | CS (Intern.) | Popul. +<br>Area +/(+)<br>Urbanis. +/(+)<br>Density + | Dummy (+)/+<br>Disparity reg.<br>p.c. income +<br>Eth.-ling.<br>fraction. (-) | P.c. income +<br>Inequality - | Federal + (Dummy) | |

Table B.12 (cont.): Overview of empirical studies on the determinants of fiscal decentralisation

| Authors | Sample | Econ. scale/ Spillovers | Hetero-geneity | Demand/ Prefer. | Instit. | Other |
|---|---|---|---|---|---|---|
| Bahl/Nath (1986) | CS (Devel.) | Urbanisat. + | | P.c. income + | | |
| Vaubel (1996) | CS (Inter./ Indust.) | Popul. (+)<br>Area (+)/+ | Dummy (+)<br>Eth.-ling. fraction. (+)<br>Disparity reg. p.c. income (+) | Per cap. income: + | Referen. +<br>Fed. (Dummy) +<br>Age federal +<br>Subnat. part. +<br>Indep. court + | |
| Wallis/ Oates (1988) | CSTS/CS (USA) | Popul. +<br>Area (+)<br>Urbanis. + | Race, econ. (%white,%farm) +/- | | | |
| Matsusaka (1995) | CSTS (USA) | | | | Referen. + | |
| Baker (2000) | CS (USA) | Popul. +<br>Area + | | P.c. income +<br>Poverty (-) | Subnat. part. - (veto central) | Young p. (+)<br>Old p. + |
| Strumpf/Oberholzer-Gee (2002) | CSTS (USA) | | Relig./ethn. + | | | |
| Giertz (1983) | CS (USA) | Popul. + | | P.c. income (+) (median inc.) | | |
| Mullen (1980) | CS (USA) | Popul. +<br>Urbanis. + | | P.c. income + (median inc.) | | |
| Litvack/Oates (1970) | CS (USA) | Popul. +<br>Urbanis. + | | | | Southern - |
| Garret/Rodden (2003) | CSTS (Inter.) | Popul. (+)<br>Area (+)<br>Urbanis. (+) | Eth.-ling. fraction. (+) | P.c. income (+)<br>Trade open. -<br>Finan. open. - | Fed. (Dummy) +<br>Democracy + | History: +<br>Cen. gov. surplus exp. + / rev. - |

Note: cross-sectional time-series (CSTS), cross-section (CS), time series (TS), significant +/-, not significant (+)/(-).

Table B.13: Index of subnational representation in the upper chamber

| | Definition | Score |
|---|---|---|
| (A) Method selection (0-1) | no subnational representation | 0.0 |
| | limited subnat. repres.: either indirectly elected by electoral college as collective representatives of subnat. entities, coopted by the other members of the upper chamber, or directly elected on a regional basis with guaranteed minimum repres. | 0.2 |
| | representatives of subnat. entities: appointed by central govern. on regional basis, or directly elected on quasi-territ. basis | 0.4 |
| | representatives of subnat. entities: directly elected by the citizens of the regions | 0.6 |
| | representatives of subnat. entities: indir. elected by regional legislatures | 0.8 |
| | representatives of subnat. entities: appointed by regional govern. | 1.0 |
| (B) Symmetry repres. (0-1) | Ratio of legislative seats of smallest region to those of largest region | |
| (C) Degree overrepr. (0-1) | = 1 – ratio of population share of smallest region to its share of seats in the legislature | |

The *index of subnational representation in the upper chamber* (0-2) takes account of the method of selection of the subnational representatives as a whole (A), and the degree of representation of the individual subnational units (B, C). Scores ranging from 0 to 1 are allocated to each of the three aspects. In case of mixed methods of selection, the score for each form is weighted with the corresponding share of representatives. With respect to symmetry of representation, a value of 1 denotes equal representation of all sub-units. The degree of overrepresentation of small sub-units is lowest in case of perfect proportional representation, which takes the value of 0.

Some notes on the entities considered in the calculation of the degree of representation: in Australia and Canada only states and provinces; in Belgium only French and Flemish communities (before 1994: only representatives indirectly elected by the provinces); in Spain only representatives indirectly elected by the regional parliaments. The composite index is finally constructed by summing up the scores for the method of selection and the arithmetic average of symmetry of representation and degree of overrepresentation: (A)+[(B)+(C)]/2.

Table B.14: Indices of participation of subnational entities in central decision-making

| | (A) Form of representation | Score (0-1) | (B) Power of legisl. initiation | Score (0-1) | (C) Veto power | Score (0-3) |
|---|---|---|---|---|---|---|
| Dir. | none | 0.0 | none | 0 | none | 0.00 |
| part. | region. legislat. | 0.5 | = 1 – required | 0-1 | suspens. veto | 1.00 |
| | region. elector. | 1.0 | major. regions | | absol. veto, quorum | |
| | | | each region | 1 | of regions to agree: | |
| | | | | | absolute majority | 2.00 |
| | | | | | two-thirds | 2.25 |
| | | | | | three-quarters | 2.50 |
| | | | | | four-fifths | 2.75 |
| | | | | | unanimity | 3.00 |
| Indir. | *index subn.* | | none | 0 | none | 0.00 |
| part. | *repr. upper h.* | | equal powers to | 1 | suspen. veto, quorum | |
| | (method select.) | | lower chamber | | lower cham. to overrule: | |
| | | | | | simple majority | 1.00 |
| | | | | | two-thirds | 1.25 |
| | | | | | three-quarters | 1.50 |
| | | | | | unanimity | 1.75 |
| | | | | | absol. veto, quorum | |
| | | | | | upper cham. to agree: | |
| | | | | | absolute majority | 2.00 |
| | | | | | two-thirds | 2.25 |
| | | | | | three-quarters | 2.50 |
| | | | | | four-fifths | 2.75 |
| | | | | | unanimity | 3.00 |

The *indices of direct/indirect participation of subnational entities in central decision-making* (0-4) take into account the form of representation of subnational entities and the power of decision with respect to the different issues of centralised decision-making. The method of selection of subnational representatives to the upper chamber described above determines the form of representation of subnational entities in indirect decision-making. With respect to power of decision-making, we further distinguish between the power to initiate legislation and the power to veto decisions, thereby giving the veto power a stronger weight. In case of different decision-making procedures for issues belonging to the same policy area, average scores are calculated. The indices are constructed for each policy area by multiplying form of representation by the sum of legislative initiation and veto powers: (A)·[(B)+(C)]. The composite index of participation covering all issues of national decision-making is then derived as the mean value of the average degree of participation in the assignment of competencies (expenditure and revenue powers) and the average degree of participation in other issues of national legislation (constitutional amendments not concerning subnational entities, national financial and non-financial legislation).

Table B.15: Indirect participation of subnational entities in central decision-making, 2003

| | Assignment expen. powers | | | | Assignment revenue powers | | | | Const. amendm. (not concerning subnat. entities) | | | |
|---|---|---|---|---|---|---|---|---|---|---|---|---|
| | Form | Legis. init. | Veto | *Total* | Form | Legis. init. | Veto | *Total* | Form | Legis. init. | Veto | *Total* |
| | (0-1) | (0-1) | (0-3) | *(0-4)* | (0-1) | (0-1) | (0-3) | *(0-4)* | (0-1) | (0-1) | (0-3) | *(0-4)* |
| AUS | 0.60 | 1.00 | 2.00 | *1.80* | 0.60 | 1.00 | 2.00 | *1.80* | 0.60 | 1.00 | 2.00 | *1.80* |
| AUT | 0.80 | 1.00 | 2.25 | *2.60* | 1.00[c] | 1.00 | 1.00 | *2.00* | 0.80 | 1.00 | 1.00 | *1.60* |
| BEL | 0.49 | 1.00 | 2.25 | *1.59* | 0.49 | 1.00 | 2.25 | *1.59* | 0.49 | 1.00 | 2.25 | *1.59* |
| CAN | 0.40 | 1.00 | 0.00 | *0.40* | 0.40 | 1.00 | 0.00 | *0.40* | 0.40 | 1.00 | 0.00 | *0.40* |
| FRA | 0.20 | 1.00 | 1.00 | *0.40* | 0.20 | 1.00 | 1.00 | *0.40* | 0.20 | 1.00 | 2.00 | *0.60* |
| GER | 1.00 | 1.00 | 2.25 | *3.25* | 1.00 | 1.00 | 2.25 | *3.25* | 1.00 | 1.00 | 2.25 | *3.25* |
| ITA | 0.20 | 1.00 | 2.00 | *0.60* | 0.20 | 1.00 | 2.00 | *0.60* | 0.20 | 1.00 | 2.00 | *0.60* |
| NED | 0.20 | 0.00 | 2.00 | *0.40* | 0.20 | 0.00 | 2.00 | *0.40* | 0.20 | 0.00 | 2.25 | *0.45* |
| SPA | 0.32 | 1.00 | 1.13[b] | *0.68* | 1.00[c] | 1.00 | 1.00 | *2.00* | 0.32 | 1.00 | 1.25 | *0.72* |
| SWI | 0.60 | 1.00 | 2.00 | *1.80* | 0.60 | 1.00 | 2.00 | *1.80* | 0.60 | 1.00 | 2.00 | *1.80* |
| USA | 0.60 | 1.00 | 2.25 | *1.95* | 0.60 | 1.00 | 2.25 | *1.95* | 0.60 | 1.00 | 2.25 | *1.95* |

| | National finan. legisl. | | | | National non-finan. legisl. | | | | All[a] |
|---|---|---|---|---|---|---|---|---|---|
| | Form | Legis. init. | Veto | *Total* | Form | Legis. init. | Veto | *Total* | |
| | (0-1) | (0-1) | (0-3) | *(0-4)* | (0-1) | (0-1) | (0-3) | *(0-4)* | *(0-4)* |
| AUS | 0.00 | 0.00 | 0.00 | *0.00* | 0.60 | 1.00 | 2.00 | *1.80* | **1.50** |
| AUT | 0.00 | 0.00 | 0.00 | *0.00* | 0.80 | 1.00 | 1.00 | *1.60* | **1.68** |
| BEL | 0.00 | 0.20 | 0.00 | *0.00* | 0.49 | 1.00 | 1.00 | *0.98* | **1.22** |
| CAN | 0.40 | 0.00 | 0.00 | *0.00* | 1.40 | 1.00 | 0.00 | *0.40* | **0.33** |
| FRA | 0.20 | 0.00 | 1.00 | *0.20* | 0.20 | 1.00 | 1.00 | *0.40* | **0.40** |
| GER | 1.00 | 0.00 | 1.55[b] | *1.55* | 1.00 | 1.00 | 1.55[b] | *2.55* | **2.85** |
| ITA | 0.20 | 1.00 | 2.00 | *0.60* | 0.20 | 1.00 | 2.00 | *0.60* | **0.60** |
| NED | 0.20 | 0.00 | 2.00 | *0.40* | 0.20 | 0.00 | 2.00 | *0.40* | **0.41** |
| SPA | 0.32 | 1.00 | 1.00 | *0.64* | 0.32 | 1.00 | 1.00 | *0.64* | **1.00** |
| SWI | 0.60 | 1.00 | 2.00 | *1.80* | 0.60 | 1.00 | 2.00 | *1.80* | **1.80** |
| USA | 0.60 | 0.00 | 2.00 | *1.20* | 0.60 | 1.00 | 2.00 | *1.80* | **1.80** |

Note: [a] mean value of the average degree of participation in the assignment of competencies and the average degree of participation in other issues of national legislation. [b] these are average veto power scores which represent different decision-making procedures according to the issues involved. Germany: on average 55% of ordinary laws had to be approved by the regional chamber in the past (score 2.0). Spain: mean value considering that a veto of the upper chamber can be overridden by a two-thirds majority in the lower chamber in case of provisions stipulated in the constitution (score 1.25), and by simple majority in case of provisions laid down by simple law (score 1.0). [c] the value of 1.0 is assigned to the form of representation in Austria and Spain, since sub-central governments negotiate the distribution of funds and taxing powers directly with the central government.

Table B.16: Direct participation of subnational entities in central decision-making, 2003

| | Assignment expen. powers | | | | Assignment revenue powers | | | | Const. amendm. (not concerning subn. ent.) | | | |
|---|---|---|---|---|---|---|---|---|---|---|---|---|
| | Form | Legis. init. | Veto | *Total* | Form | Legis. init. | Veto | *Total* | Form | Legis. init. | Veto | *Total* |
| | (0-1) | (0-1) | (0-3) | *(0-4)* | (0-1) | (0-1) | (0-3) | *(0-4)* | (0-1) | (0-1) | (0-3) | *(0-4)* |
| AUS | 1.00 | 0.00 | 2.00 | *2.00* | 1.00 | 0.00 | 2.00 | *2.00* | 1.00 | 0.00 | 2.00 | *2.00* |
| AUT | 0.00 | 0.00 | 0.00 | *0.00* | 0.00 | 0.00 | 0.00 | *0.00* | 0.00 | 0.00 | 0.00 | *0.00* |
| BEL | 0.00 | 0.00 | 0.00 | *0.00* | 0.00 | 0.00 | 0.00 | *0.00* | 0.00 | 0.00 | 0.00 | *0.00* |
| CAN | 0.50 | 1.00 | 3.00[c] | *2.00* | 0.50 | 1.00 | 3.00[c] | *2.00* | 0.00 | 0.00 | 0.00 | *0.00* |
| FRA | 0.00 | 0.00 | 0.00 | *0.00* | 0.00 | 0.00 | 0.00 | *0.00* | 0.00 | 0.00 | 0.00 | *0.00* |
| GER | 0.00 | 0.00 | 0.00 | *0.00* | 0.00 | 0.00 | 0.00 | *0.00* | 0.00 | 0.00 | 0.00 | *0.00* |
| ITA | 0.00 | 0.00 | 0.00 | *0.00* | 0.50 | 1.00 | 0.00 | *0.50* | 0.00 | 0.00 | 0.00 | *0.00* |
| NED | 0.00 | 0.00 | 0.00 | *0.00* | 0.00 | 0.00 | 0.00 | *0.00* | 0.00 | 0.00 | 0.00 | *0.00* |
| SPA | 0.63[b] | 1.00 | 1.50[b] | *1.63*[b] | 0.00 | 0.00 | 0.00 | *0.00* | 0.50 | 1.00 | 0.00 | *0.50* |
| SWI | 1.00 | 0.00 | 2.00 | *2.00* | 1.00 | 0.00 | 2.00 | *2.00* | 1.00 | 0.00 | 2.00 | *2.00* |
| USA | 0.50 | 0.33 | 2.50 | *1.42* | 0.50 | 0.33 | 2.50 | *1.42* | 0.50 | 0.33 | 2.50 | *1.42* |

| | National finan. legisl. | | | | National non-finan. legisl. | | | | All[a] |
|---|---|---|---|---|---|---|---|---|---|
| | Form | Legis. init. | Veto | *Total* | Form | Legis. init. | Veto | *Total* | |
| | (0-1) | (0-1) | (0-3) | *(0-4)* | (0-1) | (0-1) | (0-3) | *(0-4)* | *(0-4)* |
| AUS | 0.00 | 0.00 | 0.00 | *0.00* | 0.00 | 0.00 | 0.00 | *0.00* | ***1.33*** |
| AUT | 0.00 | 0.00 | 0.00 | *0.00* | 0.00 | 0.00 | 0.00 | *0.00* | ***0.00*** |
| BEL | 0.00 | 0.00 | 0.00 | *0.00* | 0.00 | 0.00 | 0.00 | *0.00* | ***0.00*** |
| CAN | 0.00 | 0.00 | 0.00 | *0.00* | 0.00 | 0.00 | 0.00 | *0.00* | ***1.00*** |
| FRA | 0.00 | 0.00 | 0.00 | *0.00* | 0.00 | 0.00 | 0.00 | *0.00* | ***0.00*** |
| GER | 0.00 | 0.00 | 0.00 | *0.00* | 0.00 | 0.00 | 0.00 | *0.00* | ***0.00*** |
| ITA | 0.00 | 0.00 | 0.00 | *0.00* | 0.50 | 1.00 | 0.00 | *0.50* | ***0.21*** |
| NED | 0.00 | 0.00 | 0.00 | *0.00* | 0.00 | 0.00 | 0.00 | *0.00* | ***0.00*** |
| SPA | 0.00 | 0.00 | 0.00 | *0.00* | 0.50 | 1.00 | 0.00 | *0.50* | ***0.57*** |
| SWI | 0.75[b] | 1.00 | 1.00[b] | *1.75*[b] | 0.75[b] | 1.00 | 1.00[b] | *1.75*[b] | ***1.92*** |
| USA | 0.00 | 0.00 | 0.00 | *0.00* | 0.00 | 0.00 | 0.00 | *0.00* | ***0.95*** |

Note: [a] mean value of the average degree of participation in the assignment of competencies and the average degree of participation in other issues of national legislation. [b] average scores which represent different decision-making procedures. Spain: mean value considering that in certain regions changes of the autonomy statute are approved by the legislature and the regional voters (form 0.75, veto 2.0), and, otherwise, the regional legislatures have only a suspensive veto (form 0.5, veto 1.0), the ultimate decision having the national parliament. Switzerland: the indices for national legislation equally take into account that cantonal legislatures have the power to initiate national legislation (form 0.5, veto 0) and that a double majority of the electorate at the national and the cantonal level is required in referendums on certain bills (form 1.0, veto power 2.0). [c] Provinces in Canada are assigned the maximum veto power since they have the right to opt out in case of disagreeing with constitutional amendments concerning them.

Table B.17: Indices of direct democracy at the national level

| | (A) Objects submitted to referendum | Score (0-1) | (B) Power of initiat. | Score (0-1) | (C) Effect of referen. | Score (0-1) |
|---|---|---|---|---|---|---|
| Legisl. | none, ruled out | 0.00 | unanimity | 0 | non-bind. | 0 |
| referen. | specif. ad hoc law, | 0.25 | facultat. referen. | 0-1 | binding | 1 |
| | exceptional cases | | (= 1 – required major. | | | |
| | specif. in constit. | 0.50 | for initiat. national, | | | |
| | all objects | 1.00 | regional parliaments) | | | |
| | | | compulsory referen. | 1 | | |
| Const. | none, ruled out | 0.00 | unanimity | 0 | non-bind. | 0 |
| referen. | specif. ad hoc law, | 0.25 | facultat. referen. | 0-1 | binding | 1 |
| | exceptional cases | | (= 1 – required major. | | | |
| | total const. revision | 0.50 | for initiat. national, | | | |
| | partial const. revis. | 1.00 | regional parliaments) | | | |
| | | | compulsory referen. | 1 | | |
| Legisl. | none, ruled out | 0.00 | none | 0.00 | non-bind. | 0 |
| popular | legisl. petition, no | 0.25 | % of electorate: | | binding | 1 |
| initiat. | compulsory referen. | | >10% | 0.25 | | |
| | specif. in constit. | 0.50 | 5%-10% | 0.50 | | |
| | all objects | 1.00 | 1%-5% | 0.75 | | |
| | | | 0%-1% | 1.00 | | |
| Const. | none, ruled out | 0.00 | none | 0.00 | non-bind. | 0 |
| popular | specif. ad hoc law, | 0.25 | % of electorate: | | binding | 1 |
| initiat. | exceptional cases | | >10% | 0.25 | | |
| | total const. revision | 0.50 | 5%-10% | 0.50 | | |
| | partial const. revis. | 1.00 | 1%-5% | 0.75 | | |
| | | | 0%-1% | 1.00 | | |

The *indices of direct democracy* (0-3) take into account the range of specific objects which can be submitted to a vote, the power of initiation in terms of the legal threshold and the effect of the consultation. In case of various legal provisions falling into the same category, the instrument with the highest score is preferred. With respect to referendums initiated by ad hoc laws, we distinguish whether provisions for the organisation are stipulated in the constitution or not. In case of the first, a higher degree of direct democratic control is assigned by considering additionally the majority needed for initiation; otherwise not.

The extent of direct democratic control is evaluated for each instrument by summing up these three criterions, each being equally weighted: (A)+(B)+(C). The composite index of direct democracy at the national level is then derived as the non weighted average of the six legal instruments considered here.

Table B.18: Direct democracy at the national level (1), 2003

| | Legislative referendum (non-financial) | | | | (financial) | | | | Constitutional referendum | | | |
|---|---|---|---|---|---|---|---|---|---|---|---|---|
| | Object (0-1) | Init. (0-1) | Effect (0-1) | *Total (0-3)* | Object (0-1) | Init. (0-1) | Effect (0-1) | *Total (0-3)* | Object (0-1) | Init. (0-1) | Effect (0-1) | *Total (0-3)* |
| AUS | 0.00 | 0.00 | 0.00 | *0.00* | 0.00 | 0.00 | 0.00 | *0.00* | 1.00 | 1.00 | 1.00 | *3.00* |
| AUT | 1.00 | 0.50 | 1.00 | *2.50* | 1.00 | 0.50 | 1.00 | *2.50* | 1.00 | 0.67 | 1.00 | *2.67* |
| BEL | 0.25 | 0.00 | 0.00 | *0.25* | 0.00 | 0.00 | 0.00 | *0.00* | 0.00 | 0.00 | 0.00 | *0.00* |
| CAN | 0.00 | 0.00 | 0.00 | *0.00* | 0.00 | 0.00 | 0.00 | *0.00* | 0.25 | 0.00 | 0.00 | *0.25* |
| DEN | 1.00 | 0.67 | 1.00 | *2.67* | 0.00 | 0.00 | 0.00 | *0.00* | 1.00 | 1.00 | 1.00 | *3.00* |
| FIN | 0.25 | 0.50 | 0.00 | *0.75* | 0.25 | 0.50 | 0.00 | *0.75* | 0.00 | 0.00 | 0.00 | *0.00* |
| FRA | 0.50 | 0.00 | 1.00 | *1.50* | 0.00 | 0.00 | 0.00 | *0.00* | 1.00 | 0.00 | 1.00 | *2.00* |
| GER | 0.00 | 0.00 | 0.00 | *0.00* | 0.00 | 0.00 | 0.00 | *0.00* | 0.00 | 0.00 | 0.00 | *0.00* |
| GRE | 0.50 | 0.40 | 1.00 | *1.90* | 0.00 | 0.00 | 0.00 | *0.00* | 0.00 | 0.00 | 0.00 | *0.00* |
| ICL | 0.25 | 1.00 | 1.00 | *2.25* | 0.00 | 0.00 | 0.00 | *0.00* | 0.25 | 1.00 | 1.00 | *2.25* |
| IRL | 0.50 | 0.50 | 1.00 | *2.00* | 0.00 | 0.00 | 0.00 | *0.00* | 1.00 | 1.00 | 1.00 | *3.00* |
| ITA | 0.50 | 0.75 | 1.00 | *2.25* | 0.00 | 0.00 | 0.00 | *0.00* | 1.00 | 0.67 | 1.00 | *2.67* |
| JAP | 0.00 | 0.00 | 0.00 | *0.00* | 0.00 | 0.00 | 5.00 | *0.00* | 1.00 | 1.00 | 1.00 | *3.00* |
| LUX | 0.25 | 0.50 | 0.00 | *0.75* | 0.00 | 0.00 | 0.00 | *0.00* | 0.00 | 0.00 | 0.00 | *0.00* |
| NED | 0.00 | 0.00 | 0.00 | *0.00* | 0.00 | 0.00 | 0.00 | *0.00* | 0.00 | 0.00 | 0.00 | *0.00* |
| NEZ | 0.50 | 1.00 | 1.00 | *2.50* | 0.00 | 0.00 | 0.00 | *0.00* | 0.00 | 0.00 | 0.00 | *0.00* |
| NOR | 0.25 | 0.50 | 0.00 | *0.75* | 0.00 | 0.00 | 0.00 | *0.00* | 0.00 | 0.00 | 0.00 | *0.00* |
| POR | 0.50 | 0.00 | 1.00 | *1.50* | 0.00 | 0.00 | 0.00 | *0.00* | 0.00 | 0.00 | 0.00 | *0.00* |
| SPA | 0.50 | 0.50 | 0.00 | *1.00* | 0.00 | 0.00 | 0.00 | *0.00* | 1.00 | 0.90 | 1.00 | *2.90* |
| SWE | 0.25 | 0.50 | 0.00 | *0.75* | 0.25 | 0.50 | 0.00 | *0.75* | 1.00 | 0.67 | 1.00 | *2.67* |
| SWI | 1.00 | 0.69 | 1.00 | *2.69* | 1.00 | 0.69 | 1.00 | *2.69* | 1.00 | 1.00 | 1.00 | *3.00* |
| UK | 0.25 | 0.00 | 0.00 | *0.25* | 0.00 | 0.00 | 0.00 | *0.00* | 0.00 | 0.00 | 0.00 | *0.00* |
| USA | 0.00 | 0.00 | 0.00 | *0.00* | 0.00 | 0.00 | 0.00 | *0.00* | 0.00 | 0.00 | 0.00 | *0.00* |

Table B.19: Direct democracy at the national level (2), 2003

| | Legislative popular initiative (non-financial) | | | | (financial) | | | | Constit. pop. initiative | | | | All[a] | Practice[b] |
|---|---|---|---|---|---|---|---|---|---|---|---|---|---|---|
| | Object (0-1) | Init. (0-1) | Effect (0-1) | *Total (0-3)* | Object (0-1) | Init. (0-1) | Effect (0-1) | *Total (0-3)* | Object (0-1) | Init. (0-1) | Effect (0-1) | *Total (0-3)* | *(0-3)* | |
| AUS | 0.00 | 0.00 | 0.00 | *0.00* | 0.00 | 0.00 | 0.00 | *0.00* | 0.00 | 0.00 | 0.00 | *0.00* | ***0.50*** | 0.58 |
| AUT | 0.25 | 0.75 | 0.00 | *1.00* | 0.25 | 0.75 | 0.00 | *1.00* | 0.00 | 0.00 | 0.00 | *0.00* | ***1.61*** | 0.06 |
| BEL | 0.00 | 0.00 | 0.00 | *0.00* | 0.00 | 0.00 | 0.00 | *0.00* | 0.00 | 0.00 | 0.00 | *0.00* | ***0.04*** | 0.00 |
| CAN | 0.00 | 0.00 | 0.00 | *0.00* | 0.00 | 0.00 | 0.00 | *0.00* | 0.00 | 0.00 | 0.00 | *0.00* | ***0.04*** | 0.03 |
| DEN | 0.00 | 0.00 | 0.00 | *0.00* | 0.00 | 0.00 | 0.00 | *0.00* | 0.00 | 0.00 | 0.00 | *0.00* | ***0.95*** | 0.24 |
| FIN | 0.00 | 0.00 | 0.00 | *0.00* | 0.00 | 0.00 | 0.00 | *0.00* | 0.00 | 0.00 | 0.00 | *0.00* | ***0.25*** | 0.03 |
| FRA | 0.00 | 0.00 | 0.00 | *0.00* | 0.00 | 0.00 | 0.00 | *0.00* | 0.00 | 0.00 | 0.00 | *0.00* | ***0.58*** | 0.12 |
| GER | 0.00 | 0.00 | 0.00 | *0.00* | 0.00 | 0.00 | 0.00 | *0.00* | 0.00 | 0.00 | 0.00 | *0.00* | ***0.00*** | 0.00 |
| GRE | 0.00 | 0.00 | 0.00 | *0.00* | 0.00 | 0.00 | 0.00 | *0.00* | 0.00 | 0.00 | 0.00 | *0.00* | ***0.32*** | 0.07 |
| ICL | 0.00 | 0.00 | 0.00 | *0.00* | 0.00 | 0.00 | 0.00 | *0.00* | 0.00 | 0.00 | 0.00 | *0.00* | ***0.75*** | 0.00 |
| IRL | 0.00 | 0.00 | 0.00 | *0.00* | 0.00 | 0.00 | 0.00 | *0.00* | 0.00 | 0.00 | 0.00 | *0.00* | ***0.83*** | 0.73 |
| ITA | 0.50 | 0.75 | 1.00 | *2.25* | 0.00 | 0.00 | 0.00 | *0.00* | 1.00 | 0.67 | 1.00 | *2.67* | ***1.64*** | 1.67 |
| JAP | 0.00 | 0.00 | 0.00 | *0.00* | 0.00 | 0.00 | 0.00 | *0.00* | 0.00 | 0.00 | 0.00 | *0.00* | ***0.50*** | 0.00 |
| LUX | 0.00 | 0.00 | 0.00 | *0.00* | 0.00 | 0.00 | 0.00 | *0.00* | 0.00 | 0.00 | 0.00 | *0.00* | ***0.13*** | 0.00 |
| NED | 0.00 | 0.00 | 0.00 | *0.00* | 0.00 | 0.00 | 0.00 | *0.00* | 0.00 | 0.00 | 0.00 | *0.00* | ***0.00*** | 0.00 |
| NEZ | 1.00 | 0.50 | 0.00 | *1.50* | 0.00 | 0.00 | 0.00 | *0.00* | 0.00 | 0.00 | 0.00 | *0.00* | ***0.67*** | 0.46 |
| NOR | 0.00 | 0.00 | 0.00 | *0.00* | 0.00 | 0.00 | 0.00 | *0.00* | 0.00 | 0.00 | 0.00 | *0.00* | ***0.13*** | 0.06 |
| POR | 0.50 | 0.00 | 1.00 | *1.50* | 0.00 | 0.00 | 0.00 | *0.00* | 0.00 | 0.00 | 0.00 | *0.00* | ***0.50*** | 0.11 |
| SPA | 0.25 | 0.75 | 0.00 | *1.00* | 0.00 | 0.00 | 0.00 | *0.00* | 0.00 | 0.00 | 0.00 | *0.00* | ***0.82*** | 0.11 |
| SWE | 0.00 | 0.00 | 0.00 | *0.00* | 0.00 | 0.00 | 0.00 | *0.00* | 0.00 | 0.00 | 0.00 | *0.00* | ***0.70*** | 0.06 |
| SWI | 1.00 | 0.75 | 1.00 | *2.75* | 1.00 | 0.75 | 1.00 | *2.75* | 1.00 | 0.75 | 1.00 | *2.75* | ***2.77*** | 8.42 |
| UK | 0.00 | 0.00 | 0.00 | *0.00* | 0.00 | 0.00 | 0.00 | *0.00* | 0.00 | 0.00 | 0.00 | *0.00* | ***0.04*** | 0.03 |
| USA | 0.00 | 0.00 | 0.00 | *0.00* | 0.00 | 0.00 | 0.00 | *0.00* | 0.00 | 0.00 | 0.00 | *0.00* | ***0.00*** | 0.00 |

Note: [a] average score of the six indices. [b] average number of referendums per year (1970-2002).

Table B.20: OLS estimates of fiscal decentralisation, self-financed expenditure (incl. social security), 23 OECD countries, 1970-2001

| | Dep. var.: Degree of expen. decentralisation (indic. ED2) | | | | | | |
|---|---|---|---|---|---|---|---|
| | (1) | (2) | (3) | (4) | (5) | (6) | (7) |
| *Population* | -.022*** | -.015** | -.012*** | -.020*** | -.016*** | -.023*** | -.030*** |
| | (.006) | (.007) | (.004) | (.005) | (.005) | (.005) | (.004) |
| *Area* | .037*** | .043*** | .026*** | .031*** | .025*** | .034*** | .026*** |
| | (.006) | (.005) | (.005) | (.006) | (.006) | (.006) | (.005) |
| *Urbanisation* | -.331*** | -.384*** | -.263*** | -.391*** | -.366*** | -.347*** | -.414*** |
| | (.062) | (.074) | (.053) | (.061) | (.064) | (.069) | (.074) |
| *Fractionalisation* | .218*** | .215*** | .203*** | .170*** | .151*** | .181*** | .221*** |
| | (.046) | (.040) | (.032) | (.034) | (.040) | (.047) | (.051) |
| *Regional disparity* | .203** | .111 | -.027 | .003 | .036 | .085 | .162** |
| | (.090) | (.087) | (.071) | (.080) | (.085) | (.079) | (.072) |
| *Per capita income* | .192*** | .207*** | .101*** | .146*** | .150*** | .146*** | .131*** |
| | (.024) | (.033) | (.028) | (.026) | (.026) | (.026) | (.028) |
| *Catholic* | -.117*** | -.115*** | -.168*** | -.156*** | -.156*** | -.141*** | -.198*** |
| | (.029) | (.023) | (.026) | (.022) | (.023) | (.023) | (.033) |
| *Legal origin* | .065** | .047 | -.022 | .018 | .007 | .022 | .013 |
| | (.027) | (.029) | (.016) | (.019) | (.018) | (.020) | (.018) |
| *Dependency ratio* | .225 | .556 | .463 | .456 | .575* | .464 | .198 |
| | (.413) | (.469) | (.312) | (.348) | (.342) | (.355) | (.333) |
| *Growth rate* | -.258 | -.285* | -.112 | -.173 | -.121 | -.161 | -.080 |
| | (.175) | (.157) | (.105) | (.121) | (.117) | (.123) | (.109) |
| *Election* | -.006 | -.004 | -.008** | -.010*** | -.010*** | -.009** | -.007* |
| | (.004) | (.004) | (.003) | (.004) | (.003) | (.004) | (.004) |
| *Left government* | .029* | .017 | .004 | .004 | .001 | .004 | .002 |
| | (.016) | (.016) | (.013) | (.014) | (.014) | (.014) | (.014) |
| *Presidential regime* | | -.088*** | -.053*** | -.074*** | -.065*** | -.073*** | -.082*** |
| | | (.025) | (.019) | (.020) | (.020) | (.020) | (.020) |
| *Electoral system* | | | | | | | .843*** |
| | | | | | | | (.202) |
| *Direct democracy* | | .002 | -.012 | -.020* | -.028*** | -.028** | -.029 |
| | | (.016) | (.009) | (.011) | (.011) | (.013) | (.013) |
| *Federal* | | | .163*** | | | | |
| | | | (.016) | | | | |
| *Subnat. represent.* | | | | .105*** | | | |
| | | | | (.014) | | | |
| *Subnat. particip.*[a] | | | | | .059*** | .043** | .028 |
| *(direct)* | | | | | (.009) | (.019) | (.020) |
| *Subnat. particip.*[a] | | | | | .043*** | .058*** | .081*** |
| *(indirect)* | | | | | (.008) | (.009) | (.010) |
| No. obs. | 483 | 483 | 483 | 483 | 483 | 483 | 483 |
| adj. $R^2$ | .666 | .703 | .838 | .802 | .810 | .798 | .816 |

Note: See Table 3.2 for further details.

Table B.21: Alternative OLS estimates of fiscal decentralisation, direct expenditure (incl. social security), 23 OECD countries, 1970-2001

| | Dep. var.: Degree of expenditure decentralisation (indic. ED1) | | | | | | | |
|---|---|---|---|---|---|---|---|---|
| | (1) | (2) | (3) | (4) | (5) | (6) | (7) | (8) |
| *Popul.* | -.004 | -.006 | -.006 | -.007 | -.004 | -.011*** | -.007 | -.006 |
| | (.006) | (.006) | (.006) | (.006) | (.006) | (.004) | (.005) | (.006) |
| *Area* | .028*** | .027*** | .039*** | .038*** | .036*** | .017*** | .033*** | .026*** |
| | (.005) | (.006) | (.005) | (.005) | (.006) | (.005) | (.006) | (.006) |
| *Urban.* | -.218*** | -.246*** | -.178*** | -.239*** | -.364*** | -.448*** | -.305*** | -.238*** |
| | (.074) | (.077) | (.069) | (.070) | (.059) | (.078) | (.075) | (.077) |
| *Fract.* | .070 | .069 | .128*** | .106*** | .154*** | .141*** | .192*** | .069 |
| | (.043) | (.042) | (.036) | (.041) | (.037) | (.036) | (.048) | (.045) |
| *Reg.disp.* | .298* | .224** | .212** | .243*** | .165 | .148* | .207** | .229** |
| | (.157) | (.102) | (.088) | (.089) | (.116) | (.084) | (.096) | (.091) |
| *P.c.inc.* | .114*** | .144*** | .137*** | .168*** | .196*** | .158*** | .161*** | .145*** |
| | (.038) | (.027) | (.030) | (.026) | (.023) | (.028) | (.032) | (.028) |
| *Catholic* | -.154*** | -.150*** | -.155*** | -.137*** | -.149*** | -.246*** | -.184*** | -.149*** |
| | (.031) | (.029) | (.027) | (.028) | (.031) | (.029) | (.030) | (.032) |
| *Legal* | .019 | .041 | .059*** | .067*** | .067** | .095*** | .081*** | .042* |
| | (.033) | (.026) | (.023) | (.023) | (.027) | (.022) | (.026) | (.023) |
| *Depen.* | -.841* | -.692* | -1.028*** | -.849** | -.625* | -.561 | -.798* | -.699* |
| | (.432) | (.401) | (.363) | (.388) | (.370) | (.399) | (.418) | (.394) |
| *Growth* | -.097 | -.076 | -.054 | -.141 | -.257* | -.071 | -.179 | -.081 |
| | (.145) | (.136) | (.142) | (.140) | (.139) | (.125) | (.132) | (.138) |
| *Elect.* | -.008** | -.008* | -.005 | -.005 | -.005 | -.005 | -.005 | -.008* |
| | (.004) | (.004) | (.004) | (.004) | (.004) | (.004) | (.004) | (.004) |
| *Left* | .032** | .031** | .030* | .037** | .038** | .032** | .030* | .030** |
| | (.015) | (.015) | (.016) | (.016) | (.016) | (.015) | (.016) | (.015) |

Table B.21 (cont.): Alternative OLS estimates of fiscal decentralisation

| | Dep. var.: Degree of expenditure decentralisation (indic. ED1) | | | | | | | |
|---|---|---|---|---|---|---|---|---|
| | (1) | (2) | (3) | (4) | (5) | (6) | (7) | (8) |
| *Mobil.* | .002 | | | | | | | |
| | (.002) | | | | | | | |
| *Gov.frag.* | | .008 | | | | | | |
| | | (.034) | | | | | | |
| *Presid.* | -.093*** | -.093*** | -.087*** | -.095*** | -.112*** | -.109*** | -.088*** | -.090*** |
| | (.025) | (.027) | (.022) | (.022) | (.019) | (.023) | (.025) | (.026) |
| *Major.* | | | | | | | | -.003 |
| | | | | | | | | (.025) |
| *Dir.dem.*[a] | -.014 | -.021 | .042*** | | | -.023 | .011 | -.020 |
| | (.018) | (.016) | (.012) | | | (.015) | (.013) | (.014) |
| *Refer.*[b] | | | | .010** | -.015 | | | |
| | | | | (.004) | (.024) | | | |
| *Reg.parl.*[c] | | | | | | .127*** | .064*** | |
| | | | | | | (.019) | (.022) | |
| No. obs. | 475 | 482 | 482 | 482 | 482 | 482 | 482 | 482 |
| adj. $R^2$ | .782 | .779 | .753 | .743 | .737 | .793 | .749 | .779 |

Note: See Table 3.2 for details. Different specifications: [a] average of the indices of referendums and popular initiatives on financial matters at the national level (3); [b] average number of referendums per year during 1970-2002 (4), and dummy variable for legal provisions concerning the conduct of national referendums on constitutional and legislative issues (5); [c] dummy variable for upper chamber of parliament consisting either of representatives elected or delegated on a regional basis no matter whether they represent the subnational entities (6), or only of representatives of the subnational entities delegated by the regional governments or legislatures (7).

Table B.22: Alternative OLS estimates of fiscal decentralisation, tax revenue, 23 OECD countries, 1965-2001

| | Dep. var.: Degree of tax decentralisation (indic. TD1) | | | | | | | |
|---|---|---|---|---|---|---|---|---|
| | (1) | (2) | (3) | (4) | (5) | (6) | (7) | (8) |
| *Popul.* | -.003 | -.007 | -.020*** | -.025*** | -.017*** | -.016*** | -.014*** | -.002 |
| | (.005) | (.005) | (.006) | (.006) | (.006) | (.005) | (.005) | (.005) |
| *Area* | .029*** | .026*** | .049*** | .052*** | .046*** | .050*** | .046*** | .030*** |
| | (.006) | (.006) | (.005) | (.006) | (.006) | (.006) | (.006) | (.006) |
| *Urban.* | -.337*** | -.256*** | -.324*** | -.234*** | -.539*** | -.440*** | -.493*** | -.302*** |
| | (.073) | (.068) | (.084) | (.080) | (.067) | (.087) | (.077) | (.074) |
| *Fract.* | .185*** | .204*** | .398*** | .312*** | .433*** | .434*** | .352*** | .195*** |
| | (.056) | (.053) | (.058) | (.058) | (.054) | (.050) | (.052) | (.055) |
| *Reg.disp.* | .137 | .144 | -.023 | .043 | -.083 | .014 | .041 | .073 |
| | (.108) | (.088) | (.086) | (.088) | (.107) | (.091) | (.086) | (.086) |
| *P.c.inc.* | .238*** | .240*** | .188*** | .181*** | .249*** | .240*** | .264*** | .236*** |
| | (.032) | (.025) | (.027) | (.025) | (.025) | (.028) | (.029) | (.024) |
| *Catholic* | -.115*** | -.130*** | -.205*** | -.168*** | -.203*** | -.190*** | -.172*** | -.127*** |
| | (.026) | (.026) | (.033) | (.030) | (.033) | (.036) | (.030) | (.027) |
| *Legal* | -.016 | -.049*** | .030 | .027 | .034 | .039 | .036 | -.040* |
| | (.024) | (.018) | (.021) | (.024) | (.026) | (.027) | (.027) | (.023) |
| *Depen.* | 1.323*** | 1.239*** | .773* | .656 | 1.203*** | 1.078** | 1.198*** | 1.337*** |
| | (.377) | (.348) | (.402) | (.409) | (.384) | (.439) | (.419) | (.359) |
| *Growth* | -.219* | -.317** | -.229 | -.208 | -.468** | -.458** | -.497*** | -.292** |
| | (.129) | (.130) | (.168) | (.169) | (.185) | (.188) | (.184) | (.128) |
| *Elect.* | -.003 | -.002 | -.003 | -.003 | -.002 | -.002 | -.001 | -.002 |
| | (.004) | (.004) | (.004) | (.004) | (.004) | (.005) | (.004) | (.004) |
| *Left* | -.008 | .020 | -.026 | -.016 | -.016 | -.017 | -.008 | -.008 |
| | (.014) | (.014) | (.016) | (.017) | (.016) | (.016) | (.015) | (.014) |

Table B.22 (cont.): Alternative OLS estimates of fiscal decentralisation

| | Dep. var.: Degree of tax decentralisation (indic. TD1) | | | | | | | |
|---|---|---|---|---|---|---|---|---|
| | (1) | (2) | (3) | (4) | (5) | (6) | (7) | (8) |
| *Mobil.* | .000 | | | | | | | |
| | (.001) | | | | | | | |
| *Gov.frag.* | | -.084*** | | | | | | |
| | | (.030) | | | | | | |
| *Presid.* | -.516*** | -.030 | -.041** | -.028 | -.070*** | -.056*** | -.081*** | -.050*** |
| | (.017) | (.019) | (.020) | (.020) | (.018) | (.019) | (.019) | (.018) |
| *Major.* | | | | | | | | .000 |
| | | | | | | | | (.025) |
| *Dir.dem.*[a] | -.029* | -.027** | -.047*** | | | .021 | -.011 | -.035*** |
| | (.015) | (.013) | (.016) | | | (.017) | (.014) | (.013) |
| *Refer.*[b] | | | | .025*** | -.018 | | | |
| | | | | (.004) | (.021) | | | |
| *Reg.parl.*[c] | | | | | | .038* | -.123*** | |
| | | | | | | (.021) | (.020) | |
| No. obs. | 538 | 549 | 549 | 549 | 549 | 549 | 549 | 549 |
| adj. $R^2$ | .848 | .854 | .768 | .786 | .753 | .756 | .781 | .847 |

Note: See Table 3.3 for details. Different specifications: [a] average of the indices of referendums and popular initiatives on financial matters at the national level (3); [b] average number of referendums per year during 1970-2002 (4), and dummy variable for legal provisions concerning the conduct of national referendums on constitutional and legislative issues (5); [c] dummy variable for upper chamber of parliament consisting either of representatives elected or delegated on a regional basis no matter whether they represent the subnational entities (6), or only of representatives of the subnational entities delegated by the regional governments or legislatures (7).

Table B.23: OLS estimates of fiscal decentralisation (institutions 1), tax revenue, 3-year-averages, 23 OECD countries, 1965-2001

| | Dep. var.: Degree of tax decentralisation | | | | | | | |
|---|---|---|---|---|---|---|---|---|
| | Total tax revenue (TD3) | | | | Auton. own tax rev. (TD1) | | | |
| | (1) | (2) | (3) | (4) | (5) | (6) | (7) | (8) |
| *Population* | -.013 | -.004 | .001 | -.008 | -.023* | -.019 | -.018 | -.019 |
| | (.017) | (.016) | (.013) | (.016) | (.013) | (.012) | (.012) | (.013) |
| *Area* | .040** | .047*** | .028* | .034* | .041*** | .045*** | .043*** | .045*** |
| | (.016) | (.015) | (.016) | (.018) | (.014) | (.013) | (.015) | (.014) |
| *Urbanisation* | -.412** | -.480** | -.333** | -.497*** | -.467** | -.472*** | -.456*** | -.472*** |
| | (.193) | (.188) | (.152) | (.168) | (.180) | (.165) | (.156) | (.167) |
| *Fractionalis.* | .295* | .280** | .222** | .213* | .450*** | .434*** | .427*** | .433*** |
| | (.147) | (.117) | (.101) | (.120) | (.139) | (.123) | (.130) | (.133) |
| *Reg. disparity* | .346 | .210 | .042 | .071 | .076 | .015 | -.003 | .012 |
| | (.220) | (.173) | (.156) | (.174) | (.177) | (.161) | (.156) | (.160) |
| *P.c. income* | .280*** | .299*** | .201*** | .247*** | .232*** | .234*** | .224*** | .233*** |
| | (.068) | (.083) | (.059) | (.064) | (.068) | (.066) | (.061) | (.061) |
| *Catholic* | -.120 | -.116* | -.140** | -.142** | -.213** | -.212*** | -.215** | -.213** |
| | (.074) | (.056) | (.062) | (.054) | (.078) | (.075) | (.077) | (.076) |
| *Legal origin* | .009 | -.016 | -.094** | -.050 | .054 | .043 | .035 | .042 |
| | (.068) | (.069) | (.041) | (.050) | (.055) | (.055) | (.051) | (.052) |
| *Depen. ratio* | .798 | 1.213 | 1.192* | 1.316* | .988 | 1.146* | 1.144* | 1.148* |
| | (.747) | (.816) | (.686) | (.764) | (.621) | (.593) | (.583) | (.608) |
| *Growth rate* | -.433 | -.453 | -.134 | -.227 | -.356 | -.334 | -.300 | -.330 |
| | (.332) | (.348) | (.209) | (.245) | (.300) | (.294) | (.241) | (.255) |
| *Election* | .010 | .011 | -.006 | -.004 | .003 | .004 | .002 | .003 |
| | (.011) | (.010) | (.010) | (.009) | (.008) | (.009) | (.009) | (.009) |
| *Left govern.* | .028 | .013 | -.007 | -.005 | -.009 | -.018 | -.020 | -.018 |
| | (.025) | (.027) | (.023) | (.023) | (.020) | (.023) | (.021) | (.020) |
| *Presid. regime* | | -.110* | -.080* | -.105** | | -.056 | -.053 | -.056 |
| | | (.059) | (.041) | (.049) | | (.037) | (.191) | (.037) |
| *Dir. democracy* | | .003 | -.020 | -.030 | | .011 | .008 | .010 |
| | | (.046) | (.031) | (.036) | | (.037) | (.039) | (.042) |
| *Federal* | | | .201*** | | | | .022 | |
| | | | (.047) | | | | (.062) | |
| *Subnat. repres.* | | | | .125** | | | | .002 |
| | | | | (.047) | | | | (.047) |
| No. obs. | 186 | 186 | 186 | 186 | 186 | 186 | 186 | 186 |
| adj. $R^2$ | .605 | .639 | .766 | .720 | .726 | .737 | .737 | .736 |

Note: Robust heteroscedasticity consistent standard errors (White) accounting for the clustering of observations are in parentheses. The degree of tax decentralisation is measured as the share of sub-central government total tax revenue, and, alternatively, autonomous own tax revenue, in consolidated general government tax revenue, excluding social security (source: OECD, Revenue Statistics, own calculations, see Table 2.3). See Table 3.3 for further details.

Table B.24: OLS estimates of fiscal decentralisation (institutions 2), tax revenue, 3-year-averages, 23 OECD countries, 1965-2001

| | Dep. var.: Degree of tax decentralisation | | | | | | | |
|---|---|---|---|---|---|---|---|---|
| | Total tax revenue (TD3) | | | | Auton. own tax rev. (TD1) | | | |
| | (1) | (2) | (3) | (4) | (5) | (6) | (7) | (8) |
| *Population* | -.010 | -.011 | -.020 | .003 | -.002 | -.003 | -.006 | -.012 |
| | (.014) | (.147) | (.014) | (.017) | (.011) | (.010) | (.010) | (.013) |
| *Area* | .030 | .036* | .027 | .027 | .026 | .030** | .027** | .024 |
| | (.019) | (.019) | (.016) | (.020) | (.017) | (.012) | (.012) | (.016) |
| *Urbanisation* | -.454** | -.435** | -.508** | -.312 | -.296* | -.287* | -.313* | -.294* |
| | (.209) | (.197) | (.208) | (.209) | (.149) | (.142) | (.153) | (.147) |
| *Fractionalis.* | .227 | .212 | .297 | .088 | .223 | .199 | .210 | .230 |
| | (.180) | (.171) | (.193) | (.172) | (.158) | (.125) | (.129) | (.140) |
| *Reg. disparity* | .168 | .178 | .297 | .262 | .019 | .109 | .151 | .070 |
| | (.177) | (.186) | (.193) | (.172) | (.145) | (.129) | (.135) | (.154) |
| *P.c. income* | .240*** | .242*** | .243*** | .241*** | .219*** | .235*** | .236*** | .172*** |
| | (.067) | (.065) | (.067) | (.069) | (.058) | (.050) | (.052) | (.055) |
| *Catholic* | -.144** | -.125* | -.181** | -.061 | -.145** | -.128** | -.148** | -.153** |
| | (.067) | (.062) | (.084) | (.061) | (.063) | (.054) | (.069) | (.070) |
| *Legal origin* | -.049 | -.052 | -.060 | -.089 | -.047 | -.042 | -.045 | -.035 |
| | (.056) | (.049) | (.042) | (.059) | (.039) | (.031) | (.029) | (.046) |
| *Depen. ratio* | 1.499* | 1.323 | 1.014 | 1.050 | 1.351* | 1.339** | 1.228* | .972 |
| | (.734) | (.786) | (.797) | (.783) | (.655) | (.592) | (.608) | (.583) |
| *Growth rate* | -.250 | -.226 | -.036 | -.299 | -.162 | -.122 | -.053 | -.171 |
| | (.247) | (.240) | (.195) | (.265) | (.188) | (.177) | (.156) | (.203) |
| *Election* | -.002 | -.002 | .008 | .001 | -.001 | .003 | .006 | -.007 |
| | (.009) | (.010) | (.008) | (.010) | (.008) | (.008) | (.007) | (.008) |
| *Left govern.* | -.005 | -.002 | -.007 | .004 | -.003 | -.010 | -.011 | -.027 |
| | (.026) | (.026) | (.024) | (.026) | (.021) | (.019) | (.018) | (.022) |
| *Presid. regime* | -.095* | -.103* | -.115** | -.097 | -.042 | -.046 | -.050 | -.042 |
| | (.052) | (.052) | (.053) | (.059) | (.030) | (.029) | (.030) | (.040) |
| *Electoral system* | | | 1.137* | | | | .409 | |
| | | | (.579) | | | | (.408) | |
| *Dir. democracy* | -.037 | -.044 | -.045 | -.015 | -.014 | -.036 | -.036 | -.008 |
| | (.040) | (.045) | (.041) | (.039) | (.035) | (.029) | (.029) | (.028) |
| *Subnat. part.*[a] | .046 | .067 | .046 | | .117** | .193*** | .185*** | |
| *(direct)* | (.061) | (.076) | (.070) | | (.056) | (.052) | (.051) | |
| *Subnat. part.*[a] | .067*** | .065** | .093*** | | -.031 | -.064*** | -.054** | |
| *(indirect)* | (.023) | (.029) | (.030) | | (.019) | (.016) | (.021) | |
| *Centr. tax comp.* | | | | -.190* | | | | -.202** |
| | | | | (.102) | | | | (.076) |
| No. obs. | 186 | 186 | 186 | 186 | 186 | 186 | 186 | 186 |
| adj. $R^2$ | .728 | .717 | .738 | .686 | .787 | .834 | .836 | .795 |

Note: [a] the following alternative indices have been used: decision-making on assignment of revenue powers (1) and (5), and on all policy areas (2)-(3) and (6)-(7). See Tables 3.3 and B.23 for further details.

Table B.25: Fixed effects (within) estimates, self-financed expenditure (incl. social security), OECD countries, 1970-2001

| | Dep. var.: Degree of expenditure decentralisation (indic. ED2) | | | | | | |
|---|---|---|---|---|---|---|---|
| | (1) | (2) | (3) | (4) | (5) | (6) | (7) |
| *Population* | .040 | .062 | .051 | .030 | .030 | .134* | .105 |
| | (.089) | (.089) | (.090) | (.090) | (.088) | (.077) | (.094) |
| *Urbanisation* | -.137 | -.161* | -.127 | -.134 | -.156* | -.165* | -.110 |
| | (.093) | (.095) | (.091) | (.092) | (.090) | (.099) | (.099) |
| *Regional disparity* | -.203*** | -.197*** | -.213*** | -.203*** | -.185*** | -.139*** | -.173*** |
| | (.058) | (.059) | (.060) | (.059) | (.057) | (.047) | (.055) |
| *Per capita income* | .006 | -.009 | -.007 | .011 | .006 | -.028 | -.008 |
| | (.034) | (.039) | (.036) | (.035) | (.036) | (.032) | (.036) |
| *Growth rate* | -.029 | .007 | -.026 | -.021 | -.000 | -.022 | -.046 |
| | (.063) | (.065) | (.063) | (.064) | (.058) | (.054) | (.062) |
| *Unemployment* | -.352*** | -.305** | -.372*** | -.334*** | -.369*** | -.444*** | -.397*** |
| | (.131) | (.139) | (.121) | (.129) | (.121) | (.119) | (.114) |
| *Election* | -.004** | -.004** | -.004** | -.004** | -.004** | -.004* | -.004** |
| | (.002) | (.002) | (.002) | (.002) | (.002) | (.002) | (.002) |
| *Coldwar* | -.006 | -.006 | -.007 | -.007 | -.007 | -.007 | -.004 |
| | (.006) | (.006) | (.006) | (.006) | (.006) | (.006) | (.006) |
| *Trade openness* | .103** | | .124*** | .105** | -.010 | .079** | .122*** |
| | (.042) | | (.044) | (.042) | (.058) | (.036) | (.044) |
| *Finan. openness* | | .051 | | | | | |
| | | (.045) | | | | | |
| *EU · EU exp.* | .004 | .005 | | | .009** | -.009 | |
| | (.005) | (.006) | | | (.004) | (.013) | |
| *EU trade* | | | .099 | | | | -.135 |
| | | | (.061) | | | | (.130) |
| *EU polit. integr.* | | | | .001 | | | |
| | | | | (.003) | | | |

Table B.25 (cont.): Fixed effects (within) estimates, self-financed expenditure

| | Dep. var.: Degree of expenditure decentralisation (indic. ED2) | | | | | | |
|---|---|---|---|---|---|---|---|
| | (1) | (2) | (3) | (4) | (5) | (6) | (7) |
| *Fractional* · *Trade openness* | | | | | .287* (.153) | | |
| *Fractional* · (*EU* · *EU exp.*) | | | | | | .123*** (.038) | |
| *Fractional* · *EU trade* | | | | | | | .769** (.313) |
| *Referendum* · *Trade openness* | | | | | -.029 (.019) | | |
| *Referendum* · (*EU* · *EU exp.*) | | | | | | -.012 (.014) | |
| *Referendum* · *EU trade* | | | | | | | .014 (.026) |
| *Regional parliam.* · *Trade openness* | | | | | -.149* (.082) | | |
| *Regional parliam.* · (*EU* · *EU exp.*) | | | | | | -.009 (.008) | |
| *Regional parliam.* · *EU trade* | | | | | | | -.032 (.153) |
| No. obs. (countries) | 485 (23) | 458 (22) | 483 (23) | 485 (23) | 485 (23) | 485 (23) | 483 (23) |
| Adj. $R^2$ | .960 | .959 | .960 | .960 | .962 | .965 | .961 |
| Within $R^2$ | .218 | .167 | .224 | .215 | .276 | .319 | .261 |

Note: See Table 4.3 for further details.

Table B.26: Fixed effects (within) estimates, total own revenue (incl. social security), OECD countries, 1970-2001

| | Dep. var.: Degree of revenue decentralisation (indic. RD3) | | | | | | |
|---|---|---|---|---|---|---|---|
| | (1) | (2) | (3) | (4) | (5) | (6) | (7) |
| *Population* | .001 | .049 | .016 | -.010 | -.013 | .088 | .060 |
| | (.097) | (.097) | (.096) | (.096) | (.096) | (.086) | (.098) |
| *Urbanisation* | -.196** | -.223** | -.195** | .189** | -.232*** | -.219** | -.185** |
| | (.087) | (.090) | (.086) | (.087) | (.083) | (.090) | (.091) |
| *Regional disparity* | -.176*** | -.164*** | -.180*** | -.172*** | -.163*** | -.130*** | -.147*** |
| | (.057) | (.057) | (.058) | (.057) | (.056) | (.048) | (.055) |
| *Per capita income* | .019 | -.000 | .008 | .024 | .023 | -.015 | .008 |
| | (.036) | (.038) | (.037) | (.036) | (.038) | (.034) | (.037) |
| *Growth rate* | -.001 | .045 | -.008 | .010 | .013 | .005 | -.023 |
| | (.065) | (.066) | (.066) | (.066) | (.060) | (.057) | (.066) |
| *Unemployment* | .026 | .086 | .002 | .053 | .013 | .060 | .025 |
| | (.113) | (.122) | (.110) | (.110) | (.107) | (.114) | (.107) |
| *Election* | -.003* | -.004** | -.003* | -.003* | -.003* | -.003 | -.003** |
| | (.002) | (.002) | (.002) | (.002) | (.002) | (.002) | (.002) |
| *Coldwar* | -.007 | -.007 | -.007 | -.008 | -.007 | -.008 | -.004 |
| | (.006) | (.006) | (.006) | (.006) | (.006) | (.006) | (.006) |
| *Trade openness* | .107** | | -.115** | .108** | .015 | .083** | .114** |
| | (.043) | | (.048) | (.043) | (.054) | (.037) | (.047) |
| *Finan. openness* | | .055 | | | | | |
| | | (.046) | | | | | |
| *EU · EU exp.* | -.001 | -.001 | | | .003 | -.003 | |
| | (.005) | (.006) | | | (.004) | (.011) | |
| *EU trade* | | | .049 | | | | -.161 |
| | | | (.060) | | | | (.117) |
| *EU polit. integr.* | | | | -.003 | | | |
| | | | | (.002) | | | |

Table B.26 (cont.): Fixed effects (within) estimates, total own revenue

| | Dep. var.: Degree of revenue decentralisation (indic. RD3) | | | | | | |
|---|---|---|---|---|---|---|---|
| | (1) | (2) | (3) | (4) | (5) | (6) | (7) |
| *Fractional* | | | | | .231 | | |
| · *Trade openness* | | | | | (.155) | | |
| *Fractional* | | | | | | .107*** | |
| · (*EU* · *EU exp.*) | | | | | | (.038) | |
| *Fractional* | | | | | | | .639** |
| · *EU trade* | | | | | | | (.294) |
| *Referendum* | | | | | -.009 | | |
| · *Trade openness* | | | | | (.016) | | |
| *Referendum* | | | | | | -.022* | |
| · (*EU* · *EU exp.*) | | | | | | (.013) | |
| *Referendum* | | | | | | | .026 |
| · *EU trade* | | | | | | | (.021) |
| *Regional parliam.* | | | | | -.184** | | |
| · *Trade openness* | | | | | (.073) | | |
| *Regional parliam.* | | | | | | -.009 | |
| · (*EU* · *EU exp.*) | | | | | | (.008) | |
| *Regional parliam.* | | | | | | | -.013 |
| · *EU trade* | | | | | | | (.153) |
| No. obs. (countries) | 485 (23) | 458 (22) | 483 (23) | 485 (23) | 485 (23) | 485 (23) | 483 (23) |
| Adj. $R^2$ | .961 | .960 | .961 | .961 | .963 | .965 | .962 |
| Within $R^2$ | .192 | .145 | .195 | .198 | .240 | .277 | .222 |

Note: See Table 4.3 for further details. Source for own revenue data: IMF, Government Finance Statistics Yearbook (except for: BEL – Banque Nationale de Belgique, JAP – OECD, National Accounts). Own calculations.

Table B.27: Fixed effects (within) estimates, direct expenditure (excl. social security), OECD countries, 1970-2001

| | Dep. var.: Degree of expenditure decentralisation (indic. ED1) | | | | | | |
|---|---|---|---|---|---|---|---|
| | (1) | (2) | (3) | (4) | (5) | (6) | (7) |
| *Population* | -.213** | -.221** | -.117 | -.214** | -.236** | -.032 | .004 |
| | (.098) | (.103) | (.099) | (.096) | (.098) | (.099) | (.109) |
| *Urbanisation* | -.150 | -.148 | -.105 | -.160 | -.148 | -.171 | -.061 |
| | (.125) | (.128) | (.106) | (.132) | (.120) | (.159) | (.099) |
| *Regional disparity* | -.239*** | -.241*** | -.295*** | -.246*** | -.204*** | -.131** | -.196*** |
| | (.075) | (.071) | (.080) | (.077) | (.067) | (.053) | (.060) |
| *Per capita income* | .120*** | .071 | .030 | .122*** | .123*** | .050 | .030 |
| | (.038) | (.047) | (.045) | (.038) | (.037) | (.038) | (.041) |
| *Growth rate* | -.076 | -.034 | -.104 | -.083 | -.058 | -.069 | -.146* |
| | (.100) | (.111) | (.088) | (.097) | (.097) | (.090) | (.076) |
| *Unemployment* | -.203 | -.263 | -.335 | -.232 | -.201 | -.341 | -.384** |
| | (.288) | (.265) | (.229) | (.277) | (.273) | (.218) | (.187) |
| *Election* | -.004 | -.003 | -.003 | -.004 | -.004 | -.003 | -.003 |
| | (.003) | (.003) | (.003) | (.003) | (.003) | (.003) | (.003) |
| *Coldwar* | -.028*** | -.025*** | -.031*** | -.027*** | -.030*** | -.027*** | -.025*** |
| | (.008) | (.008) | (.007) | (.008) | (.007) | (.007) | (.007) |
| *Trade openness* | .016 | | .127*** | .013 | -.069 | -.022 | .126*** |
| | (.039) | | (.046) | (.040) | (.079) | (.039) | (.041) |
| *Finan. openness* | | .146** | | | | | |
| | | (.071) | | | | | |
| *EU · EU exp.* | .016 | .008 | | | .023** | -.018 | |
| | (.012) | (.009) | | | (.012) | (.014) | |
| *EU trade* | | | .531*** | | | | .118 |
| | | | (.177) | | | | (.122) |
| *EU polit. integr.* | | | | .011 | | | |
| | | | | (.007) | | | |

Table B.27 (cont.): Fixed effects (within) estimates, direct expenditure

| | Dep. var.: Degree of expenditure decentralisation (indic. ED1) | | | | | | |
|---|---|---|---|---|---|---|---|
| | (1) | (2) | (3) | (4) | (5) | (6) | (7) |
| *Fractional* · *Trade openness* | | | | | .247 (.162) | | |
| *Fractional* · (*EU* · *EU exp.*) | | | | | | .218*** (.062) | |
| *Fractional* · *EU trade* | | | | | | | 1.602*** (.488) |
| *Referendum* · *Trade openness* | | | | | -.079** (.034) | | |
| *Referendum* · (*EU* · *EU exp.*) | | | | | | -.008 (.013) | |
| *Referendum* · *EU trade* | | | | | | | -.042 (.037) |
| *Regional parliam.* · *Trade openness* | | | | | -.228* (.120) | | |
| *Regional parliam.* · (*EU* · *EU exp.*) | | | | | | -.011 (.011) | |
| *Regional parliam.* · *EU trade* | | | | | | | -.546*** (.166) |
| No. obs. (countries) | 459 (22) | 432 (21) | 457 (22) | 459 (22) | 459 (22) | 459 (22) | 457 (22) |
| Adj. $R^2$ | .952 | .953 | .959 | .953 | .955 | .962 | .965 |
| Within $R^2$ | .306 | .333 | .413 | .324 | .355 | .456 | .509 |

Note: See Table 4.3 for further details.

Table B.28: Fixed effects (within) estimates, self-financed expenditure (excl. social security), OECD countries, 1970-2001

| | Dep. var.: Degree of expenditure decentralisation (indic. ED2) | | | | | | |
|---|---|---|---|---|---|---|---|
| | (1) | (2) | (3) | (4) | (5) | (6) | (7) |
| *Population* | -.117 | -.069 | -.099 | -.125 | -.136 | -.021 | -.062 |
| | (.100) | (.100) | (.101) | (.101) | (.098) | (.085) | (.107) |
| *Urbanisation* | -.171** | -.198** | -.164** | -.168** | -.182** | -.207*** | -.164** |
| | (.082) | (.079) | (.078) | (.082) | (.071) | (.079) | (.082) |
| *Regional disparity* | -.204*** | -.182*** | -.216*** | -.203*** | -.174*** | -.166*** | -.174*** |
| | (.060) | (.055) | (.062) | (.059) | (.056) | (.052) | (.055) |
| *Per capita income* | .084** | .059*** | .068 | .088** | .088** | .045 | .072* |
| | (.039) | (.044) | (.042) | (.039) | (.040) | (.036) | (.042) |
| *Growth rate* | -.041 | .001 | -.043 | -.034 | -.009 | -.043 | -.061 |
| | (.074) | (.076) | (.074) | (.073) | (.068) | (.067) | (.071) |
| *Unemployment* | -.340** | -.308* | -.368** | -.324** | -.356** | -.446*** | -.386*** |
| | (.159) | (.165) | (.145) | (.156) | (.144) | (.142) | (.135) |
| *Election* | -.005** | -.005** | -.004** | -.005** | -.004** | -.004* | -004** |
| | (.002) | (.002) | (.002) | (.002) | (.002) | (.002) | (.002) |
| *Coldwar* | -.024*** | -.022*** | -.024*** | -.024*** | -.026*** | -.026*** | -.022*** |
| | (.007) | (.007) | (.007) | (.008) | (.007) | (.007) | (.008) |
| *Trade openness* | .098** | | .119** | .099** | -.006 | .075* | .119** |
| | (.047) | | (.050) | (.047) | (.058) | (.041) | (.049) |
| *Finan. openness* | | .100** | | | | | |
| | | (.051) | | | | | |
| *EU · EU exp.* | .002 | -.002 | | | .008* | .011 | |
| | (.006) | (.006) | | | (.005) | (.011) | |
| *EU trade* | | | .094 | | | | -.023 |
| | | | (.070) | | | | (.111) |
| *EU polit. integr.* | | | | -.000 | | | |
| | | | | (.003) | | | |

Table B.28 (cont.): Fixed effects (within) estimates, self-financed expenditure

| | Dep. var.: Degree of expenditure decentralisation (indic. ED2) | | | | | | |
|---|---|---|---|---|---|---|---|
| | (1) | (2) | (3) | (4) | (5) | (6) | (7) |
| *Fractional* | | | | | .282* | | |
| · *Trade openness* | | | | | (.167) | | |
| *Fractional* | | | | | | .108*** | |
| · (*EU* · *EU exp.*) | | | | | | (.040) | |
| *Fractional* | | | | | | | .516 |
| · *EU trade* | | | | | | | (.326) |
| *Referendum* | | | | | -.057*** | | |
| · *Trade openness* | | | | | (.020) | | |
| *Referendum* | | | | | | -.032** | |
| · (*EU* · *EU exp.*) | | | | | | (.015) | |
| *Referendum* | | | | | | | -.020 |
| · *EU trade* | | | | | | | (.024) |
| *Regional parliam.* | | | | | -.185** | | |
| · *Trade openness* | | | | | (.090) | | |
| *Regional parliam.* | | | | | | -.016** | |
| · (*EU* · *EU exp.*) | | | | | | (.007) | |
| *Regional parliam.* | | | | | | | -.418** |
| · *EU trade* | | | | | | | (.187) |
| No. obs. (countries) | 467 (23) | 440 (22) | 465 (23) | 467 (23) | 467 (23) | 467 (23) | 465 (23) |
| Adj. $R^2$ | .967 | .968 | .967 | .967 | .969 | .971 | .968 |
| Within $R^2$ | .330 | .318 | .333 | .329 | .387 | .409 | .356 |

Note: See Table 4.3 for further details.

Table B.29: Fixed effects (within) estimates, total own revenue (excl. social security), OECD countries, 1970-2001

| | Dep. var.: Degree of revenue decentralisation (indic. RD3) | | | | | | |
|---|---|---|---|---|---|---|---|
| | (1) | (2) | (3) | (4) | (5) | (6) | (7) |
| *Population* | -.097 | -.039 | -.077 | -.104 | -.119 | -.019 | -.058 |
| | (.113) | (.110) | (.110) | (.112) | (.112) | (.096) | (.115) |
| *Urbanisation* | -.227** | -.262*** | -.236*** | -.219** | -.252*** | -.263*** | -.240*** |
| | (.091) | (.086) | (.090) | (.090) | (.082) | (.082) | (.092) |
| *Regional disparity* | -.167*** | -.142** | -.170*** | -.162*** | -.143** | -.156*** | -.145** |
| | (.061) | (.056) | (.062) | (.059) | (.059) | (.052) | (.059) |
| *Per capita income* | .074* | .058 | .065 | .076* | .081* | .039 | .068 |
| | (.044) | (.047) | (.045) | (.043) | (.046) | (.041) | (.046) |
| *Growth rate* | -.039 | .009 | -.056 | -.029 | -.020 | -.042 | -.066 |
| | (.077) | (.077) | (.081) | (.077) | (.072) | (.069) | (.082) |
| *Unemployment* | .110 | .167 | .075 | .140 | .097 | .013 | .062 |
| | (.135) | (.147) | (.137) | (.131) | (.131) | (.137) | (.137) |
| *Election* | -.004* | -.005** | -.004* | -.004* | -.004* | -.003 | -.004* |
| | (.002) | (.002) | (.002) | (.002) | (.002) | (.002) | (.002) |
| *Coldwar* | -.021*** | -.021*** | -.020*** | -.022*** | -.023*** | -.025*** | -.019** |
| | (.008) | (.008) | (.008) | (.008) | (.008) | (.007) | (.008) |
| *Trade openness* | .114** | | .109* | .116** | .026 | .090* | .110* |
| | (.054) | | (.059) | (.054) | (.060) | (.046) | (.059) |
| *Finan. openness* | | .084 | | | | | |
| | | (.058) | | | | | |
| *EU · EU exp.* | -.007 | -.011 | | | -.002 | .021** | |
| | (.007) | (.007) | | | (.006) | (.010) | |
| *EU trade* | | | -.009 | | | | -.078 |
| | | | (.080) | | | | (.125) |
| *EU polit. integr.* | | | | -.006** | | | |
| | | | | (.003) | | | |

Table B.29 (cont.): Fixed effects (within) estimates, total own revenue

| | Dep. var.: Degree of revenue decentralisation (indic. RD3) | | | | | | |
|---|---|---|---|---|---|---|---|
| | (1) | (2) | (3) | (4) | (5) | (6) | (7) |
| *Fractional* | | | | | .237 | | |
| · *Trade openness* | | | | | (.186) | | |
| *Fractional* | | | | | | .082* | |
| · (*EU* · *EU exp.*) | | | | | | (.042) | |
| *Fractional* | | | | | | | .280 |
| · *EU trade* | | | | | | | (.354) |
| *Referendum* | | | | | -.036* | | |
| · *Trade openness* | | | | | (.020) | | |
| *Referendum* | | | | | | -.050*** | |
| · (*EU* · *EU exp.*) | | | | | | (.017) | |
| *Referendum* | | | | | | | -.004 |
| · *EU trade* | | | | | | | (.024) |
| *Regional parliam.* | | | | | -.208** | | |
| · *Trade openness* | | | | | (.092) | | |
| *Regional parliam.* | | | | | | -.015 | |
| · (*EU* · *EU exp.*) | | | | | | (.009) | |
| *Regional parliam.* | | | | | | | -.261 |
| · *EU trade* | | | | | | | (.196) |
| No. obs. (countries) | 467 (23) | 440 (22) | 465 (23) | 467 (23) | 467 (23) | 467 (23) | 465 (23) |
| Adj. $R^2$ | .963 | .962 | .962 | .963 | .965 | .967 | .962 |
| Within $R^2$ | .284 | .264 | .280 | .295 | .324 | .364 | .286 |

Note: See Tables 4.3 and B.26 for further details.

Table B.30: Sensitivity analysis with Belgium and Spain: Fixed effects (within) estimates, direct expenditure (incl. social security), 1970-2001

| | Dep. var.: Degree of expen. decentralis. (indic. ED1) | | | | | |
|---|---|---|---|---|---|---|
| | (1) | (2) | (3) | (4) | (5) | (6) |
| *Population* | .033 | -.035 | -.039 | -.046 | -.041 | .041 |
| | (.079) | (.077) | (.091) | (.084) | (.085) | (.077) |
| *Urbanisation* | -.204** | -.195** | -.237** | -.204** | -.206** | -.237** |
| | (.093) | (.089) | (.097) | (.090) | (.088) | (.102) |
| *Regional disparity* | -.185*** | -.197*** | -.173*** | -.163*** | -.168*** | -.114** |
| | (.062) | (.062) | (.059) | (.056) | (.057) | (.049) |
| *Per capita income* | .029 | .002 | .048* | .062** | .059** | .030 |
| | (.025) | (.028) | (.028) | (.025) | (.025) | (.023) |
| *Growth rate* | .009 | .018 | -.014 | -.100* | -.102* | -.080 |
| | (.072) | (.076) | (.072) | (.054) | (.055) | (.052) |
| *Unemployment* | -.216 | -.284 | -.193 | -.464*** | -.475*** | .524*** |
| | (.201) | (.185) | (.195) | (.106) | (.104) | (.103) |
| *Election* | -.003 | -.002 | -.003 | -.002 | -.002 | -.001 |
| | (.002) | (.002) | (.002) | (.002) | (.002) | (.001) |
| *Coldwar* | -.002 | -.001 | -.002 | -.006 | -.005 | -.006 |
| | (.005) | (.006) | (.005) | (.005) | (.005) | (.005) |
| *Trade openness* | -.034 | | -.053 | .044 | .044 | .010 |
| | (.027) | | (.062) | (.032) | (.033) | (.027) |
| *Finan. openness* | | .063 | | | | |
| | | (.046) | | | | |
| *EU · EU exp.* | .014* | .011* | .017** | -.002 | | -.015 |
| | (.007) | (.006) | (.008) | (.004) | | (.012) |
| *EU trade* | | | | | .003 | |
| | | | | | (.066) | |
| *Fractional · Trade openness* | | | .213 | | | |
| | | | (.170) | | | |
| *Fractional · (EU × EU exp.)* | | | | | | .122*** |
| | | | | | | (.034) |
| *Referendum · Trade openness* | | | -.037 | | | |
| | | | (.028) | | | |
| *Referendum · (EU × EU exp.)* | | | | | | -.006 |
| | | | | | | (.010) |
| *Regional parliam. · Trade openness* | | | -.200** | | | |
| | | | (.095) | | | |
| *Regional parliam. · (EU × EU exp.)* | | | | | | -.003 |
| | | | | | | (.006) |
| No. obs. (countries) | 455 (22) | 428 (21) | 455 (22) | 465 (22) | 463 (22) | 465 (22) |
| Adj. $R^2$ | .964 | .966 | .965 | .974 | .974 | .977 |
| Within $R^2$ | .152 | .174 | .190 | .257 | .257 | .345 |

Note: (1)-(3) BEL excluded, (4)-(6) SPA excluded. See Table 4.3 for further details.

Table B.31: Fixed effects (within) estimates, total tax revenue, OECD countries, 1965-2001

| | Dep. var.: Degree of tax decentralisation (indic. TD3) | | | | | | |
|---|---|---|---|---|---|---|---|
| | (1) | (2) | (3) | (4) | (5) | (6) | (7) |
| *Population* | -.262* | -.273** | -.236 | -.267* | -.266** | -.011 | -.206 |
| | (.138) | (.136) | (.143) | (.145) | (.127) | (.099) | (.155) |
| *Urbanisation* | -.273** | -.252** | -.267** | -.267** | -.263*** | -.267** | -.270** |
| | (.117) | (.103) | (.114) | (.116) | (.100) | (.127) | (.118) |
| *Regional disparity* | -.264*** | -.280*** | -.260*** | -.261*** | -.225*** | -.215*** | -.243*** |
| | (.090) | (.093) | (.091) | (.088) | (.086) | (.074) | (.088) |
| *Per capita income* | .066* | .080* | .055 | .067 | .065* | .001 | .055 |
| | (.039) | (.045) | (.042) | (.041) | (.037) | (.030) | (.043) |
| *Growth rate* | -.129 | -.109 | -.145 | -.127 | -.077 | -.093 | -.155 |
| | (.091) | (.091) | (.099) | (.089) | (.073) | (.075) | (.101) |
| *Unemployment* | .326** | .233 | .289* | .326** | .221 | .212 | .291* |
| | (.152) | (.173) | (.161) | (.149) | (.145) | (.150) | (.158) |
| *Election* | -.003 | -.004 | -.003 | -.003 | -.003* | -.002 | -.003 |
| | (.002) | (.003) | (.002) | (.002) | (.002) | (.002) | (.002) |
| *Coldwar* | -.019** | -.013 | -.018** | -.019** | -.021** | -.021** | -.016* |
| | (.009) | (.008) | (.009) | (.009) | (.009) | (.009) | (.009) |
| *Trade openness* | .087* | | .104* | .088* | -.015 | .061 | .097 |
| | (.053) | | (.060) | (.053) | (.058) | (.044) | (.062) |
| *Finan. openness* | | .078 | | | | | |
| | | (.063) | | | | | |
| *EU · EU exp.* | -.003 | -.005 | | | .005 | .001 | |
| | (.006) | (.007) | | | (.006) | (.017) | |
| *EU trade* | | | .023 | | | | -.114 |
| | | | (.081) | | | | (.146) |
| *EU polit. integr.* | | | | -.002 | | | |
| | | | | (.003) | | | |

Table B.31 (cont.): Fixed effects (within) estimates, total tax revenue

| | Dep. var.: Degree of tax decentralisation (indic. TD3) | | | | | | |
|---|---|---|---|---|---|---|---|
| | (1) | (2) | (3) | (4) | (5) | (6) | (7) |
| *Fractional* · *Trade openness* | | | | | .341* (.195) | | |
| *Fractional* · (*EU* · *EU exp.*) | | | | | | .176*** (.059) | |
| *Fractional* · *EU trade* | | | | | | | .420 (.447) |
| *Referendum* · *Trade openness* | | | | | -.081 (.052) | | |
| *Referendum* · (*EU* · *EU exp.*) | | | | | | -.046* (.023) | |
| *Referendum* · *EU trade* | | | | | | | .022 (.028) |
| *Regional parliam.* · *Trade openness* | | | | | -.138** (.063) | | |
| *Regional parliam.* · (*EU* · *EU exp.*) | | | | | | -.000 (.010) | |
| *Regional parliam.* · *EU trade* | | | | | | | -.037 (.181) |
| No. obs. (countries) | 548 (23) | 522 (22) | 535 (23) | 548 (23) | 548 (23) | 548 (23) | 535 (23) |
| Adj. $R^2$ | .941 | .940 | .940 | .941 | .944 | .947 | .940 |
| Within $R^2$ | .172 | .156 | .176 | .173 | .226 | .270 | .182 |

Note: See Table 4.3 for further details.

Fig. B.1: Allocation of total public expenditure (including social security) by fiscal tiers, Germany, 1881-2001

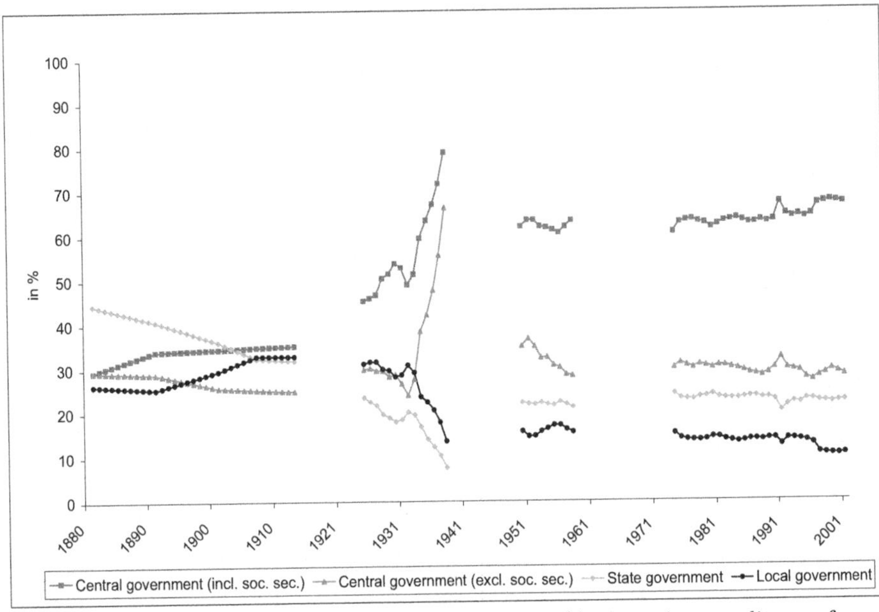


Note: Public expenditure by level of government in % of total expenditure of consolidated government, including social security, and excluding payments to the EU. No social security figures are available for the period 1959-1973. Due to different expenditure definitions, the time series 1881-1959 and 1974-2001 are not strictly comparable. See Appendix C for data sources and definitions.

Table B.32: Allocation of public expenditure by government function and level of government, Germany, 1913-2001

| | Administration & Other | | | | Law & Order | | | | Economic Services | | | | out of which Transp. & Commun. | | | | Other | | | |
|---|---|---|---|---|---|---|---|---|---|---|---|---|---|---|---|---|---|---|---|---|
| | C | S | L | T | C | S | L | T | C | S | L | T | C | S | L | T | C | S | L | T |
| 1913 | 9.9 | 49.6 | 40.4 | 1.3 | 0.5 | 83.2 | 16.3 | 1.1 | 5.3 | 35.1 | 59.6 | 1.7 | 6.2 | 29.8 | 64.0 | 1.6 | 4.2 | 67.3 | 28.5 | 0.3 |
| 1925-1932 | 40.5 | 20.7 | 38.8 | 2.3 | 0.8 | 87.1 | 12.1 | 2.1 | 18.3 | 25.3 | 56.4 | 2.5 | 15.2 | 18.0 | 66.9 | 2.0 | 29.9 | 48.8 | 21.3 | 0.7 |
| 1950-1955 | 25.1 | 40.6 | 34.3 | 1.9 | 5.8 | 59.5 | 34.8 | 0.8 | 34.1 | 32.5 | 33.4 | 0.1 | 28.1 | 32.3 | 39.6 | 1.6 | 36.9 | 32.5 | 30.6 | 3.6 |
| 1985-1990 | 22.0 | 36.6 | 41.4 | 2.0 | 9.4 | 64.1 | 26.5 | 1.1 | 47.5 | 29.6 | 22.9 | 0.0 | 44.7 | 29.3 | 26.1 | 1.6 | 49.0 | 29.7 | 21.3 | 3.2 |
| 1996-2001 | 20.3 | 36.8 | 42.9 | 2.0 | 10.2 | 60.7 | 29.2 | 1.2 | 55.5 | 25.8 | 18.7 | 0.1 | 43.2 | 27.7 | 29.1 | 1.4 | 59.6 | 25.2 | 15.1 | 4.0 |

| | Education | | | | out of which School | | | | University | | | | Other | | | | Science & Research | | | |
|---|---|---|---|---|---|---|---|---|---|---|---|---|---|---|---|---|---|---|---|---|
| | C | S | L | T | C | S | L | T | C | S | L | T | C | S | L | T | C | S | L | T |
| 1913 | 0.3 | 35.8 | 63.9 | 2.4 | 0.1 | 33.2 | 66.8 | 2.2 | 1.2 | 96.3 | 2.4 | 0.2 | | | | | | | | |
| 1925-1932 | 1.2 | 51.1 | 47.7 | 3.8 | 0.2 | 50.7 | 49.0 | 3.1 | 0.5 | 96.3 | 3.2 | 0.3 | | | | | | | | |
| 1950-1955 | 2.3 | 61.5 | 36.2 | 2.5 | 0.1 | 56.0 | 43.9 | 2.0 | 0.4 | 99.6 | 0.0 | 0.4 | | | | | 42.2 | 40.2 | 17.6 | 0.1 |
| 1985-1990 | 13.2 | 71.8 | 15.0 | 5.5 | 0.0 | 76.7 | 23.3 | 3.0 | 5.8 | 94.2 | 0.0 | 1.4 | 28.7 | 44.4 | 26.9 | 0.5 | 76.8 | 20.9 | 2.3 | 0.7 |
| 1996-2001 | 10.6 | 69.2 | 20.2 | 5.5 | 0.0 | 71.6 | 28.4 | 3.4 | 9.5 | 90.5 | 0.0 | 1.2 | 23.1 | 39.0 | 37.9 | 0.4 | 69.8 | 28.1 | 2.2 | 0.5 |

| | Social Services (incl. Soc. Security) | | | | out of which Social Assistance & War Damage Compens. | | | | Health | | | | Housing | | | | Communal Services | | | |
|---|---|---|---|---|---|---|---|---|---|---|---|---|---|---|---|---|---|---|---|---|
| | C | S | L | T | C | S | L | T | C | S | L | T | C | S | L | T | C | S | L | T |
| 1913 | 88.6 | 1.5 | 9.9 | 4.1 | 21.7 | 10.4 | 68.0 | 0.6 | 0.4 | 20.6 | 79.0 | 0.5 | 12.5 | 25.0 | 62.5 | 0.1 | 0.0 | 5.5 | 94.5 | 0.6 |
| 1925-1932 | 81.3 | 3.1 | 15.6 | 14.9 | 67.2 | 5.2 | 27.5 | 8.4 | 2.8 | 14.3 | 82.9 | 0.5 | 6.0 | 25.7 | 68.3 | 0.0 | 0.0 | 6.8 | 93.2 | 0.5 |
| 1950-1955 | 87.8 | 7.6 | 4.5 | 13.0 | 72.8 | 17.0 | 10.2 | 8.1 | 0.9 | 31.5 | 67.6 | 1.1 | 45.7 | 36.7 | 17.6 | 0.0 | 0.0 | 12.6 | 87.4 | 0.8 |
| 1985-1990 | 89.5 | 3.9 | 6.6 | 25.0 | 64.6 | 13.1 | 22.3 | 7.7 | 3.9 | 25.6 | 70.5 | 2.4 | 13.0 | 55.5 | 31.5 | 0.3 | 0.3 | 7.6 | 92.1 | 1.2 |
| 1996-2001 | 89.9 | 4.3 | 5.8 | 30.4 | 65.2 | 14.8 | 20.0 | 8.8 | 13.8 | 35.5 | 50.7 | 1.1 | 15.4 | 52.1 | 32.5 | 0.7 | 0.7 | 2.9 | 96.5 | 1.0 |

Note: Public expenditure of central (C), state (S) and local (L) government in % of total public expenditure, and total (T) public expenditure in % of net national product, by government function, as reported in financial statistics; period averages. Defence, social security, debt service and financial transfers are not considered. See Appendix C for data sources and definitions and the breakdown by government functions.

Table B.33: Allocation of public expenditure by level of government, Germany, 1881-2001

| | Publ. expen. (incl. soc. sec.) | | | | Publ. expen. (excl. soc. sec.) | | | |
|---|---|---|---|---|---|---|---|---|
| | Total[a] | Central (share) | State (share) | Local (share) | Total[a] | Central (share) | State (share) | Local (share) |
| 1881 | 10.6 | 29.3 | 44.4 | 26.3 | 10.6 | 29.3 | 44.4 | 26.3 |
| 1891 | 12.3 | 34.0 | 40.7 | 25.4 | 12.2 | 30.4 | 42.9 | 26.8 |
| 1901 | 13.4 | 34.4 | 36.1 | 29.5 | 13.3 | 28.2 | 39.5 | 32.3 |
| 1907 | 13.5 | 34.9 | 32.2 | 32.9 | 13.4 | 28.0 | 35.7 | 36.4 |
| 1913 | 14.8 | 35.2 | 31.9 | 32.9 | 14.7 | 27.8 | 35.5 | 36.7 |
| 1925-1932 | 25.0 | 49.5 | 20.3 | 30.2 | 24.7 | 38.8 | 23.9 | 37.4 |
| 1933-1938 | 30.3 | 65.4 | 13.4 | 21.2 | 30.1 | 57.0 | 14.8 | 28.2 |
| 1950-1955 | 37.0 | 62.4 | 21.9 | 15.7 | 26.1 | 51.3 | 29.0 | 19.6 |
| 1985-1990 | 52.4 | 63.1 | 23.2 | 13.7 | 34.6 | 44.0 | 35.2 | 20.8 |
| 1996-2001 | 57.9 | 66.9 | 22.3 | 10.8 | 36.3 | 46.2 | 36.3 | 17.5 |

Note: Public expenditure by level of government, in % of consolidated public expenditure (excluding EU payments) according to financial statistics, including or excluding social security. [a] public expenditure of consolidated general government (excluding EU payments) according to national income statistics, including or excluding social security, in % of net national product at market prices (note that social security expenditures are understated before 1950). Period averages. See Appendix C for data sources and definitions.

Table B.34: Allocation of tax revenue by level of government, Germany, 1881-2001

| | Tax revenue | | |
|---|---|---|---|
| | Central (share) | State (share) | Local (share) |
| 1881 | 39.0 | 35.1 | 25.9 |
| 1891 | 48.5 | 26.5 | 25.0 |
| 1901 | 44.3 | 25.6 | 30.1 |
| 1907 | 44.3 | 23.6 | 32.1 |
| 1913 | 40.3 | 22.6 | 37.2 |
| 1925-1932 | 46.7 | 23.1 | 30.3 |
| 1933-1938 | 61.4 | 14.8 | 23.8 |
| 1950-1955 | 61.1 | 27.3 | 11.6 |
| 1985-1990 | 48.7 | 38.0 | 13.4 |
| 1996-2001 | 48.8 | 39.6 | 11.6 |

Note: Tax revenue by level of government, in % of consolidated tax revenue (excluding social security and EU payments) according to financial statistics. Period averages. See Appendix C for data sources and definitions.

Fig. B.2: Composition of central government expenditure by government function, Germany, 1881-2001

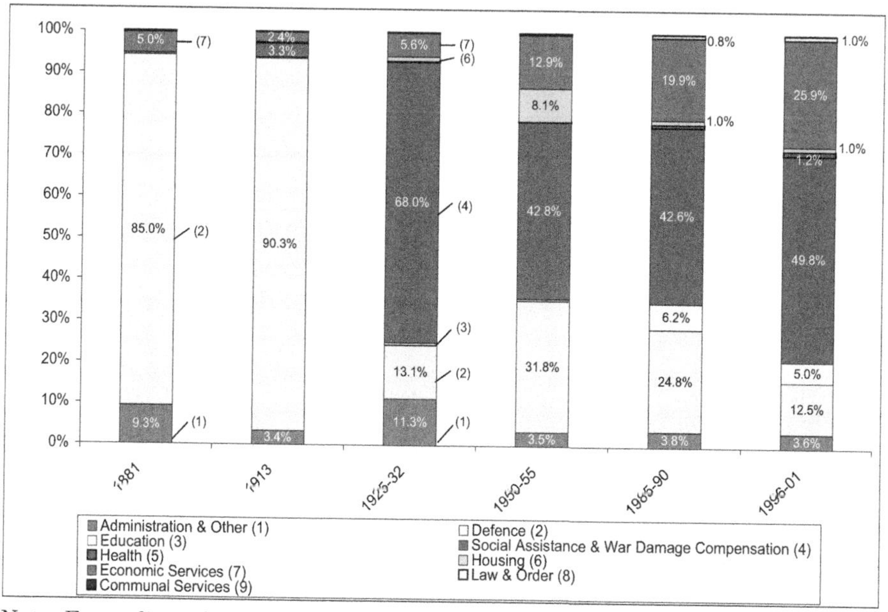


Note: Expenditure by government function in % of total central government expenditure (excluding social security), as reported in national financial statistics; period averages. Debt service and financial transfers are excluded, too. See Appendix C for data sources and definitions.

Fig. B.3: Composition of state government expenditure by government function, Germany, 1913-2001

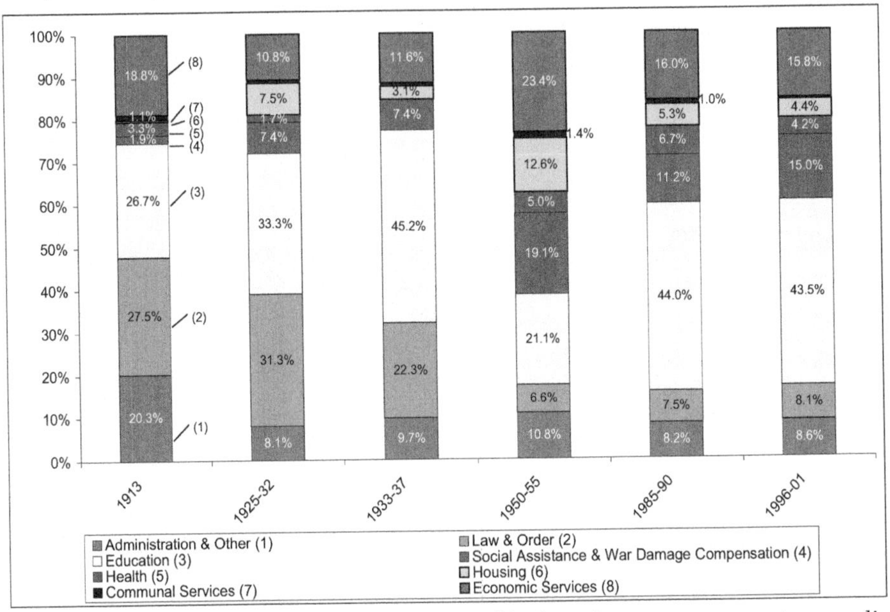


Note: Expenditure by government function in % of total state government expenditure, as reported in national financial statistics; period averages. Debt service and financial transfers are excluded. See Appendix C for data sources and definitions.

Fig. B.4: Composition of local government expenditure by government function, Germany, 1913-2001

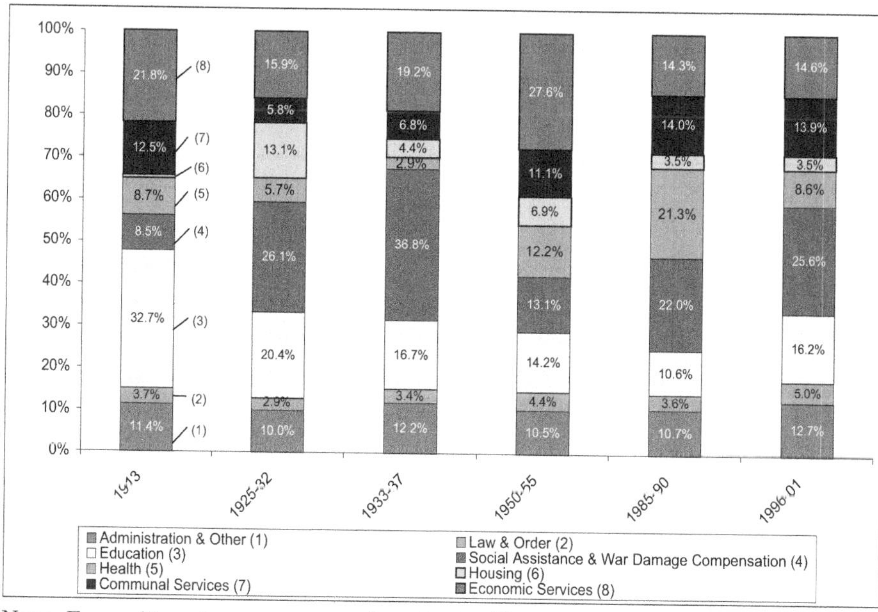


Note: Expenditure by government function in % of total local government expenditure, as reported in national financial statistics; period averages. Debt service and financial transfers are excluded. See Appendix C for data sources and definitions.

Table B.35: OLS estimates of fiscal decentralisation, expenditure on other economic services, Germany, 1950-2001

| | Dep. var.: Degree of expen. decentr. (indic. ED2) | | | | |
|---|---|---|---|---|---|
| | (1) | (2) | (3) | (4) | (5) |
| $Decentr_{t-1}$ | .468*** | .478*** | .416*** | .524*** | .463*** |
| | (.119) | (.119) | (.088) | (.113) | (.113) |
| $Per\ capita\ income_{t-1}$ | .181 | .330 | .252* | .148 | .190 |
| | (.147) | (.265) | (.134) | (.121) | (.142) |
| $Population_{t-1}$ | | -1.009** | | | |
| | | (.432) | | | |
| $Density_{t-1}$ | -1.072** | | -.978** | -.993** | -1.005* |
| | (.483) | | (.364) | (.421) | (.546) |
| $Urbanisation_{t-1}$ | | -2.053 | | | |
| | | (1.990) | | | |
| $Growth\ rate_t$ | -.046 | -.049 | -.034 | -.051 | -.052 |
| | (.118) | (.241) | (.103) | (.112) | (.117) |
| $Trade\ openness_{t-1}$ | | | .303*** | | |
| | | | (.099) | | |
| $EU\ exp._{t-1}$ | | | | .023 | |
| | | | | (.014) | |
| $EU\ trade_{t-1}$ | | | | | -.109 |
| | | | | | (.187) |
| *Re-unification* | -.127*** | .265* | -.062** | -.112*** | -.116** |
| | (.044) | (.137) | (.028) | (.042) | (.055) |
| *Postwar* | .017 | | .039* | .003 | .024 |
| | (.018) | | (.020) | (.013) | (.017) |
| *Trend* | -.002 | | -.008** | -.003 | -.002 |
| | (.003) | | (.003) | (.003) | (.003) |
| No. obs. | 49 | 39 | 49 | 49 | 49 |
| $R^2$ | .897 | .787 | .914 | .901 | .897 |
| adj. $R^2$ | .879 | .747 | .897 | .881 | .877 |
| BG(1) | 7.123 | 3.743 | 0.699 | 6.031 | 6.148 |
| BG(2) | 7.580 | 4.071 | 1.084 | 6.504 | 6.388 |

Note: Due to serial correlation, Newey-West heteroscedasticity and autocorrelation consistent standard errors (L=3) are reported in parentheses. ***, **, and * indicate significance at the 1%, 5% and 10% level, respectively.

Table B.36: OLS estimates of fiscal decentralisation, expenditure on transport and communication, Germany, 1950-2001

| | Dep. var.: Degree of expen. decentr. (indic. ED2) | | | | |
|---|---|---|---|---|---|
| | (1) | (2) | (3) | (4) | (5) |
| *Decentr*$_{t-1}$ | .632*** | .651*** | .632*** | .651*** | .624*** |
| | (.115) | (.114) | (.119) | (.107) | (.122) |
| *Per capita income*$_{t-1}$ | .126** | .214* | .126** | .123** | .127** |
| | (.061) | (.112) | (.062) | (.060) | (.060) |
| *Population*$_{t-1}$ | | -.824*** | | | |
| | | (.222) | | | |
| *Density*$_{t-1}$ | -.764*** | | -.763*** | -.750*** | -.752*** |
| | (.245) | | (.244) | (.234) | (.245) |
| *Urbanisation*$_{t-1}$ | | -1.296 | | | |
| | | (.855) | | | |
| *Growth rate*$_t$ | .192 | .391* | .192 | .191 | .189 |
| | (.144) | (.202) | (.147) | (.139) | (.144) |
| *Trade openness*$_{t-1}$ | | | .003 | | |
| | | | (.043) | | |
| *EU exp.*$_{t-1}$ | | | | .006 | |
| | | | | (.007) | |
| *EU trade*$_{t-1}$ | | | | | -.030 |
| | | | | | (.080) |
| *Re-unification* | -.042*** | .263*** | -.042*** | -.040*** | -.039*** |
| | (.015) | (.072) | (.013) | (.014) | (.014) |
| *Postwar* | .011 | | .011 | .009 | .012* |
| | (.008) | | (.007) | (.009) | (.007) |
| *Trend* | -.002 | | -.002 | -.002 | -.002 |
| | (.001) | | (.001) | (.001) | (.001) |
| No. obs. | 49 | 39 | 49 | 49 | 49 |
| $R^2$ | .962 | .871 | .962 | .962 | .962 |
| adj. $R^2$ | .955 | .847 | .954 | .955 | .954 |
| BG(1) | 3.228 | 5.294 | 3.377 | 3.706 | 3.258 |
| BG(2) | 4.927 | 6.861 | 5.614 | 5.150 | 5.167 |

Note: Due to serial correlation, Newey-West heteroscedasticity and autocorrelation consistent standard errors (L=3) are reported in parentheses. ***, **, and * indicate significance at the 1%, 5% and 10% level, respectively.

Table B.37: OLS estimates of fiscal decentralisation, total tax revenue, Germany, 1950-2001

| | Dep. var.: Degree of tax decentralisation (indic. TD3) | | | | | |
|---|---|---|---|---|---|---|
| | (1) | (2) | (3) | (4) | (5) | (6) |
| *Decentr*$_{t-1}$ | .510*** | .743*** | .523*** | .512*** | .516*** | .471*** |
| | (.130) | (.081) | (.115) | (.135) | (.107) | (.110) |
| *Per capita income*$_{t-1}$ | .048 | .056 | .055 | .046 | .053 | .113*** |
| | (.034) | (.044) | (.034) | (.035) | (.035) | (.036) |
| *Population*$_{t-1}$ | | .063 | | | | |
| | | (.067) | | | | |
| *Density*$_{t-1}$ | -.094 | | -.066 | -.099*** | -.046 | .037 |
| | (.093) | | (.090) | (.094) | (.090) | (.085) |
| *Urbanisation*$_{t-1}$ | | -.277 | | | | |
| | | (.373) | | | | |
| *Growth rate*$_t$ | .036 | -.015 | .040 | .034 | .033 | .032 |
| | (.055) | (.050) | (.053) | (.055) | (.055) | (.051) |
| *Unemployment*$_{t-1}$ | | | | | | .449*** |
| | | | | | | (.115) |
| *Trade openness*$_{t-1}$ | | | .042 | | | |
| | | | (.045) | | | |
| *EU exp.*$_{t-1}$ | | | | .003 | | |
| | | | | (.007) | | |
| *EU trade*$_{t-1}$ | | | | | -.067 | |
| | | | | | (.072) | |
| *Re-unification* | -.017 | -.016 | -.006 | -.017 | -.009 | .009 |
| | (.012) | (.019) | (.015) | (.012) | (.013) | (.009) |
| *Postwar* | .014* | | -.011 | -.016* | -.010 | -.018** |
| | (.007) | | (.008) | (.008) | (.010) | (.007) |
| *Trend* | .000 | | -.000 | .000 | .000 | -.003*** |
| | (.001) | | (.001) | (.001) | (.001) | (.001) |
| No. obs. | 49 | 39 | 49 | 49 | 49 | 49 |
| $R^2$ | .971 | .953 | .972 | .971 | .971 | .976 |
| adj. $R^2$ | .966 | .944 | .966 | .965 | .966 | .972 |
| BG(1) | 7.433 | 0.007 | 5.722 | 6.201 | 6.219 | 5.032 |
| BG(2) | 7.942 | 0.008 | 5.778 | 6.441 | 6.865 | 5.058 |

Note: Due to serial correlation, Newey-West heteroscedasticity and autocorrelation consistent standard errors (L=3) are reported in parentheses. ***, **, and * indicate significance at the 1%, 5% and 10% level, respectively.

# C

# Data Sources and Definitions

## Panel Analysis for OECD Countries (1965-2001)

### *Variables*

**Area** Natural log of geographic area in 1000 $km^2$. [Source: Eurostat; OECD; World Bank]

**Catholic** Proportion of population that is Roman Catholic. [Source: CIA World Factbook; Encyclopaedia Britannica (1989), World Data Annual]

**Central tax competency** Dummy=1 for ultimate competency of the central government in terms of tax legislation. [Source: See *subnational representation*. Own calculations]

**Coldwar** Military expenditure in % of gross national product of Warsaw Treaty Organisation countries relative to NATO countries. [Source: U.S. Arms Control and Disarmament Agency. Own calculations]

**Degree of fiscal decentralisation** Sub-central government expenditure (revenue) as a share of consolidated general government expenditure (revenue). Different measurement concepts. [Source for public expenditure data: IMF, Government Finance Statistics Yearbook. Source for tax revenue data: OECD, Revenue Statistics. Own calculations]

**Dependency ratio** Proportion of population aged below 15 or above 64. [Source: OECD, Labour Force Statistics. Own calculations]

**Direct democracy (financial)** Average of the indices of referendums and popular initiatives on financial matters at the national level (0-3), see description above. [Source: See *direct democracy (all)*]

**Direct democracy (all)** Average of all indices of direct democracy at the national level (0-3), see description above. [Source: Research and Documentation Centre on Direct Democracy (http://c2d.unige.ch); Kaufmann and Waters (2004); Hug and Tsebelis (2002); national constitutions, available form the International Constitutional Law Project, at http://www.oefre.unibe.ch/law/icl/. Own calculations]

**Election** Dummy=1 for national election. [Source: Ismayr (1999); Mackie and Rose (1991); http://www.polisci.com]

**Electoral system** Ghallagher index of disproportionality of electoral systems.

$$D = \sqrt{0.5 \cdot \sum_{i=1}^{N} (v_i - s_i)^2}$$

where $v_i$ is the percentage of votes and $s_i$ the percentage of seats received by party $i$. The lower the value, the more proportional is the electoral system, with 0 indicating perfect proportional representation. Average for the period 1970-2001. [Source: Own calculations based on electoral results, see above]

**EU** Dummy=1 for membership in the European Union. [Source: Own compilation]

**EU expenditure** Expenditure of the European Union in % of total public expenditure of EU member countries. [Source: Europäische Kommission (2000)]

**EU political integration** Index of integration in the European Union (0-6): 0 (none), 1 (free-trade agreement), 2 (European Economic Area), 3 (customs union), 4 (European Community/European Union), 5 (European Monetary System), 6 (European Economic and Monetary Union). [Source: Own calculations]

**EU trade** Exports plus imports to/from EU15 as a share of foreign trade. [Source: OECD, Statistical Compendium Database. Own calculations]

**Federal** Dummy=1 for federal state. [Source: Own calculations]

**Financial openness** Index of financial openness (re-scaled 0-1). [Source: Quinn and Inclan (1997); Armingeon et al. (2004)]

**Fractionalisation** Greenberg index of linguistic diversity (0-1).

$$F = 1 - \sum_{i=1}^{n} p_i^2$$

where $p_i$ is the population share of the language group $i$. The index varies from 0, indicating the lowest degree of fractionalisation, to 1, indicating the highest. [Source: Ethnologue project at http://www.ethnologue.com]

**Government fragmentation** Index of party fragmentation of the central government.

$$GF = 1 - \sum_{i=1}^{N} s_i^2$$

where $s_i$ is the share of party $i$ in total seats of the government coalition in the legislature. [Source: Own calculations based on party classification and electoral and government statistics, see above]

**Growth rate** Rate of growth of real GDP per capita. [Source: IMF, International Financial Statistics. Own calculations]

**Left government** Share of leftist parties (communist, socialist, social-democrat, ecologist) in total seats of the government coalition in the legislature. [Source for the classification of the parties: Castles and Mair (1982), Ware (1996), Armingeon et al. (2004), Lane et al. (1997); own compilation. Source for the data: Ismayr (1999), Mackie and Rose (1991), Woldendorp et al. (1998), Lane et al. (1997), http://www.polisci.com. Own calculations]

**Legal origin** Dummy=1 for legal system based on English common law. [Source: CIA World Factbook]

**Majority rule** Dummy=1 for electoral system based on majority or plurality rule (lower chamber). [Source: Lane et al. (1997); Armingeon et al. (2004)]

**Mobility** Number of inter-regional migrants per 1000 inhabitants; average for the period 1965-2001. [Source: Eurostat, REGIO Database, and Regional Accounts; national statistics. Own calculations]

**Per capita income** Natural log of real GDP per capita, in prices of 1995, in ECU/EUR. [Source: IMF, International Financial Statistics. Own calculations]

**Population** Natural log of population in 1000. [Source: IMF; World Bank]

**Presidential regime** Dummy=1 for presidential regime, i.e. regimes where the elected executive is not accountable to the legislature through a vote of confidence. [Source: Lane and Ersson (1987); Lane et al. (1997)]

**Referendum (dummy)** Dummy=1 for legal provisions concerning the conduct of national referendums on constitutional and legislative issues. [Source: See *direct democracy (all)*]

**Referendum (practice)** Average number of referendums per year during 1970-2002. [Source: Research and Documentation Centre on Direct Democracy (http://c2d.unige.ch)]

**Regional** Dummy=1 for regional ethnically, linguistic or culturally distinct minorities. [Source: Classification according to Gurr (1993), the Ethnologue project at http://www.ethnologue.com, and the electoral score of regionalist parties. Own calculations]

**Regional disparity** Coefficient of variation of regional gross domestic product, gross value added, or income per capita. [Source: Eurostat, REGIO Database, and, Regional Accounts; national statistics. Own calculations]

**Regional parliament** Dummy=1 for upper chamber of parliament consisting only of representatives delegated by regional governments or legislatures. [Source: See *sub-national representation*]

**Subnational decision-making (direct/indirect)** Indices of direct and indirect participation of subnational entities in central decision-making, see description above. [Source: See *sub-national representation*]

**Subnational representation** Index of subnational representation in the upper chamber, see description above. [Source: CIA World Fact Book, Council of Europe (1997), Ismayr (1999), Tsebelis and Money (1997); national constitutions, available form the International Constitutional Law Project, at http://www.oefre.unibe.ch/law/icl/. Own calculations]

**Trade openness** Exports plus imports as a share of gross domestic product. [Source: IMF, International Financial Statistics. Own calculations]

**Unemployment** Rate of unemployment. [Source: OECD, Labour Force Statistics]

**Urbanisation** Fraction of urban population. [Source: Eurostat; OECD; World Bank]

## Time Series Analysis for Germany (1850-2003/1950-2001)

### *Variables*

**Degree of expenditure decentralisation (total)** Public expenditure (financial statistics) by level of government, as per cent of total expenditure of consolidated government (excluding EU payments), including/excluding social security. *Lastenausgleichfonds* and *ERP-Vermögen* are allocated to the central government. Partly different expenditure concepts, not strictly comparable. Excluding social security: 1881-1913 direct expenditure, 1925-2001 self-financed expenditure. Including social security: 1881-1958 direct expenditure, 1974-2001 self-financed expenditure, missing social security data for the years in between. [Source: 1881-1958 direct expenditure (partly interpolated figures), Andic and Veverka (1963); 1925-2001 self-financed expenditure, Kraus (1983), Statistisches Bundesamt (1961, 1972, 1996, 2000, 2001). Own calculations]

**Degree of expenditure decentralisation (government functions)** Public expenditure (financial statistics) by government function and level of government, including/excluding social security. Partly different expenditure concepts, not strictly comparable. Including social security: 1881-1958 direct expenditure, 1974-2001 self-financed expenditure. Excluding social security: 1881-1937 direct expenditure, 1950-2001 self-financed expenditure. Data for transport & communication, other economic services, school, and university in terms of self-expenditure are derived for 1913-1932 from Statistisches Bundesamt (1972). [Source: 1881-1958 direct expenditure (partly interpolated figures), Andic and Veverka (1963); 1950-2001 self-financed expenditure (partly interpolated figures), Stat. Bundesamt (1996, 2000, 2001). Own calculations]

**Degree of tax decentralisation** Tax revenue (financial statistics) by level of government, as per cent of total tax revenue of consolidated general government, excluding social security. Figures for 1881-1913 are interpolated. [Source: 1881-1949 data compiled by Kraus (1983) from national statistics; 1950-2001 Stat. Bundesamt (1972, 1996, 2000, 2001). Own calculations]

**Density** Natural log of population density, inhabitants per $km^2$. [Source: IMF; World Bank]

**Dependency ratio** Proportion of population aged below 15 or above 64. [Source: OECD, Labour Force Statistics. Own calculations]

**Election** See panel analysis for OECD countries.

**Employment agriculture** Fraction of working force employed in agriculture. [Source: Sachverständigenrat (2004), interpolated figures. Own calculations]

**EU expenditure** See panel analysis for OECD countries.

**EU trade** Exports plus imports to/from EU15 as a share of foreign trade. [Source: Sachverständigenrat (1997, 2002, 2004). Own calculations]

**Financial openness** See panel analysis for OECD countries.

**Growth rate** Rate of growth of real GDP per capita. [Source: 1950-69 Stat. Bundesamt (1991a), 1970-2002 Sachverständigenrat (2002, 2004). Own calculations]

**Left government** See panel analysis for OECD countries.

**Per capita income** Natural log of real GDP per capita, in prices of 1995 and in EUR, partly reckoned back. [Source: 1950-69 Stat. Bundesamt (1991a), 1970-2002 Sachverständigenrat (2002, 2004). Own calculations]

**Population** See panel analysis for OECD countries.

**Size of the public sector** Public expenditure (national income statistics) including/excluding social security, as per cent of net national product. Total public expenditures reported by Hoffmann (1965) for 1850-1938 include public consumption, current transfers, interest payments, and partly net public investment. Note that social security is understated, including only administrative expenditure for this period. [Source: 1850-1938 Hoffmann (1965), 1950-1969 Stat. Bundesamt (1991a, 1991b), 1970-2003 Sachverständigenrat (2003) drawing on data from Stat. Bundesamt. Own calculations]

**Trade openness** Exports plus imports as a share of gross domestic product. [Source: 1950-69 Stat. Bundesamt (1991a), 1970-2002 Sachverständigenrat (2002, 2004). Own calculations]

**Unemployment** Rate of unemployment. [Source: Sachverständigenrat (1997, 2002, 2004)]

**Urbanisation** See panel analysis for OECD countries.

### *Territory*

1850-1913 German *Kaiserreich*, frontiers of 1913 (until 1870 without Elsass-Lothringen)

1925-1938 Germany, frontiers of 1925 (without Austria and Sudetenland, since 1934 with Saarland)

1950-2003 Federal Republic of Germany, until 1990 without German Democratic Republic (until 1959 also without Saarland and West Berlin)

### *Classification of government functions, 1881-2001*

Administration & Other: general government, internal, tax and other administration, other unallocated functions

Law & Order: public security, police, courts, attorneys, prisons

Defence

Education: schools (general, vocational), universities, science & research (extra-university), other education (support of education, etc.)

Social Assistance & War Damage Compensation: social welfare, family benefits, youth welfare, war effects, other social affairs

Social Security: unemployment, health, invalidity and retirement insurance

Health: hospitals, other health affairs, sports and recreation, environmental protection

Housing: housing, area planning, city development

Economic/Trading Services: transport and communication (railways, public transportation, roads), other economic services (regional and economic development, public enterprises, food and agriculture, other manufacturing services, real estate, capital income)

Communal/Environmental Services

# D

# Descriptive Statistics

Table D.1: Time Series Analysis for Germany (1950-2001)

| Variable | Mean | Std.Dev. | Min. | Max. |
|---|---|---|---|---|
| Degree of fiscal decentralisation: | | | | |
| ED2, self-finan. expen. (excl. soc. sec.) | .530 | .029 | .455 | .566 |
| ED2, self-finan. expen. (excl. soc. sec. and defence) | .587 | .023 | .537 | .627 |
| ED2, self-finan. expen. (other economic services) | .514 | .076 | .341 | .632 |
| ED2, self-finan. expen. (transport, communications) | .592 | .073 | .493 | .736 |
| TD3, total tax revenue | .467 | .044 | .377 | .522 |
| Population | 11.040 | .149 | 10.820 | 11.319 |
| Density | 5.452 | .064 | 5.303 | 5.537 |
| Urbanisation | .826 | .036 | .761 | .880 |
| Per capita income | 9.585 | .448 | 8.506 | 10.091 |
| Dependency ratio | .331 | .015 | .304 | .364 |
| Employment agriculture | .088 | .062 | .024 | .246 |
| Unemployment | .056 | .040 | .005 | .127 |
| Growth rate | .033 | .034 | -.071 | .137 |
| Election | .255 | .440 | .000 | 1.000 |
| Left government | .323 | .419 | .000 | 1.000 |
| Government fragmentation | .286 | .106 | .000 | .500 |
| Trade openness | .467 | .108 | .265 | .686 |
| Financial openness | .898 | .233 | .107 | 1.000 |
| EU | .824 | .385 | .000 | 1.000 |
| EU expenditure | 1.231 | .899 | .000 | 2.400 |
| EU trade | .485 | .066 | .351 | .615 |

Table D.2: Panel Analysis for OECD Countries (1965-2001)

| Variable | Mean | Std.Dev. | Min. | Max. |
|---|---|---|---|---|
| ED1, direct expenditure (incl. soc. sec.) | .321 | .154 | .031 | .626 |
| ED1, direct expenditure (excl. soc. sec.) | .420 | .184 | .041 | .789 |
| ED2, self-financed expenditure (incl. soc. sec.) | .219 | .135 | .009 | .543 |
| ED2, self-financed expenditure (excl. soc. sec.) | .280 | .167 | .013 | .649 |
| RD3, own revenue (incl. soc. sec.), IMF | .225 | .140 | .027 | .545 |
| RD3, own revenue (excl. soc. sec.), IMF | .283 | .173 | .037 | .666 |
| TD1, autonomous own tax revenue | .191 | .166 | .000 | .615 |
| TD3, total tax revenue | .233 | .172 | .001 | .645 |
| Population | 9.348 | 1.624 | 5.257 | 12.560 |
| Area | 5.413 | 1.849 | 1.099 | 9.208 |
| Urbanisation | .737 | .140 | .239 | .972 |
| Fractionalisation | .246 | .201 | .000 | .650 |
| Regional disparity | .196 | .087 | .000 | .452 |
| Per capita income | 9.588 | .460 | 8.150 | 10.698 |
| Catholic | .401 | .358 | .001 | .940 |
| Legal origin | .262 | .440 | .000 | 1.000 |
| Dependency ratio | .347 | .026 | .299 | .429 |
| Mobility | 18.192 | 10.484 | 2.405 | 45.793 |
| Unemployment | .054 | .041 | .000 | .241 |
| Growth rate | .026 | .029 | -.105 | .272 |
| Election | .291 | .455 | .000 | 1.000 |
| Left government | .340 | .402 | .000 | 1.000 |
| Government fragmentation | .270 | .282 | .000 | .794 |
| Coldwar | 2.117 | .594 | 1.150 | 2.680 |
| Trade openness | .645 | .373 | .093 | 2.907 |
| Financial openness | .782 | .194 | .214 | 1.000 |
| EU | .448 | .498 | .000 | 1.000 |
| EU expenditure | 1.732 | .562 | .300 | 2.400 |
| EU trade | .544 | .202 | .072 | .865 |
| EU political integration | 2.233 | 2.301 | .000 | 6.000 |
| Presidential regime | .155 | .362 | .000 | 1.000 |
| Electoral system | .056 | .039 | .013 | .181 |
| Referendum (dummy) | .634 | .482 | .000 | 1.000 |
| Direct democracy (all) | .551 | .672 | .000 | 2.770 |
| Direct democracy (financial) | .226 | .657 | .000 | 2.720 |
| Direct democracy (practice) | .575 | 1.751 | .000 | 8.424 |
| Federal | .277 | .448 | .000 | 1.000 |
| Regional parliament | .090 | .287 | .000 | 1.000 |
| Subnational representation | .460 | .608 | .000 | 1.655 |
| Subnat. part. (dir.): expen. powers | .383 | .752 | .000 | 2.000 |
| Subnat. part. (dir.): reven. powers | .358 | .719 | .000 | 2.000 |
| Subnat. part. (dir.): all policies | .261 | .525 | .000 | 1.917 |
| Subnat. part. (indir.): expen. powers | .664 | .961 | .000 | 3.250 |
| Subnat. part. (indir.): reven. powers | .631 | .931 | .000 | 3.250 |
| Subnat. part. (indir.): all policies | .559 | .807 | .000 | 2.850 |
| Central tax competency | .774 | .418 | .000 | 1.000 |

# List of Figures


2.1 Degree of expenditure decentralisation (including social security), 1996-2001 ... 24
2.2 Degree of expenditure decentralisation (excluding social security), 1996-2001 ... 25
2.3 Degree of tax autonomy of sub-central government, 1996-2001 .. 28
2.4 Degree of tax decentralisation, 1996-2001 ... 29
2.5 Degree of revenue decentralisation, 1996-2001 ... 30
2.6 Trends in expenditure decentralisation (including social security), 1970-2001 ... 32
2.7 Trends in expenditure decentralisation (excluding social security), 1970-2001 ... 33
2.8 Trends in tax decentralisation, 1965-2001 ... 37
2.9 Trends in revenue decentralisation, 1975-2001 ... 38

3.1 Indirect participation of subnational entities in central decision-making, 2003 ... 53
3.2 Direct participation of subnational entities in central decision-making, 2003 ... 55
3.3 Direct democracy at the national level (referendums), 2003 ... 58
3.4 Direct democracy at the national level (initiatives), 2003 ... 59
3.5 Direct democracy at the national level (all instruments), 2003 ... 60

5.1 Growth of the public sector in Germany, 1850-2003 ... 126
5.2 Allocation of total public expenditures (excluding social security) by fiscal tiers, Germany, 1881-2001 ... 130
5.3 Allocation of total tax revenue (excluding social security) by fiscal tiers, Germany, 1881-2001 ... 132
5.4 Degree of centralisation by government function, Germany, 1913-2001 ... 135

B.1 Allocation of total public expenditure (including social security) by fiscal tiers, Germany, 1881-2001 . . . . . 194
B.2 Composition of central government expenditure by government function, Germany, 1881-2001 . . . . . 197
B.3 Composition of state government expenditure by government function, Germany, 1913-2001 . . . . . 198
B.4 Composition of local government expenditure by government function, Germany, 1913-2001 . . . . . 199

# List of Tables

2.1 Classification of subnational taxes (in decreasing order of control over revenue sources) . . . 20
2.2 Taxes of sub-central levels of government according to the degree of autonomy, 2001 . . . 27
2.3 Degree of tax autonomy of sub-central government, 1965-2001 . . 36

3.1 Representation of subnat. entities at the national level, 2003 . . . 50
3.2 OLS estimates of fiscal decentralisation, direct expenditure (incl. social security), 23 OECD countries, 1970-2001 . . . 73
3.3 OLS estimates of fiscal decentralisation (institutions 1), tax revenue, 23 OECD countries, 1965-2001 . . . 77
3.4 OLS estimates of fiscal decentralisation (institutions 2), tax revenue, 23 OECD countries, 1965-2001 . . . 78

4.1 Degree of economic openness, and trade with EU countries, 1970-2001 . . . 96
4.2 The budget of the European Union, 1960-2001 . . . 97
4.3 Fixed effects (within) estimates for fiscal decentralisation, direct expenditure (incl. social security), OECD countries, 1970-2001 . . . 103
4.4 Fixed effects (within) estimates for fiscal decentralisation, autonomous own tax revenue, OECD countries, 1965-2001 . . . 106
4.5 Quantile (median) estimates for fiscal decentralisation, direct expenditure (incl. social security), OECD countries, 1970-2001 . 109
4.6 Quantile (median) estimates for fiscal decentralisation, autonomous own tax revenue, OECD countries, 1965-2001 . . . 111

5.1 Trends in public sector growth and decentralisation, Germany . . 134
5.2 OLS estimates of fiscal decentralisation, self-financed expenditure (excl. social security), Germany, 1950-2001 . . . 140

B.1 Levels of government in OECD countries ... 153
B.2 Fiscal decentralisation in OECD countries (competencies, polit. autonomy) ... 154
B.3 Fiscal decentralisation in OECD countries (finan. autonomy) ... 156
B.4 Degree of expenditure decentralisation, 1970-2001 ... 157
B.5 Own revenue of sub-central government, 1970-2001 ... 158
B.6 Degree of revenue autonomy of sub-central government, 1975-2001 ... 159
B.7 Decentralisation trends, fixed effects estimates, 23 OECD countries, 1965-2001 ... 160
B.8 Degree of tax decentralisation (indic. TD1), annual figures, 1965-2001 ... 161
B.9 Degree of tax decentralisation, 1965-2001 ... 162
B.10 Degree of revenue decentralisation (indic. RD1), annual figures, 1975-2001 ... 163
B.11 Degree of revenue decentralisation, 1975-2001 ... 164
B.12 Overview of empirical studies on the determinants of fiscal decentralisation ... 165
B.13 Index of subnational representation in the upper chamber ... 167
B.14 Indices of participation of subnational entities in central decision-making ... 168
B.15 Indirect participation of subnational entities in central decision-making, 2003 ... 169
B.16 Direct participation of subnational entities in central decision-making, 2003 ... 170
B.17 Indices of direct democracy at the national level ... 171
B.18 Direct democracy at the national level (1), 2003 ... 172
B.19 Direct democracy at the national level (2), 2003 ... 173
B.20 OLS estimates of fiscal decentralisation, self-financed expenditure (incl. social security), 23 OECD countries, 1970-2001 ... 174
B.21 Alternative OLS estimates of fiscal decentralisation, direct expenditure (incl. social security), 23 OECD countries, 1970-2001 ... 175
B.22 Alternative OLS estimates of fiscal decentralisation, tax revenue, 23 OECD countries, 1965-2001 ... 177
B.23 OLS estimates of fiscal decentralisation (institutions 1), tax revenue, 3-year-averages, 23 OECD countries, 1965-2001 ... 179
B.24 OLS estimates of fiscal decentralisation (institutions 2), tax revenue, 3-year-averages, 23 OECD countries, 1965-2001 ... 180
B.25 Fixed effects (within) estimates, self-financed expenditure (incl. social security), OECD countries, 1970-2001 ... 181
B.26 Fixed effects (within) estimates, total own revenue (incl. social security), OECD countries, 1970-2001 ... 183

B.27 Fixed effects (within) estimates, direct expenditure (excl. social security), OECD countries, 1970-2001 . . . . . 185
B.28 Fixed effects (within) estimates, self-financed expenditure (excl. social security), OECD countries, 1970-2001 . . . . . 187
B.29 Fixed effects (within) estimates, total own revenue (excl. social security), OECD countries, 1970-2001 . . . . . 189
B.30 Sensitivity analysis with Belgium and Spain: Fixed effects (within) estimates, direct expenditure (incl. social security), 1970-2001 . . . . . 191
B.31 Fixed effects (within) estimates, total tax revenue, OECD countries, 1965-2001 . . . . . 192
B.32 Allocation of public expenditure by government function and level of government, Germany, 1913-2001 . . . . . 195
B.33 Allocation of public expenditure by level of government, Germany, 1881-2001 . . . . . 196
B.34 Allocation of tax revenue by level of government, Germany, 1881-2001 . . . . . 196
B.35 OLS estimates of fiscal decentralisation, expenditure on other economic services, Germany, 1950-2001 . . . . . 200
B.36 OLS estimates of fiscal decentralisation, expenditure on transport and communication, Germany, 1950-2001 . . . . . 201
B.37 OLS estimates of fiscal decentralisation, total tax revenue, Germany, 1950-2001 . . . . . 202

D.1 Time Series Analysis for Germany (1950-2001) . . . . . 211
D.2 Panel Analysis for OECD Countries (1965-2001) . . . . . 212

# References


Ades, A. F. and E. L. Glaeser (1999), Evidence on Growth, Increasing Returns, and the Extent of the Market, *The Quarterly Journal of Economics* 114(3), 1025–1045.

Aghion, P., A. Alesina, and F. Trebbi (2004), Endogenous Political Institutions, *Quarterly Journal of Economics* 119(2), 565–611.

Albers, W. (1964), Das Popitz'sche Gesetz der Anziehungskraft des übergeordneten Haushalts, in: F. Neumark (Ed.), *Strukturwandlungen einer wachsenden Wirtschaft*, Berlin.

Alesina, A. (2002), *The Size of Countries: Does It Matter?*, Harvard Institute of Economic Research Discussion Paper No. 1975.

Alesina, A. and R. Perotti (1998), Economic Risk and Political Risk in Fiscal Unions, *The Economic Journal* Vol. 108(449), 989–1008.

Alesina, A. and E. Spolaore (1997), On the Number and Size of Nations, *The Quarterly Journal of Economics* 112(4), 1027–1056.

Alesina, A. and E. Spolaore (2003), *The Size of Nations*, Cambridge (MA).

Alesina, A. and R. Wacziarg (1998), Openness, Country Size and Government, *Journal of Public Economics* 69, 305–321.

Alesina, A., E. Spolaore, and R. Wacziarg (2000), Economic Integration and Political Disintegration, *American Economic Review* 90(5), 1276–1296.

Alesina, A., I. Angeloni, and F. Etro (2001a), *Institutional Rules for Federations*, NBER Working Paper No. 8646.

Alesina, A., I. Angeloni, and F. Etro (2003), *International Unions*, Harvard Institute of Economic Research Discussion Paper No. 2001.

Alesina, A., I. Angeloni, and L. Schuknecht (2001b), *What Does the European Union Do?*, NBER Working Paper No. 8647.

Alesina, A., A. Devleeschauwer, W. Easterly, S. Kurlat, and R. Wacziarg (2003), Fractionalization, *Journal of Economic Growth* 8(2), 155–194.

Alesina, A., R. Baqir, and W. Easterly (1999), Public Goods and Ethnic Divisions, *The Quarterly Journal of Economics* 114(4), 1243–1284.

Amin, A. and N. Thrift (1999), Living in the Global, in: Amin, A. and N. Thrift (Eds.), *Globalization, Institutions, and Regional Development in Europe*, New York.

Andic, S. and J. Veverka (1963), The Growth of Government Expenditure in Germany Since the Unification (1871), *Finanzarchiv* N.F. 23(2), 169–278.

Arellano, M. (1987), Computing Robust Standard Errors for Within-Groups Estimators, *Oxford Bulletin of Economics and Statistics* 49(4), 431–434.

Arikan, G. G. (2004), Fiscal Decentralization: A Remedy for Corruption?, *International Tax and Public Finance* 11, 175–195.

Armingeon, K., P. Leimgruber, M. Beyeler, and S. Menegale (2004), *Comparative Political Data Set 1960-2002*, Institute of Political Science, University of Berne.

Aschauer, D. A. (1989), Is Public Expenditure Productive?, *Journal of Monetary Economics* 23, 177–200.

Bahl, R. and S. Nath (1986), *Public Expenditure Decentralization in Developing Countries*, Environmental and Planning C: Government and Policy, Vol. 4, 405–418.

Bahl, R. (1999), *Implementation Rules for Fiscal Decentralization*, Andrew Young School of Policy Studies, Georgia State University, unpublished manuscript.

Baker, S. H. (2000), Does Enhanced Veto Authority Centralize Government?, *Public Choice* 104, 63–79.

Baldwin, R. E. and P. Krugman (2002), *Agglomeration, Integration and Tax Harmonization*, NBER Working Paper No. 9290.

Baron, D. P. and J. A. Ferejohn (1989), Bargaining in Legislatures, *The American Political Science Review* 83(4), 1181–1206.

Barro, R. J. (1990), Government Spending in a Simple Model of Endogenous Growth, *Journal of Political Economy* 98(5), S103–S125.

Behnisch, A., T. Buettner, and D. Stegarescu (2002), *Public Sector Centralization and Productivity Growth: Reviewing the German Experience*, ZEW Discussion Paper No. 02-03, Mannheim.

Besley, T. and A. Case (2002), *Political Institutions and Policy Choices: Evidence from the United States*, Institute for Fiscal Studies, WP 02/13.

Besley, T. and S. Coate (2000), *Issue Unbundling via Citizens' Initiatives*, NBER Working Paper No. 8036.

Besley, T. and S. Coate (2003), Centralized Versus Decentralized Provision of Local Public Goods : A Political Economy Approach, *Journal of Public Economics* 87, 2611–2637.

Bird, R. M. (1993), Threading the Fiscal Labyrinth. Some Issues in Fiscal Decentralization, *National Tax Journal* 46(2), 207–227.

Bird, R. M. (2003), *Asymmetric Fiscal Decentralization: Glue or Solvent?*, Andrew Young School of Policy Studies Working Paper 03-09, Georgia State University.

Blais, A., D. Blake, and S. Dion (1993), Do Parties Make a Difference? Parties and the Size of Government in Liberal Democracies, *American Journal of Political Science* 37(1), 40–62.

Blankart, C. B. (1999), Die schleichende Zentralisierung der Staatstätigkeit: Eine Fallstudie, *Zeitschrift für Wirtschafts- und Sozialwissenschaften* 119, 331–350.

Blankart, C. B. (2000), The Process of Government Centralization: A Constitutional View, *Constitutional Political Economy* 11, 27–39.

Blankart, C. B. (2001), Popitz Law, Bryce's Law and Government Centralization in Prussia and in Germany, *Journal of Public Finance and Public Choice* 19(1), 71–81.

Bolton, P. and G. Roland (1996), Distributional Conflicts, Factor Mobility, and Political Integration, *American Economic Review* 86(2), 99–105.

Bolton, P. and G. Roland (1997), The Break-Up of Nations: A Political Economy Analysis *The Quarterly Journal of Economics* 112(4), 1057–1090.

Bolton, P., G. Roland, and E. Spolaore (1996), Economic Theories of the Break-Up and Integration of Nations, *European Economic Review* 40, 697–705.

Bookman, M. Z. (1992), *The Economics of Secession*, New York.

Bordignon, M. and S. Brusco (2001), Optimal Secession Rules, *European Economic Review* 45, 1811–1834.

Bradbury, J. C. and W. M. Crain (2001), Legislative Organization and Government Spending: Cross-Country Evidence, *Journal of Public Economics* 82, 309–325.

Bradbury, J. C. and W. M. Crain (2002), Bicameral Legislatures and Fiscal Policy, *Southern Economic Journal* 68(3), 646–659.

Brakman, S., H. Garretsen, and C. van Marrewijk (2002), *Locational Competition and Agglomeration: The Role of Government Spending*, CESifo Working Paper No. 775.

Brecht, A. (1932), *Internationaler Vergleich öffentlicher Ausgaben, Grundfragen der internationalen Politik 2*, Leipzig.

Brennan, G. and J. Buchanan (1980), *The Power to Tax – Analytical Foundations of a Fiscal Constitution*, Cambridge.

Breton, A. and A. Scott (1978), *The Economic Constitution of Federal States*, Toronto etc.

Buchanan, J. (1967), *Public Finance in Democratic Process*, Chapel Hill.

Buchanan, J. and G. Tullock (1962), *The Calculus of Consent. Logical Foundation of Constitutional Democracy*, Ann Arbor.

Buettner, T., R. Schwager, and D. Stegarescu (2004), Agglomeration, Population Size, and the Cost of Providing Public Services: An Empirical Analysis for German States, *Public Finance and Management* 4(4), 496–520.

Burg, P. (1992), Der Föderalismus im Kaiserreich. Politische Strukturen und Prozesse, in: Huhn, J. and P.C. Witt (Eds.), *Föderalismus in Deutschland. Traditionen und gegenwärtige Probleme*, Baden-Baden, 55–74.

Cameron, D. R. (1978), The Expansion of the Public Economy: A Comparative Analysis, *American Political Science Review* 72, 1243–1261.

Casella, A. and J. S. Feinstein (2002), Public Goods in Trade: On the Formation of Markets and Jurisdictions, *International Economic Review* 43(2), 437–462.

Castles, F. G.(Ed.) (1982), *The Impact of Parties: Politics and Policies in Democratic Capitalist States*, London etc.

Castles, F. G. and P. Mair (1982), *Left-Political Scales: Some Expert Judgements*, EUI Working Paper No. 28, San Domenico.

Committee of the Regions (1999), *Regional and Local Democracy in the European Union*, Brussels.

Committee of the Regions (2000), *Decentralisation of European Decision Making*, Brussels.

Committee of the Regions (2001), *Regional and Local Government in the European Union – Responsibilities and Resources*, Brussels.

Council of Europe (1997), *Federal and Regional States*, Collection Science and Technique of Democracy, No. 19.

Council of Europe, *Structure and Operation of Local and Regional Democracy*, various country studies, Strasbourg.

Crémer, J. and T. R. Palfrey (1996), In or Out?: Centralization by Majority Vote, *European Economic Review* 40, 43–60.

Dafflon, B. and F. Pujol (2001), Fiscal Preferences and Fiscal Performance: Swiss Cantonal Evidence, *International Public Management Review* 2(2), 54–78.

Davidson, R. and J. J. MacKinnon (1993), *Estimation and Inference in Economics*, New York etc.

Davoodi, H. and H. Zou (1998), Fiscal Decentralization and Economic Growth: A Cross-Country Study, *Journal of Urban Economics* 43, 244–257.

Döhler, E. (2002), *Autonome Besteuerungsrechte für Gliedstaaten und Gemeinden in ausgewählten föderativen Finanzverfassungen*, INFER Research Edition Vol. 7, Berlin.

Drazen, A. (2002), *Political Economy in Macroeconomics*, 2nd ed., Princeton (NJ).

Ebel, R. D. and S. Yilmaz (2003), On the Measurement and Impact of Fiscal Decentralization, in: Martinez-Vazquez, J. and J. Alm (Eds.), *Public Finance in Developing and Transitional Countries: Essays in Honor of Richard Bird*, Cheltenham, 101–126.

Edwards, J. and M. Keen (1996), Tax Competition and Leviathan, *European Economic Review* 40, 113–134.

Efron, B. and R. J. Tibshirani (1993), *An Introduction to the Bootstrap*, New York.

Elazar, D. J. (Ed.) (1994), *Federal Systems of the World: A Handbook of Federal, Confederal and Autonomy Arrangements*, 2nd ed., Harlow.

Engel, C. and J. van Ginderachter (1992), *Le pouvoir régional et local dans la Communauté Européenne*, Études de Droit des Communautés Européennes, Paris.

Esteban, J.-M. and D. Ray (1994), On the Measurement of Polarization, *Econometrica* 62(4), 819–851.

Etro, F. (2003), *Globalization and Political Economy*, CESIfo Working Paper No. 986.

Europäische Kommission (2000), *Haushaltsvademekum 2000*, Brussels.

European Commission (2002), *Inventory of Taxes in the EU*, various country studies, Brussels.

Fearon, J. D. (2003), Ethnic and Cultural Diversity by Country, *Journal of Economic Growth* 8(2), 195–222.

Feld, L. P. and G. Kirchgässner (2001), The Political Economy of Direct Legislation: Direct Democracy and Local Decision-Making, *Economic Policy* 33, 330–367.

Feld, L. P., G. Kirchgässner, and C. A. Schaltegger (2003), *Decentralized Taxation and the Size of Government: Evidence from Swiss State and Local Governments*, CESifo Working Paper No. 1087, Munich.

Feld, L. P. and J. G. Matsusaka (2003), Budget Referendums and Government Spending: Evidence from Swiss Cantons, *Journal of Public Economics* 87(12), 2703–2724.

Fisman, R. and R. Gatti (2002), Decentralization and Corruption: Evidence Across Countries, *Journal of Public Economics* 83(3), 325–345.

Fossati, A. and G. Panella (Eds.) (1999), *Fiscal Federalism in the European Union*, London etc.

Frey, B. S. and A. Stutzer (2000), Happiness, Economy and Institutions, *The Economic Journal* 110, 918–938.

Frey, B. S. and A. Stutzer (2003), *Direct Democracy: Designing a Living Constitution*, Institute for Empirical Research in Economics Working Paper No. 167, Zurich.

Garrett, G. and J. Rodden (2003), Globalization and Fiscal Decentralization, in: Kahler, M. and D. A. Lake (Eds.), *Governance in a Global Economy: Political Authority in Transition*, Princeton, 87–109.

Gerber, E. R. and J. B. Lewis (2004), Beyond the Median: Voter Preferences, District Heterogeneity, and Political Representation, *Journal of Political Economy* 112(6), 1364–1383.

Gerloff, W. (1913), *Die Finanz- und Zollpolitik des Deutschen Reiches nebst ihren Beziehungen zu Landes- und Gemeindefinanzen von der Gründung des Norddeutschen Bundes bis zur Gegenwart*, Jena.

Giannetti, M. (2002), The Effects of Integration on Regional Disparities: Convergence, Divergence or Both?, *European Economic Review* 46, 539–567.

Giertz, J. F. (1983), State-Local Centralization and Income: A Theoretical Framework and Further Empirical Results, *Public Finance/Finances Publiques* 38(3), 398–408.

Gradstein, M. (2000), *The Political Economy of Sustainable Federations*, CESifo Working Paper No. 315.

Granger, C. W. J. (1969), Investigating Causal Relations by Econometric Models and Cross-Spectral Methods, *Econometrica* 37(3), 424–438.

Granger, C. W. J. and P. Newbold (1974), Spurious Regressions in Econometrics, *Journal of Econometrics* 2, 111–120.

Greenberg, J. H. (1956), The Measurement of Linguistic Diversity, *Language* 32(1), 109–115.

Greene, W. H. (2000), *Econometric Analysis*, 4th ed., Prentice Hall.

Grossman, P. J. and E. G. West (1994), Federalism and the Growth of Government Revisited, *Public Choice* 79, 19–32.

Gurr, T. R. (1993), *Minorities at Risk*, Washington D.C.

Hansmeyer, K.-H. (1967), Das Popitzsche Gesetz von der Anziehungskraft des zentralen Etats, in: Timm, H. and C.-A. Andreae (Eds.), *Beiträge zur Theorie der öffentlichen Ausgaben*, Berlin, 197–229.

Hansmeyer, K.-H. and K. Zimmermann (1984), Das Popitzsche Gesetz und die Entwicklung der Aufgabenverteilung zwischen Bund und Ländern in den 60er und 70er Jahren, in: Koch, W. and H.-G. Petersen (Eds.), *Staat, Steuern und Finanzausgleich. Festschrift für Heinz Kolms zum 70. Geburtstag*, Berlin, 297–314.

Hesse, K. (1962), *Der unitarische Bundesstaat*, Karlsruhe.

Helliwell, J. F. (1996), Do National Borders Matter for Quebec's Trade?, *The Canadian Journal of Economics* 29(3), 507–522.

Hibbs, D. A. Jr. (1977), Political Parties and Macroeconomic Policy, *American Political Science Review* 70, 467–487

Hicks, A. M. and D. H. Swank (1992), Politics, Institutions, and Welfare Spending in Industrialized Democracies, 1960–82, *American Political Science Review* 86(3), 658–674.

Hiscox, M. J. (2003), Political Integration and Disintegration in the Global Economy, in: Kahler, M. and D. A. Lake (Eds.), *Governance in a Global Economy: Political Authority in Transition*, Princeton, 60–86.

Hoffmann, W. G. (1965), *Das Wachstum der deutschen Wirtschaft seit der Mitte des 19. Jahrhunderts*, Berlin.

Hooghe, L. and G. Marks (2001), *Multi-Level Governance and European Integration*, Lanham.

Hug, S. and G. Tsebelis (2002), Veto Players and Referendums Around the World, *Journal of Theoretical Politics* 14(4), 465-515.

Huntington, S. P. (1993), The Clash of Civilizations?, *Foreign Affairs*, 72(3) (Summer).

International Monetary Fund (IMF) (2001), *Government Finance Statistics Manual*, Washington.

Inman, R. P. and D. L. Rubinfeld (1997), Rethinking Federalism, *Journal of Economic Perspectives* 11(4), 43–64.

Ismayr, W. (1999), *Die politischen Systeme Westeuropas*, 2nd ed., Opladen.

Jehiel, P. and S. Scotchmer (2001), Constitutional Rules of Exclusion in Jurisdiction Formation, *Review of Economic Studies* 68, 393–413.

Judge, G. G., R. C. Hill, W. E. Griffiths, H. Lütkepohl, and T.-C. Lee (1988), *Introduction to the Theory and Practice of Econometrics*, New York.

Kaufman, H. (1963), *Politics and Policies in State and Local Governments*, Englewood Cliffs (NJ).

Kaufmann, B. and M. D. Waters (2004), *Direct Democracy in Europe*, Durham (NC).

Keating, M. (1998), *The New Regionalism in Western Europe. Territorial Restructuring and Political Change*, Cheltenham.

Kee, W. S. (1977), Fiscal Decentralization and Economic Development, *Public Finance Quarterly* 5(1), 79–97.

Koenker, R. and G. Bassett (1978), Regression Quantiles, *Econometrica* 46(1), 33–50.

Kraus, A. (1983), *Zentrale und dezentrale Tendenzen im Föderalismus*, Göttingen.

Krieger-Boden, C. (2000), *Globalization, Integration and Regional Specialization*, Kiel Working Paper No. 1009.

Krugman, P. (1991a), *Geography and Trade*, Cambridge (MA).

Krugman, P. (1991b), Increasing Returns and Economic Geography, *The Jounal of Political Economy* 99(3), 483–499.

Krugman, P. and A. Venables (1996), Integration, Specialization, and Adjustment, *European Economic Review* 40, 959–967.

Kuhn, T. (1993), Determinanten der Staatsausgaben: Bevölkerung und Urbanisierung, Eine Literaturübersicht, *Ifo Studien – Zeitschrift für empirische Wirtschaftsforschung* 39(1-4), 127–145.

Laitin, D. and D. Posner (2001), The Implications of Constructivism for Constructing Ethnic Fractionalization Indices, *Newsletter of the American Political Science Association Organized Section in Comparative Politics (APSA-CP)* 12(1), 13–17.

Lammers, K. (1999), Europäische Integration und räumliche Entwicklungsprozesse: Wo bleibt die nationale Ebene?, *Beihefte der Konjunkturpolitik* 49, 21–44.

La Porta, R., F. Lopez-de-Silanes, A. Shleifer, and R. Vishny (1999), The Quality of Government, *The Journal of Law, Economics, & Organization* 15(1), 222–279.

Lane, J.-E. and S. O. Ersson (1987), *Politics and Society in Western Europe*, London.

Lane, J.-E., D. McKay, and K. Newton (1997), *Political Data Handbook OECD Countries*, Oxford.

Legler, J.B., R. Sylla, and J.J. Wallis (1988), U.S. City Finances and the Growth of Government, 1850-1902, *The Journal of Economic History* Vol. XLVIII, No. 2, p.347–356.

Levin, J. (1990), Measuring the Role of Subnational Governments, in: Prud'homme, R. (Ed.), *Public Finance with Several Levels of Government*, Proceedings of the 46th Congress of the IIPF, Brussels 1990, The Hague/Koenigstein, 21–36.

Lijphart, A. (1984), *Democracies*, New Haven.

Litvack, J. M. and W. E. Oates (1970), Group Size and the Output of Public Goods. Theory and an Application to State-Local Finance in the United States, *Public Finance/Finances Publiques* 25, 42–62.

Lockwood, B. (2002), Distributive Politics and the Costs of Centralization, *The Review of Economic Studies* 69(2), 313–337.

Lockwood, B. (2004), Decentralization via Federal and Unitary Referenda, *Journal of Public Economic Theory* 6(1), 79–108.

Mackie, T. T. and R. Rose (1991), *The International Almanac of Electoral History*, 3rd ed., London.

Majone, G. (1997), From the Positive to the Regulatory State: Causes and Consequences of Changes in the Mode of Governance, *Journal of Public Policy* 17, 139–167.

Marcou, G., A. Gazaryan, and K. Svoboda (2000), *La régionalisation en Europe*, European Parliament, Directorate General for Research, Regional Policy Series Working Papers REGI 108 A XX/rev. 1, 04/2000.

Marlow, M. L. (1988), Fiscal Decentralization and Government Size, *Public Choice* 56(3), 259–269.

Matsusaka, J. G. (1995), Fiscal Effects of the Voter Initiative: Evidence from the Last 30 Years, *Journal of Political Economy* 103(3), 587–623.

Matsusaka, J. G. (2000), Fiscal Effects of the Voter Initiative in the First Half of the Twentieth Century, *Journal of Law & Economics* 43(2), 619–650.

Meltzer, A. H. and S. F. Richard (1981), A Rational Theory of the Size of Government, *Journal of Political Economy* 89(5), 914–927.

Meyer, S. (1998), Popitz' "Gesetz der Anziehungskraft des zentralen Etats" – Erklärungsansatz für Zentralisierungstendenzen im europäischen Integrationsprozess?, *WiSt* 4, 197–200.

Milesi-Ferretti, G. M., R. Perotti, and M. Rostagno (2002), Electoral Systems and Public Spending, *Quarterly Journal of Economics* 117, 609–657.

Miñana, J.-S. (1998), *Décentralisation, corresponsabilité et responsabilité fiscales: Étude de dix-huit États européens*, Cahiers économiques de Bruxelles, No. 160(4), 389–425.

Moser, P. (1999), The Impact of Legislative Institutions on Public Policy, *European Journal of Political Economy* 15, 1–33.

Mueller, D. C. (1996), *Constitutional Democracy*, Oxford.

Mullen, J. K. (1980), The Role of Income in Explaining State-Local Fiscal Decentralization, *Public Finance/Finances Publiques* 35(2), 300–308.

Musgrave, R. A. (1959), *The Theory of Public Finance: A Study in Public Economy*, Tokyo.

Nelson, M. A. (1987), Searching for Leviathan: Comment and Extension, *American Economic Review* 77(1), 198–204.

Neumark, F. (1976), Die Finanzpolitik in der Zeit vor dem I. Weltkrieg, in: Deutsche Bundesbank (Ed.), *Währung und Wirtschaft in Deutschland 1876-1975*, Frankfurt am Main, 57–111.

Newey, W. K. and K. D. West (1987), A Simple, Positive Semi-Definite, Heteroskedasticity and Autocorrelation Consistent Covariance Matrix, *Econometrica* 55(3), 703–708.

Norton, A. (1994), *International Handbook of Local and Regional Government – A Comparative Analysis of Advanced Democracies*, Aldershot.

Oates, W. E. (1972), *Fiscal Federalism*, New York.

Oates, W. E. (1985), Searching for Leviathan: An Empirical Study, *American Economic Review* 75(4), 748–757.

Oates, W. E. (1999), An Essay on Fiscal Federalism, *Journal of Economic Literature* 37, 1120–1149.

OECD (1981), *Long-Term Trends in Tax Revenues of OECD Member Countries 1955-1980*, Paris.

OECD (1997), *Managing Across Levels of Government*, Paris.

OECD (1999), *Taxing Powers of State and Local Government*, OECD Tax Policy Studies No.1, Paris.

OECD (2002a), *Fiscal Design Surveys Across Levels of Government*, OECD Tax Policy Studies No. 7, Paris.

OECD (2002b), *Fiscal Decentralization in EU Applicant States and Selected EU Member States*, Report Prepared for the Workshop on "Decentralization: Trends, Perspective and Issues at the Threshold of EU Enlargement", Denmark, October 10-11, 2002.

OECD (2003), *OECD Economic Outlook* 74, Paris.

Ohmae, K. (1995), *The End of the Nation State*, New York.

Olson, M. (1969), The Principle of "Fiscal Equivalence": The Division of Responsibilities Among Different Levels of Government, *American Economic Review* 59, 479–487.

Owens, J. P. and J. Norregaard (1991), The Role of Intermediate and Local Levels of Government: The Experience of Selected OECD Countries, in: King, D. N. and J. P. Owens (Eds.), *Fiscal Federalism in Economies in Transition*, Proceedings of a Conference Organised by the OECD, April 1991, 69–116.

Panizza, U. (1999), On the Determinants of Fiscal Centralization: Theory and Evidence, *Journal of Public Economics* 74, 97–139.

Patsouratis, V. A. (1990), Fiscal Decentralization in the EEC Countries, *Public Finances/Finances Publiques* 45(3), 423–439.

Peacock, A. T. and J. Wiseman (1961), *The Growth of Public Expenditure in the United Kingdom*, Princeton.

Peltzman, S. (1980), The Growth of Government, *The Journal of Law & Economics*, Vol. 23(2), 209–287.

Peltzman, S. (1992), Voters as Fiscal Conservatives, *Quarterly Journal of Economics* 107, 327–361.

Persson, T. (2002), Do Political Institutions Shape Economic Policy?, *Econometrica* 70(3), 883–905.

Persson, T. (2003), *Consequences of Constitutions*, NBER Working Paper No. 10170.

Persson, T., G. Roland, and G. Tabellini (2003), Comparative Politics and Public Finance, *Journal of Political Economy* 108(6), 1121–1161.

Persson, T. and G. Tabellini (1996a), Federal Fiscal Constitutions: Risk Sharing and Moral Hazard, *Econometrica* 64(3), 623–646.

Persson, T. and G. Tabellini (1996b), Federal Fiscal Constitutions: Risk Sharing and Redistribution, *Journal of Political Economy* 104, 979–1009.

Persson, T. and G. Tabellini (1999), The Size and Scope of Government: Comparative Politics with Rational Politicians, *European Economic Review* 43, 699–735.

Persson, T. and G. Tabellini (2000), *Political Economics: Explaining Economic Policy*, Cambridge (MA).

Persson, T. and G. Tabellini (2001), *Political Institutions and Policy Outcomes: What Are the Stylized Facts?*, CESifo Working Paper No. 459.

Persson, T. and G. Tabellini (2003), *Do Electoral Cycles Differ Across Political Systems?*, IGIER Working Paper No. 232.

Pfetsch, F. R. (1974), *Zur Entwicklung der Wissenschaftspolitik in Deutschland 1750-1914*, Berlin.

Pola, G. (1999), A Comparative View of Local Finances in EU Member Countries: Are There Any Lessons to Be Drawn?, in: Fossati, A. and G. Panella (Eds.), *Fiscal Federalism in the European Union*, London, 15–62.

Pommerehne, W. W. (1977), Quantitative Aspects of Federalism: A Study of Six Countries, in: Oates, W. E. (Ed.), *The Political Economy of Fiscal Federalism*, Lexington (MA).

Pommerehne, W. W. (1978), Institutional Approaches to Public Expenditure – Empirical Evidence from Swiss Municipalities, *Journal of Public Economics* 9, 255–280.

Poole, K. T. and H. Rosenthal (1996), Are Legislators Idealogues or the Agents of Constituents?, *European Economic Review* 40, 707–717.

Popitz, J. (1927), Der Finanzausgleich, in: Gerloff, W. and F. Meisel, *Handbuch der Finanzwissenschaft*, 2nd Vol., Tübingen, 338ff.

Poterba, J. (1995), Capital Budgets, Borrowing Rules, and State Capital Spending, *Journal of Public Economics* 56(2), 165–187.

Poterba, J. (1996), Budget Institutions and Fiscal Policy in the U.S. States, *American Economic Review*, 86(2), 395–400.

Pryor, F. L. (1968), *Public Expenditures in Communist and Capitalist Nations*, London.

Pujol, F. and L. Weber (2003), Are Preferences for Fiscal Discipline Endogenous?, *Public Choice* 114, 421–444

Quinn, D. P. and C. Inclan (1997), The Origins of Financial Openness: A Study of Current and Capital Account Liberalization, *American Journal of Political Science* 41(3), 771–813.

Ram, R. (1987), Wagner's Hypothesis in Time-Series and Cross-Section Perspectives: Evidence from "Real" Data for 115 Countries, *The Review of Economics and Statistics*, 69(2), 194–204.

Rahmann, B., U. Steinborn, and G. Vornholz (1994), *Empirische Analyse der Autonomie lokaler Finanzwirtschaften in der Europäischen Gemeinschaft*, Finanzwissenschaftliche Schriften 64, Frankfurt a.M.

Recktenwald, H.C. (1962), Die Entwicklung der öffentlichen Ausgaben in der Bundesrepublik, in: König, H. (Ed.), *Wandlungen der Wirtschaftsstruktur in der Bundesrepublik Deutschland*, 199–248.

Recktenwald, H.C. (1975), Umfang und Struktur der öffentlichen Ausgaben in säkularer Entwicklung, in: Andel, N., H. Haller, and F. Neumark (Eds.), *Handbuch der Finanzwissenschaft* Vol. 1, 3rd ed.

Recktenwald, H. C. (1984), Föderalismus im säkularen Wandel. Erste Ergebnisse einer empirischen Analyse, in: Koch, W. and H.-G. Petersen (Eds.), *Staat, Steuern und Finanzausgleich. Festschrift für Heinz Kolms zum 70. Geburtstag*, Berlin, 279–295.

Redoano, M. and K. Scharf (2004), The Political Economy of Policy Centralization: Direct Versus Representative Democracy, *Journal of Public Economics* 88, 799–817.

Reichsschatzamt (1908), *Denkschriftenband zur Begründung des Entwurfs eines Gesetzes betreffend Änderungen im Finanzwesen*, Berlin.

Riker, W. H. (1964), *Federalism. Origin, Operation, Significance*, Boston.

Rodrik, D. (1998), Why Do More Open Economies Have Bigger Governments?, *Journal of Political Economy* 106(5), 997–1032.

Rondinelli, D. (1999), What Is Decentralization?, in: Litvack, J. and J. Seddon (Eds.), *Decentralization Briefing Notes*, World Bank Institute, Washington.

Roubini, N. and J. D. Sachs (1989), Political and Economic Determinants of Budget Deficits in the Industrial Democracies, *European Economic Review* 33, 903–938.

Ruta, M. (2005), Economic Theories of Political (Dis)Integration, *Journal of Economic Surveys* 19(1), 1–21.

Sachverständigenrat zur Begutachtung der gesamtwirtschaftlichen Entwicklung, diverse editions, Wiesbaden.

Schaltegger, C. A. and L. P. Feld (2001), *On Government Centralization and Budget Referendums: Evidence from Switzerland*, CESifo Working Paper No. 615.

Schaltegger, C. A. and L. P. Feld (2004), *Do Large Cabinets Favor Large Governments? Evidence from Swiss Sub-Federal Jurisdictions*, CESifo Working Paper No. 1294.

Scharpf, F. W., B. Reissert, and F. Schnabel (1976), *Politikverflechtung. Theorie und Empirie des kooperativen Föderalismus in der Bundesrepublik*, Kronberg.

Schmidt, M.G. (1999), Die Europäisierung der öffentlichen Ausgaben, *ZeS-Arbeitspapier* 3/1999, Zentrum für Sozialpolitik, Bremen.

Schremmer, E. (1994), *Steuern und Staatsfinanzen während der Industrialisierung Europas: England, Frankreich, Preußen und das Deutsche Reich 1800 bis 1914*, Berlin.

Schulze, G. and H. Ursprung (1999), Globalisation of the Economy and the Nation State, *The World Economy* 22, 295–351.

Schwager, R. (1999a), Administrative Federalism and a Central Government with Regionally Based Preferences, *International Tax and Public Finance* 6, 165–189.

Schwager, R. (1999b), The Theory of Administrative Federalism: An Alternative to Fiscal Centralization and Decentralization, *Public Finance Review* 27, 282–309.

Scott, A. J. (1998), *Regions and the World Economy*, Oxford.

Seabright, P. (1996), Accountability and Decentralisation in Government: An Incomplete Contracts Model, *European Economic Review* 40, 61–89.

Shadbegian, R. J. (1999), Fiscal Federalism, Collusion, and Government Size: Evidence from the States, *Public Finance Review* 27(3), 262–281.

Sharpe, L. J. (1979), *Decentralist Trends in Western Democracies*, London etc.

Smith, B. C. (1979), The Measurement of Decentralization, *International Review of Administrative Sciences* 1, 214–222.

Spolaore, E. and A. Alesina (2001), *War, Peace and the Size of Countries*, Harvard Institute of Economic Research Discussion Paper No. 1937.

Spolaore, E. and R. Wacziarg (2002), *Borders and Growth*, NBER Working Paper No. 9223.

Statistisches Bundesamt (1961), *Statistik der Bundesrepublik Deutschland, Band 259. Öffentliche Finanzwirtschaft in den Rechnungsjahren 1957 und 1958*, Stuttgart.

Statistisches Bundesamt (1972), *Bevölkerung und Wirtschaft 1872-1972*, Stuttgart.

Statistisches Bundesamt (1991a), *Volkswirtschaftliche Gesamtrechnungen. Der Staat in den Volkswirtschaftlichen Gesamtrechnungen 1950 bis 1990* Fachserie 18, Reihe S.16, Wiesbaden.

Statistisches Bundesamt (1991b), *Volkswirtschaftliche Gesamtrechnungen. Revidierte Ergebnisse 1950 bis 1990* Fachserie 18, Reihe S.15, Wiesbaden.

Statistisches Bundesamt (1996), *Öffentliche Finanzen. Rechnungsergebnisse des öffentlichen Gesamthaushalts 1996. Fachserie 14, Reihe 3.1*, Wiesbaden.

Statistisches Bundesamt (2000), *Öffentliche Finanzen. Rechnungsergebnisse des öffentlichen Gesamthaushalts 2000. Fachserie 14, Reihe 3.1*, Wiesbaden.

Statistisches Bundesamt (2001), *Öffentliche Finanzen. Rechnungsergebnisse des öffentlichen Gesamthaushalts 2001. Fachserie 14, Reihe 3.1*, Wiesbaden.

Stephens, G. (1974), State Centralization and the Erosion of Local Autonomy, *Journal of Politics* 36(1), 44–76.

Steunenberg, B. and N. Mol (1997), Fiscal and Financial Decentralization: A Comparative Analysis of Six West European Countries, in: Lane, J.-E. (Ed.), *Public Sector Reform – Rationale, Trends and Problems*, London, 235–256.

Stirböck, C. (2002), *Relative Specialization of EU Regions: An Econometric Analysis of Sectoral Gross Fixed Capital Formation*, ZEW Discussion Paper No. 02-36.

Strange, S. (1996), *The Retreat of the State*, Cambridge.

Straubhaar, T. (1999), Glokalisierung – Die Champions League der Agglomerationen, *Wirtschaftsdienst* 1999/10.

Strumpf, K. S. and F. Oberholzer Gee (2002), Endogenous Policy Decentralization: Testing the Central Tenet of Economic Federalism, *Journal of Political Economy* 110(1), 1–58.

Stutzer, A. (1999), *Demokratieindizes für die Kantone der Schweiz*, Institute for Empirical Research in Economics Working Paper No. 23, University of Zurich.

Tanzi, V. (2001), *Pitfalls on the Road to Fiscal Decentralization*, Carnegie Endowment for International Peace Working Paper No. 19 (April).

Terhalle, F. (1952), Geschichte der deutschen öffentlichen Finanzwirtschaft vom Beginn des 19. Jahrhunderts bis zum Schlusse des Zweiten Weltkrieges, in: Gerloff, W. and F. Neumark (Eds.), *Handbuch der Finanzwissenschaft, Vol. 1*, 2nd ed., Tübingen, 273–326.

Ter-Minassian, T. (Ed.) (1997), *Fiscal Federalism in Theory and Practice*, International Monetary Fund, Washington.

Thiessen, U. (2003), Fiscal Decentralisation and Economic Growth in High-Income OECD Countries, *Fiscal Studies* 24(3), 237–274.

Tiebout, C. (1956), A Pure Theory of Local Expenditures, *Journal of Political Economy*, 64(5), 416–424.

Tilly, R. (1997), Kommunalfinanzen und -investitionen im Deutschen Kaiserreich, 1870-1914: Quantifizierungsansätze, in: Gerhard, H.-J. (Ed.), *Struktur und Dimension. Festschrift für Karl Heinrich Kaufhold zum 65.Geburtstag. Vol. 2: Neunzehntes und Zwanzigstes Jahrhundert*, VSWG Beiheft 133, 134–166.

de Tocqueville, A. (1840), *De la démocratie en Amérique II*, electronic edition.

Treisman, D. (2002), *Defining and Measuring Decentralization: A Global Perspective*, unpublished manuscript.

Tsebelis, G. and J. Money (1997), *Bicameralism*, Cambridge.

van Houten, P. (2003), Globalization and Demands for Regional Autonomy in Europe, in: Kahler, M. and D. A. Lake (Eds.), *Governance in a Global Economy: Political Authority in Transition*, Princeton, 110–135.

Vaubel, R. (1996), Constitutional Safeguards Against Centralization in Federal States: An International Cross-Section Analysis, *Constitutional Political Economy* 7(2), 79–102.

Verdier, D. and R. Breen (2001), Europeanization and Globalization – Politics Against Markets in the European Union, *Comparative Political Studies* 34(3), 227–262.

Wacziarg, R. T., E. Spolaore, and A. Alesina (2002), *Trade, Growth and the Size of Countries*, Institute Research Working Paper No. 1995, Harvard University.

Wagner, A. (1876), *Grundlegung der politischen Ökonomie. Bd. 1: Grundlagen der Volkswirtschaft*, 3rd ed., Leipzig.

Wallis, J. J. and W. E. Oates (1988), Decentralization in the Public Sector: An Empirical Study of State and Local Government, in: Rosen, H. S. (Ed.), *Fiscal Federalism: Quantitative Studies*, Chicago.

Ware, A. (1996), *Political Parties and Party Systems*, Oxford.

Wasylenko, M. (1987), Fiscal Decentralization and Economic Development, *Public Budgeting & Finance* 7(4), 57–71.

Weingast, B. R., K. A. Shepsle, and C. Johnsen (1981), The Political Economy of Benefits and Costs: A Neoclassical Approach to Distributive Politics, *Journal of Political Economy* 89, 642–664.

Wheare, K. C. (1963), *Federal Government*, 4th ed., London.

White, H. (1980), A Heteroskedasticity-Consistent Covariance Matrix Estimator and a Direct Test for Heteroskedasticity, *Econometria* 48(4), 817–838.

Witt, P.-C. (1992), Finanzen und Politik im Bundesstaat Deutschland 1871-1933, in: Huhn, J. and P.-C. Witt (Eds.), *Föderalismus in Deutschland. Traditionen und gegenwärtige Probleme*, Baden-Baden, 75–100.

Woldendorp, J., H. Keman and I. Budge (1998), Party Government in 20 Democracies: An Update (1990-1995), *European Journal of Political Research* 33, 125–164.

Wooldridge, J. M. (2002), *Econometric Analysis of Cross Section and Panel Data*, Cambridge (MA).

World Bank (2000), *World Development Report 1999/2000*, Washington D.C.

Wrede, M. (2004), Small States, Large Unitary States and Federations, *Public Choice* 119, 219–240.

Young, R. A. (1994), The Political Economy of Secession: The Case of Quebec, *Constitutional Political Economy* 5(2), 221–245.

Zantman, W. (2002), Constitutional Design and Regional Favoritism, *Journal of Public Economic Theory* 4(1), 71–93.

Zimmermann, H. (1973), Die Ausgabenintensität der öffentlichen Aufgabenerfüllung, *Finanzarchiv* N.F. 32(1), 1–20.

Zimmermann, H. (1990), Gewichtsverlagerungen im föderativen Staatsaufbau unter EG-Einfluß?, *Wirtschaftsdienst* 9, 451–456.

Printing and Binding: Strauss GmbH, Mörlenbach

The manufacturer's authorised representative in the EU is Springer Nature Customer Service Centre GmbH, Europaplatz 3, 69115 Heidelberg, Germany. If you have any concerns regarding our products, please contact ProductSafety@springernature.com

Printed and bound by CPI Group (UK) Ltd, Croydon, CR0 4YY
22/09/2026
02221064-0009